AQA Design & Technology: Product Design (3-D Design)

AS A2

Exclusively endorsed by AQA

Brian Evans
Will Potts

 Nelson Thornes

Published in 2008 by:
Nelson Thornes Ltd
Delta Place
27 Bath Road
CHELTENHAM
GL53 7TH
United Kingdom

09 10 11 12 / 10 9 8 7 6 5 4

A catalogue record for this book is available from the British Library

ISBN 978 0 7487 8257 4

Cover photograph courtesy of the Design and Technology Association
Illustrations include artwork drawn by Barking Dog Art and GreenGate Publishing
Photo research by Uniquedimension Limited
Page make-up by GreenGate Publishing, Kent

Printed and bound in China by 1010 Printing International Ltd

Acknowledgements

The authors and publisher would like to thank the following for permission to reproduce material:

p16 Deutschesee AG; p18 Procter & Gamble; p23 (top) Luca Mazzocco – Renault F1 team; p23 (bottom) ARPL Science Library; p28 Topfoto; p29 iStockphoto; p33 Science Photo Library; p40 www.frednelsonfabrication.com; p41 Science Photo Library; p46 Fotolia/David Lloyd; p50 iStockphoto; p53 Fotolia/Feng Yu; p55 iStockphoto; p57 (top) iStockphoto; p57 (bottom) public domain; p58 iStockphoto; p60 Ikea; p61 (bottom) iStockphoto; p62 iStockphoto; p64 ARPL Science Library; p65 (top) courtesy of Stafford-White.com; p65 (bottom) iStockphoto; p69 (top) Topfoto; p76 Russell Hobbs; p77 Science Photo Library/Pascal Goetgheluck; p79 public domain; p83 Ferrari SA; p84 public domain; p85 (top) www. sherylblais.com; p85 (bottom) public domain; p86 (bottom) courtesy of Hammerstroem; p99 Saltbox mill; p104 Dyson; p105 (top) public domain; p105 iStockphoto; p108 (top) public domain; p108 (middle) public domain; p108 (bottom) Carousel Design; p111 (top) public domain; p111 (bottom) public domain; p112 www.missvshanghai.com; p116 (top) public domain; p116 (bottom) www.crosscustomworks. com; p116 (bottom left) Maglite; p116 (bottom middle) public domain; p116 (bottom right) iStockphoto; p127 iStockphoto; p133 Image Content Collections; p136 (top) Image Content Collections; p136 (bottom) Image Content Collections; p147 Image Content Collections; p149 (top and middle) public domain; p149 Image Content Collections; p151 figure adapted from Advanced Design and Technology, p41 by Syd Urry, Eddie Norman, Joyce Cubitt and Mike Whittaker used by kind permission of Pearson Education Ltd; p157 United Kingdom patent Office; p159 (top) Audi GmbH; p160 EC Information Office; p162 Panasonic; p164 (top) Bang and Olufsen; p164 (bottom) Sylvania Dura-one; p165 DaimlerChrysler GmbH; p168 (top) Image Content Collections; p168 (bottom) Image Content Collections; p173 Image Content Collections; p174 public domain; p178 John Birdsall Photography; p179 (top) Science and Society Picture Library; p179 (bottom) iStockphoto; p180 public domain; p182 Apple Inc.; p183 public domain; p185 (top) Image Content Collections; p185 (bottom) www.sparkmuseum.com; p186 (top) Tetra Images/Getty Images; p186 (bottom) Phillips Electronics; p187 Logitech; p188 (top) www.mdfinternational.com; p188 (bottom) Science Photo Library/Manfred Kage; p190 Sony Corporation; p191 (top) Nokia; p191 (bottom) Sony Corporation; p192 Topfoto/Universal Pictorial Press; p196 iStockphoto; p197 John MacDougall/AFP/Getty Images; p198 (top) public domain; p198 (middle) Chip East/Reuters/Corbis; p198 (bottom) public domain; p199 (top and middle) copyright Clarice Cliff; p199 (bottom) iStockphoto; p200 (top) Topfoto; p200 (middle) Picquot Ware; p200 (bottom) Topfoto; p201 (top) Collection 'Memphis Milano'; p201 (bottom) courtesy of www.dannylane.co.uk; p202 (top) public domain; p202 (bottom) Rennie Mackintosh Society; p204 (top) Victoria and Albert Museum; p204 (bottom) public domain; p209 TRUMPF Werkzeugmaschinen GmbH & Co. KG; p211 elnicjewellery@ hotmail.com; p212 Practical Technologies LLC; p214 www. minicoindustries.com; p217 (top) United Archives AG; p217 (bottom) public domain.

Every effort has been made to contact copyright holders and we apologise if any have been overlooked. Should copyright have been unwittingly infringed in this book, the owners should contact the publishers, who will make corrections at reprint.

Contents

AQA Introduction iv

Introduction to this book vi

1 Materials, components and application ... 1

Plastics 1
Elastomers 14
Composite materials 20
Metals 29
Non-ferrous metals 31
Alloys and alloying 32
Wood 54
Veneers, laminates and composites ... 57
Glass 61
Ceramics 64
Papers and boards 67
Printing 70
'Smart' and 'modern' materials 76

2 Hand and commercial processing ... 88

Joining processes 88
Joining metals 91
Joining wood 99
Joining polymers 101
Joining ceramics 103
Corrosion, decay and degradation ... 105
Finishes and finishing processes ... 108
Properties and materials testing ... 117

3 Design, environment and ergonomics ... 124

Environmental and sustainability issues ... 124
Ergonomics and anthropometrics ... 126
Inclusive design 129
Consumer safety 130

4 Design and manufacture ... 133

Materials and components 133
Industrial materials testing 137

5 Design and market influences ... 145

Roles in the design process 145
The marketing function 146
Design methods 148
Design activity within organisations ... 149
The design process 149
Development 153
Testing and evaluation 154
Patents 156
Communication and representation of design ideas ... 158
Sustainability and environmental concerns ... 160
Safety 169
Human needs and human factors ... 173
Major developments in technology ... 178
Product life cycles and historical influences ... 193
The work of past and present designers ... 195

6 Processes and manufacture ... 206

Selecting a process 206
Modern manufacturing systems 207
ICT in manufacturing 211
ICT applications in product design and manufacture ... 213

Index ... 221

AQA introduction

Nelson Thornes has worked in partnership with AQA to ensure this book and the accompanying online resources offer you the best support for your GCSE course.

All resources have been approved by senior AQA examiners so you can feel assured that they closely match the specification for this subject and provide you with everything you need to prepare successfully for your exams.

These print and online resources together **unlock blended learning**; this means that the links between the activities in the book and the activities online blend together to maximise your understanding of a topic and help you achieve your potential.

These online resources are available on **kerboodle!** which can be accessed via the internet at **http://www.kerboodle.com/live**, anytime, anywhere. If your school or college subscribes to this service you will be provided with your own personal login details. Once logged in, access your course and locate the required activity.

For more information and help visit **http://www.kerboodle.com**

Icons in this book indicate where there is material online related to that topic. The following icons are used:

💡 Learning activity

These resources include a variety of interactive and non-interactive activities to support your learning.

✅ Progress tracking

These resources include a variety of tests that you can use to check your knowledge on particular topics (Revision Quizzes) and a range of resources that enable you to analyse and understand examination questions (On your marks).

⚡ Research support

These resources include WebQuests, in which you are assigned a task and provided with a range of web links to use as source material for research.

◤ Study Skills

These resources provide tools that help to develop skills, such as Product Analysis Exercises.

When you see an icon, go to **Kerboodle** at **www.kerboodle.com**, enter your access details and select your course. The materials are arranged in the same order as the chapters in the book, so you can easily find the resources you need.

▦ How to use this book

This book covers the specification for your course and is arranged in a sequence approved by AQA.

The book content is divided into chapters that match the sections of the AQA Product design (3-D Design) specification for Units 1 and 3 - Materials, components and application; Hand and commercial processing; Design environment and ergonomics; Design and manufacture; Design and market influences; Processes and manufacture. Chapters 1, 2 and 3 cover Unit 1 and Chapters 4, 5 and 6 cover Unit 3 from the specification.

The content of the book is designed to meet the core requirements of the AS (Unit 1) and A2 (Unit 3) written papers. The electronic resources also cover the requirements of the written papers, as well as the coursework requirements (Units 2 and 4).

The features in this book include:

Learning objectives

At the beginning of each chapter you will find a list of learning objectives that contain targets linked to the requirements of the specification.

Key terms

Terms that you will need to be able to define and understand.

Case study

Gives insights into specific products and industries

Product analysis exercise

To facilitate your understanding, investigation and analysis of materials, product types and manufacture processes. Contains a series of questions or activities for you to carry out.

Activity

Suggestions for practical investigations you can carry out.

Further reading

Links to further sources of information, including websites and other publications.

Did you know?

An extension to the main text that provides you with added bits of information.

AQA Examiner's tip

Examiner's tip

Hints from AQA examiners to help you with your study and to prepare for your exam.

Examination-style questions

Questions in the style that you can expect in your exam appear at the end of each chapter.

AQA examination questions are reproduced by permission of the Assessment and Qualifications Alliance.

After studying this chapter it is hoped you will:

A bulleted list at the end of each chapter summarising the content in an easy-to-follow way.

Web links in the book

As Nelson Thornes is not responsible for third party content online, there may be some changes to this material that are beyond our control. In order for us to ensure that the links referred to in the book are as up-to-date and stable as possible, the websites are usually homepages with supporting instructions on how to reach the relevant pages if necessary.

Please let us know at **kerboodle@nelsonthornes.com** if you find a link that doesn't work and we will do our best to redirect the link, or to find an alternative site.

Introduction to this book

The world of product design

Whether you have thought about it or not, design is a part of everyday life. From the moment you get up in the morning and decide how you are going to look, the products we use to make life easier, to the grand architectural structures we live and work in, the process of design has been applied. It is the role of the designer to use this process in a structured way in order to provide solutions to problems.

The product designer then is charged with identifying design needs or problems. These can be very broad ranging and can come from individual design problems to meeting needs identified by clients or corporate organisations. For example, having won the bid to hold the 2012 Olympics in the UK a number of problems have become apparent. These include designing and building venues for the events, accommodation for participants and spectators and transport systems for travel between these. On a smaller scale there will be sports equipment, communications and memorabilia to go along with the events. All of which product designers will need to develop.

At the other end of the broad spectrum of product design lie the needs of groups and societies such as those developing nations where the most basic needs of food, water and shelter are an everyday struggle. Other groups might include the less able in society who need help with basic functions like making a hot drink or personal care.

Designers must approach their task with an open mind. Indeed the act of designing can be a fanciful affair with what can appear to be quite extraordinary and unworkable ideas being scribbled on some scrap paper while waiting to interview a client. Yet these might be the seeds of a brilliant idea.

Sometimes it will mean thinking in a different way. Edward de Bono is probably the best known exponent of a technique called lateral thinking, an excellent tool for a designer to help think around a problem. For example, when considering the problems arthritis sufferers have lifting and pouring a kettle, rather than designing a cradle system to support the kettle, the designer might develop a single cup system like the new espresso coffee making machines.

A further technique that designers find useful is to look at existing products. This often leads to incremental design changes including redesigning in order to update the shape, function or technology used in a product.

You only have to look at products such as televisions and cars to appreciate this. A further method would be to establish those aspects of the existing product that have relevance to the current design problem. An example of this is James Dyson observing how industrial paint filter systems worked and then miniaturising the technology in the cyclonic filter used in the vacuum cleaner. Sometimes, observing how others interact with products can also lead to radical innovation.

Some product designers have become household names due, largely, to their innovative approach to design. Innovation can be apparent in the shape, form or aesthetics of a product or in the way technology has been utilised to provide better function. An example includes the work of Philippe Starck and the Alessi group in their approach to household products.

There is a clear link between design and technology and it is the role of the designer to make effective use of developing technologies in the quest for high quality products. Designers need to be familiar with the range of materials that are available and their characteristics that determine how they can be used and commercially processed. Working with materials requires an understanding of Health and Safety issues, particularly when handling and processing materials so that the workforce and environment are protected.

Challenging the designer

One of the most important challenges to the designer is in the use of materials and consumption of energy. Designers have moral, economic, social and environmental responsibilities and should select materials and processing techniques that are sustainable. Materials must be selected carefully in order to ensure future supplies; the growth in the use of managed forests is a good example of this. The same applies in the use of energy for processing and the consumption of energy when products are in use. The high use of energy and subsequent CO_2 production, as we are seeing, contributes to global warming, so the lower the energy consumption the less impact there is likely to be to the environment. This means taking advantage of low melting point materials such as aluminium alloys (for processing car engine and gearbox components) or thermoplastics (for use in internal and external car body components).

Disposal also needs to be considered carefully. Materials should be recycled where possible but this means that the materials in a product must be identifiable and able to be readily separated. A further option is the reuse of products –as in the refilling of cosmetics bottles.

Safety is very important in the design of products. One of the areas where safety becomes paramount is the interaction between the user and the product. Failure of the product due to a 'design fault' can sometimes become a legal matter and involve litigation, so the protection of the consumer is extremely important. Designers must therefore be aware of any legislation that will affect the way their products are used.

An awareness of human sizes is also an area of knowledge important to a designer. Where people interact directly with products, e.g. sitting at desks, driving a car, it is crucial that ergonomics and anthropometrics have been incorporated making their use effective and safe.

Studying product design

With the AQA specification, there is considerable flexibility in what you do for coursework. You can do 3D products (both functioning and in block model form), graphic products like a point of sale display or textile/fashion items. Whatever you choose to do, you will have the opportunity to develop skills in using the process of design. At AS level this may be achieved by a series of small projects that feature certain aspects of the design process or one single project covering the full design process. At A2 you will do a single project with a commercial focus.

Whether you complete a single large project or work on a number of smaller ones you will be working through the same stages of the process as a practicing designer, i.e.

- Identifying a design problem and writing a brief. (This may be set by your teacher).
- making it clear that you understand the brief,
- discussing the requirements with your client (teacher),
- researching factors such as target market, design styles, fashions and trends and other areas that may influence what you design,
- sketching ideas,
- selecting an idea to take forward and develop,
- using CAD and physical models to help visualise the product,
- planning for prototype manufacture and considering industrial processing,
- producing the final outcome and evaluating it.

Working in this way will help you develop designing skills in a number of areas. For example it is important

that designers have good sketching skills in order to be able to show what they mean when discussing a product. If it is available, working with CAD is a further area for you to aim to be familiar with by using it to demonstrate what a final product might look like. Your project work will help you develop your understanding of materials and making processes.

After having designed and produced a final outcome it is important to question what you have done. In the process of evaluation you should be asking yourself:

- does my product meet the points on the brief or specification?
- is it finished to a high standard?
- what would I do differently if I could go through the process again?

Taking the exam

You will take exams at both AS and A2 level. By the end of the AS year, it is important for you to have gained a good knowledge of materials processing techniques and components as well as social issues associated with design. To obtain the highest grades you will need to develop the skill to critically analyse products to identify how the functional, manufacturing, aesthetic and social issues affect choice of material and process. In your A2 year, you will need to gain a deeper understanding of materials, components and manufacturing and the ability to identify where these are applied to specific products. The really high grades go to candidates who understand current industrial practice and wider issues that affect design such as the environment, quality and consumer safety requirements, and who can discuss these with reference to specific products and industries.

This book

This book has been structured to reflect AQA's specification for A level Design & Technology: Product Design (3-D Design). In agreement with AQA, Chapters one, two and three cover AS level and chapters four, five and six cover A2.

1 Materials, components and application

Through the study of this chapter it is hoped that you will:

- become familiar with the range of materials and components available
- be able to identify materials and their main characteristics
- give reasons why material(s) and components have been used for particular applications.

The first part of this book looks at the main groups of materials, i.e. plastics, metals and woods, as well as ceramics and glass. Composite materials are also discussed along with the newer smart materials and those that can be considered modern materials. In addition, you will find reference to some manufacturing processes in this section where appropriate.

Reference has also been made to the sources of materials. This has been treated as an overview only and is meant as background information when considering appropriate use of materials.

You will need to make use of other resources – books, CD-ROMs, the internet – to find all the information you will need for success in Product Design. Some references for further reading are given in this section.

Plastics

Introduction to plastics

You will need to know about the range of plastics available, along with their general properties and characteristics. You should also be familiar with the more popular methods of manufacturing and the role of a variety of additives in the successful manufacture and use of products.

What are plastics?

Plastics are a group of materials made up of long chains of molecules. A large proportion of them are known as hydrocarbons, because the **long-chain molecules** consist of hydrogen and carbon atoms in various combinations with other atoms. Others have been derived from natural sources and are becoming more popular.

Why are plastics so popular?

Plastics are becoming more popular in the manufacture of products, and in some cases have replaced more traditional materials. For example, the domestic kettle has developed from a product manufactured from a metal (e.g. stainless steel) to a **polymer** with all the inherent benefits this material brings (lightweight, self-coloured and self-finished, electrical and thermal insulator). In addition, the processes used in the manufacture of the polymer kettle have enabled the product to become more user-friendly by incorporating all of the ergonomic issues associated with the use of the product.

Polypropylene jug kettle

Key terms

Long-chain molecule: the main constituent part of a polymer. The long-chain molecule is made up of a series of atoms – in the case of the hydrocarbons these would be made up of hydrogen and carbon along with elements such as oxygen.

Polymer: the proper term for a plastic material.

Cellulose: a constituent part of timber. Approximately 55 per cent of a tree is made up of cellulose. Note: this material can be used to produce a cellulose-based polymer.

AQA Examiner's tip

As with any subject there are specific areas that you need to become familiar with. In this subject you will need to have an understanding of the main types of plastics and their overall characteristics. In addition, you should also be able to give examples of applications where plastics are used.

AQA Examiner's tip

It is important that you become familiar with the main properties of materials. You should be able to refer to materials properties of plastics when discussing applications.

Sources of plastics

There are a number of sources of raw material used in the production of plastics (polymers).

Animal and vegetable by-products are used in the manufacture of semi-synthetic polymers. For example, **cellulose** is a natural material occurring in plant fibres. This is mixed with acetic acid to produce cellulose acetate from which products such as OHP slides are manufactured.

Casein is a further example. In this case, by-products of milk are used to create the polymer. The material is still used in the manufacture of buttons.

Coal, oil and gas are the sources for a range of purely synthetic plastics. Plastics produced from these materials are gained through the process of 'thermal cracking'. Synthetic plastics are therefore carbon-based and account for the majority of plastics used today.

Plastics can be grouped into three types.

- *Thermoplastics* These materials can be repeatedly reheated and remoulded.
- *Thermosets* (Thermosetting plastics): these undergo a chemical change resulting in them becoming permanently rigid, i.e. they cannot be reheated and reshaped.
- *Elastomers* These are polymers that have good elasticity, i.e. they can be distorted under pressure but will return to their original shape when the pressure is removed.

The figure below shows examples of the different types of polymer available for use in manufacturing products; more details of common polymers are given in Table 1.

The main types of plastics (polymers)

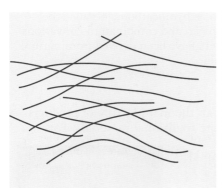

Thermoplastics

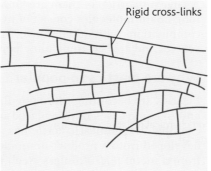

Rigid cross-links

Thermosets

Elastomers

Structure of polymers

💡 General properties of plastics

Here is a summary of the properties of plastics.

- They are good electrical and thermal insulators.
- They have a good strength to weight ratio. This does not mean they are strong materials in the same way that mild steel is strong, but that they have good strength compared to their weight.
- Generally, they have good atmospheric and chemical corrosion resistance.

Table 1 *Common polymers*

Common name	Working name	Characteristics	Common uses
Thermoplastics			
ABS	Acrylonitrile Butadiene Styrene	High impact strength, giving good toughness with good strength, scratch-resistant, lightweight and durable	Kitchen products, mobile telephone cases, PC monitor cases, safety helmets, toys, some car parts and domestic telephones
CA	Cellulose Acetate	Tough and rigid, lightweight with good strength, transparent and non flammable	Photographic film, handles for cutlery, cupboard door knobs, frames for glasses
Nylon	Polyamide	Hard, tough, resistant to wear with a low coefficient of friction	Bearings, gears, curtain rail fittings and clothing
PMMA (PolyMethyl MethAcrylate)	Acrylic	Food-safe, tough, hard, durable, easily machined	Light units, illuminated signs, lenses for car lights
PP	Polypropylene	Lightweight, food-safe, good impact resistance even at low temperatures, good chemical resistance	Kitchen products (food containers), medical equipment, string and rope
HIPS	High Impact Polystyrene	Good impact resistance, good strength and stiffness, lightweight	Toys and refrigerator linings
PS	Polystyrene	Lightweight, rigid, colourless, low impact strength	Packaging, disposable cups/plates and containers
	Expanded polystyrene	Floats, good sound and heat insulator, lightweight, low strength	Packaging, disposable cups, sound and heat insulation
LDPE	Low Density Polyethylene	Low density (lightweight), low stiffness and rigidity, good chemical resistance	Detergent bottles, toys and carrier bags
HDPE	High Density Polyethylene	High density, good stiffness, good chemical resistance	Crates, bottles, buckets and bowls
uPVC	Polyvinyl Chloride	Good chemical resistance, good resistance to weathering, rigid, hard, tough, lightweight, can be coloured	Pipes, guttering, bottles and window frames
PVC (un-plasticised, flexible)	Polyvinyl Chloride	Good chemical resistance, good resistance to weathering, rigid, hard, tough, lightweight, can be coloured	Flexible hose, e.g. hose pipes, cable insulation
PET	Polyethylene Terephthalate	Moderate chemical resistance	Fibres used to make a wide range of clothing, blow-moulded bottles for beers and soft drinks, electrical plugs and sockets, audio and video tapes, insulation tapes
PC	Polycarbonate	Good chemical resistance, expensive material	Very tough – used for protective shields, e.g. safety glasses, safety helmets, hairdryer bodies, telephone parts, vandal-proof street-light covers
Thermosets			
Epoxy resins		High strength when reinforced with fibres (GRP – glass-reinforced plastic), good chemical and wear resistance	Surface coating, encapsulation of electronic components, adhesives
Melamine formaldehyde		Rigid, good strength and hardness, scratch-resistant, can be coloured	Tableware, decorative laminates for work surfaces
Polyester resins		Rigid, brittle, good heat and chemical resistance	Casting, used in glass re-inforced plastic (e.g. boat hulls and car body parts)
Urea formaldehyde		Rigid, hard, good strength, brittle, heat-resistant, good electrical insulator	Electrical fittings, adhesives

■ They have fairly low melting temperatures, ranging from 70 to 185 °C (thermoplastics only).
■ They are lightweight.
■ They can be self-coloured, opaque, translucent or transparent, depending on the type of polymer and processing used.

Improving the properties of plastics: additives

A variety of materials can be incorporated into the polymer powder prior to processing. Some of these, e.g. fillers, can be used to give the material bulk, while others are used to condition the material (i.e. increase the mechanical properties of the material) in a similar way to **heat treatments** for metals. For example, particular additives give the material anti-static properties, make the material flame-retardant or resistant to ultraviolet light.

Fillers

Fillers are used to reduce the bulk of the plastic. They are generally cheaper than plastics and so help reduce costs. Examples of fillers include: sawdust, wood flour, crushed quartz and limestone. Some fillers can increase strength and hardness of the polymer by removing brittleness.

Flame-retardants

Flame-retardants are used to reduce the risk of combustion. Their main role is to create a chemical reaction once combustion has begun; they release agents that will stifle the combustion. An example of the use of flame-retardants is in the foams used to fill seating cushions.

Anti-static agents

Anti-static agents reduce the effects of static charges that could build up on a product, e.g. from walking on a carpet made from synthetic materials.

Plasticiser

Plasticisers are added to plastics to improve the flow properties of plastics when being moulded. They also reduce the softening temperature and go some way to making the material less brittle.

Stabilisers

Stabilisers are used to reduce the effects of ultraviolet light, i.e. by making the plastics more resistant to being 'broken down' by sunlight. This is important both from a structural and an aesthetic point of view. Stabilisers are used in products that are exposed to a lot of sunlight (such as windows, doors and conservatory components).

Applications for thermoplastics

There is a huge range of thermoplastics available. Further development of these materials extends their usefulness. Examples of improved polymers include those that have been designed to meet food quality standards. The development of polymers such as PET helps to extend the shelf life of carbonated drinks; these polymers are less permeable than previously used polymers such as PVC.

Being thermoplastic, these materials will begin to soften at raised temperatures. Again further development has helped produce materials that will withstand higher temperatures than previously used polymers, allowing motor casings to be moulded integrally. The ability to withstand higher temperatures has enabled the manufacture and use of products such

■ **Key terms**

Heat treatment: a term given to a range of processes using heat to cause a change in a metal's properties by making changes to the internal structure of the material. Annealing, hardening, tempering and normalising are the more common heat treatments.

■ Further reading
■ R. A. Higgins, *Materials for Engineers and Technicians*, Newnes.

as 'ready-meals', where the plastic container is placed in the oven with the food as it cooks – something that was unheard of a few years ago.

▧ Biodegradable plastics

Conventional oil-based plastics do not break down easily and, since the main bulk of domestic waste is made up of plastics, they have a significant effect on the environment. **Biodegradable** plastics however are designed to be degradable under the right conditions, i.e. in a biologically rich environment.

Applications

Applications for biodegradable polymers vary widely: packaging – shopping bags, food trays and some soft drinks bottles; catering – disposable pots, bowls and cutlery; gardening; and medical and sanitary products such as disposable gloves.

The majority of biodegradable plastics are derived entirely from **renewable** raw materials. For example, starch-based polymers are produced from wheat, corn and potatoes and are used in the manufacture of capsules for medicines.

Polylactides (PLA) is another type of polymer derived from natural resources. This polymer is transparent and has similar properties to polyethylene and polypropylene and, as such, can be processed in similar ways to these conventional thermoplastics. Applications include packaging in the form of bottles and films for carrier bags and gardening products such as plant pots. They are also used in the manufacture of disposable nappies. Certain types of PLA have been used successfully in medical implants and in sutures, because of their ability to dissolve over time.

PHAs and PHBs

Biodegradable plastics can also be produced naturally by using bacteria to aid in fermenting plant sugars. These polymers are called polyhydroxyalkanoate (or PHA), also known as **Biopol**. The plastic is harvested from bacteria grown in cultures. The most popular of this type of polymer is PHB (poly-beta-hydroxybutyrate) and variations of this polymer are used in packaging since it has similar properties to polypropylene. PHAs have wide-ranging applications in the area of medicine in the form of dispersible fixatives such as films, screws, and bone plates and are also used for applying slow-release medication. Although stable in the environment these polymers are fully compostible, i.e. they will break down completely when in contact with micro-organisms in the soil.

Oxo-degradable polymers

Oxo-degradable polymers have additives that promote short **degradation** times, e.g. less than five years. These additives will help the polymer break down into a fine powder from the effects of heat, oxygen, moisture and even mechanical stress, making it more readily digestible by micro-organisms.

Photo-degradable polymers will break down when exposed to ultraviolet (UV) light making them more readily biodegradable.

It is possible to help conventional polymers break down more readily by including an additive such as 'bio-batch'. This additive can be used with polymers such as PE, PP, PVC, PET or PS and its inclusion will enable the material to degrade in a much shorter period of time (again fewer than five years) rather than the possible 100 years predicted for conventional oil-based products.

■ Key terms

Biodegradable: a term given to materials that will break down with the aid of natural processes such as sunlight and rain.

Renewables: materials that are extracted from managed sources, such as Scandinavian pine taken from forests where trees are replaced by saplings as they are felled.

Biopol: a polymer made from natural cellulose, which can be used to make biodegradable packaging.

Degradation: the deterioration of polymers.

Water-soluble polymers

One of the areas of biodegradation that is coming increasingly to the fore is that of water-soluble polymers. Products such as liquid detergent pouches make use of the water-soluble properties of these materials to dispense the detergent only when in contact with warm water. Other applications include laundry bags where the dirty laundry is held by the material until it is placed in a large washing machine thereby protecting, for example, hospital staff.

The cost of producing biodegradable polymers remains more expensive than conventional polymers and this is reflected in the cost of products made from these materials. However, with increasing interest in these materials, scales of production are likely to increase, thus bringing costs down.

Processing plastics

Thermoplastics can be processed in a number of ways depending on the shape of the product being manufactured, while thermosets are limited by the manufacturing methods used. The diagram below gives an overview of these methods.

We will now consider some of the more common moulding and forming processes for thermoplastics. Joining processes will not be covered here. For more on joining for polymers see p101.

■ **Further reading**

■ Norman, Cubitt, Urry and Whittaker, *A Level Design and Technology, Third Edition*, Longman.

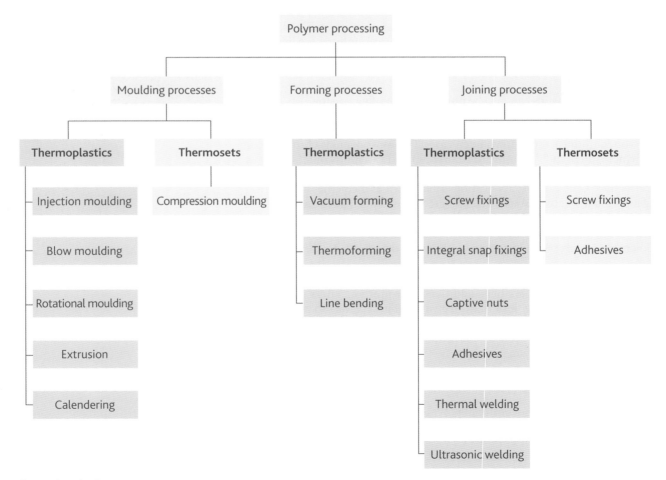

Processing plastics

Injection moulding

This process is most commonly associated with thermoplastics and is used to produce complex three-dimensional (3-D) shapes.

Stages of the process:

Step 1 Plastic granules (plus any other additives and colours mixed with them) are placed in the hopper. The granule mixture falls through the hopper onto the Archimedean screw.

Step 2 The screw is rotated via the motor and gearbox. This action forces the polymer forwards towards the heaters, where it becomes softened to the point where it is ready to be injected into the mould.

Step 3 The hydraulic ram forces the softened polymer through the feedhole into the mould. Pressure from the ram ensures the mould cavity has been filled.

Step 4 When sufficient time has passed to allow the polymer to cool and solidify (a matter of seconds), the mould halves are opened. As they open, ejector pins are activated to release the product from the mould.

Step 5 Once emptied, the mould is then closed ready to begin another cycle.

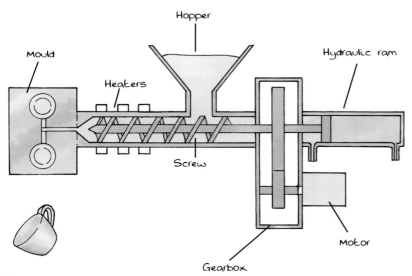

💡 *Injection moulding*

■ **Key terms**

Injection moulding: a method of processing thermoplastic materials. Products generally have complex 3-D shapes.

■ **Activity**

1 Identify three items produced by injection moulding.

2 Identify the signs that suggest a product has been injection moulded.

3 State the materials used to manufacture the products.

AQA **Examiner's tip**

It is a good idea to practice producing appropriate line diagrams that are fully labelled in order to obtain the best marks when answering exam questions that ask you to produce your own notes and diagrams.

Advantages and disadvantages of injection moulding

Advantages

■ Very complex 3-D shapes can be produced.

■ High volumes can be produced with consistent quality.

■ Metal inserts can be included in the item being produced.

Disadvantages

■ Initial set-up costs are high.

■ Moulds are expensive.

■ Key terms

Blow moulding: a process of manufacturing thermoplastic materials into re-entrant shapes with a single opening. Examples include soft drinks bottles, detergent bottles, etc.

Parison: the extruded tube of thermoplastic material used in the process of blow moulding.

■ Activity

1 Identify three different products that have been manufactured by blow moulding. Identify the materials used in these products.

2 State the main characteristics of products that are produced in this way.

Blow moulding

This process is used in the manufacture of bottles and other containers. Objects produced are usually hollow and have a narrow neck.

Stages of the process:

Step 1 A tube of heated and softened polymer is extruded vertically downwards. This tube is called a **Parison**.

Step 2 The mould halves close, trapping the upper end of the Parison, effectively sealing it.

Step 3 Hot air is then blown into the Parison forcing it out to follow the shape of the mould.

Step 4 The mould effectively cools the polymer allowing it to be released from the mould.

Step 5 The mould halves are opened and the product is extracted.

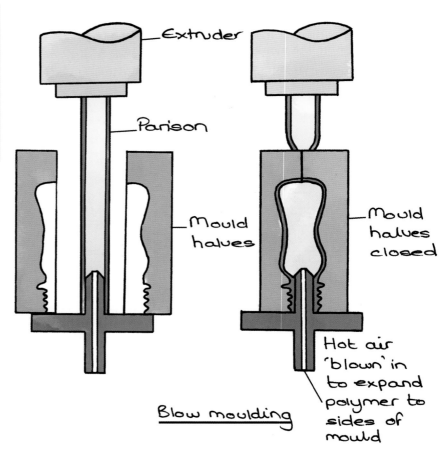

Blow moulding

💡 *Blow moulding*

Advantages and disadvantages of blow moulding

Advantages

■ Once set up, blow moulding is a rapid method of producing hollow objects with narrow necks.

■ Non-circular shapes can be produced.

Disadvantages

■ Moulds can be expensive.

■ It's difficult to produce re-entrant shapes, i.e. shapes that do not allow easy extraction from the mould (e.g. a dovetail joint).

■ Triangular-shaped bottles are difficult to produce.

Rotational moulding

Rotational moulding is used in the manufacture of 3-D hollow products, such as footballs, road cones and large storage tanks (up to 3 m³ capacity).

Stages of the process:

The machines used have a number of arms that rotate about a fixed central point. Moulds are attached to the end of each arm and are rotated continuously. The only time the moulds do not rotate is when they are at the starting point and end point of the process.

Step 1 Once the moulds have been loaded with a precise weight of thermoplastic powder (e.g. polyethylene) the mould halves are clamped together.

Step 2 The moulds are then rotated about the arm spindle and the whole arm is rotated towards a heated chamber where the thermoplastic material is heated to its melting point. The continuously rotating mould ensures that the thermoplastic covers all of the mould.

Step 3 The next stage of the process is the cooling chamber where the material is cooled ready to be extracted from the mould.

Step 4 The mould is then returned to the starting point where the mould halves are separated and the product removed.

Cycle times vary as they depend on the required wall thickness of the material.

Advantages and disadvantages of rotational moulding

Advantages

■ One-piece mouldings can be produced.

■ It is ideal for both rigid, tough shapes and flexible shapes.

■ A large range of sizes is possible, from small medical components to large storage tanks.

■ Surface **textures** can be applied to the finished products from textures applied in the mould.

■ Moulds tend to be cheaper than those for injection or blow moulding, since high pressures are not required.

■ Cheaper moulds allow lower production runs.

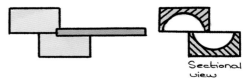

1. Open mould is filled with plastic powder.

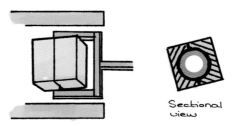

2. Mould is heated and the plastic melts, coating the inside.

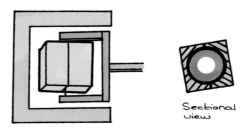

3. Mould is cooled to set the plastic.

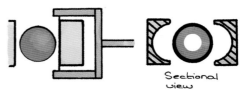

4. Mould is opened and the product removed.

Rotational moulding

💡 *Rotational moulding*

Disadvantages

- Only hollow shapes can be produced in this way. More complex 3-D shapes would either be blow moulded or injection moulded.

Thermoforming and vacuum forming

Thermoforming is a relatively new process, but is very closely related to **vacuum forming**. Where vacuum forming relies solely on a vacuum to 'pull' the softened polymer around a mould, thermoforming uses an outer mould to help in the process – this allows a greater level of detail, such as lettering, symbols and sharp edges, to be achieved.

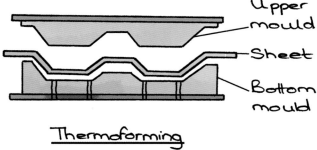

Thermoforming

The thermoforming process

Sheet material is heated to just above its softening point and then held securely in a frame between the two mould halves. The mould halves close and at the same time a vacuum is applied through the lower mould. The upper mould ensures the required amount of detail is achieved.

Advantages and disadvantages of thermoforming

Advantages

- It's a low-cost process.
- It's good for smooth shapes with additional detail.

Disadvantages

- Deep moulds result in a thinning of the wall thickness where it has been stretched.
- It's limited to simple designs.
- Trimming is usually needed.

Extrusion

Extrusion is the process used where products with a continuous cross-section are required.

In essence, the process forces molten plastic through a die that has the required cross-sectional shape.

Stages of the process:

Step 1 Thermoplastic powder is placed in the hopper; this powder then falls onto the rotating Archimedean screw, which in turn pushes the material towards a heated section of the extruder.

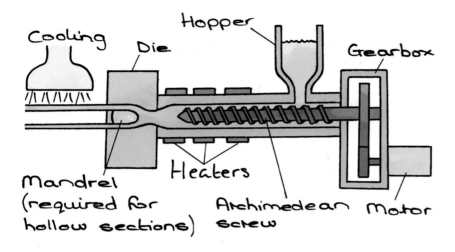

Plastic extrusion

Step 2 The heaters soften the plastic, which is then forced through the die by the rotating screw.

Step 3 On exiting the die, the plastic product is then cooled using a water jet.

Step 4 Further along the transfer table, the product is cut to the required length.

Wires can be insulated with the aid of a special mandrel arrangement that allows the wire to pass through.

Advantages and disadvantages of extrusion

■ Extrusion has the advantage of generally being a low-cost process that requires only simple dies.

■ Its main disadvantage is that it can only produce continuous cross-sectional shapes.

Calendaring

Calendaring is used for the manufacture of thermoplastic film, sheet and coating materials. In the main, materials such as PE, PVC, ABS and cellulose acetate would be processed in this way. Shopping bags made from LDPE would have been calendared.

Stages of the process:

Calendaring involves rolling out a mass of pre-mixed plastic material between large rollers to form a continuous film of accurate thickness.

Step 1 The rollers are heated to just above the softening point of the thermoplastic.

Step 2 During the rolling process, the plastic 'dough' is forced through the gap roller. These rollers determine the thickness of the material.

Step 3 The final roller is the 'chill' roller that cools the material.

 Activity

Identify three products produced by extrusion. Sketch the cross-section of each of the products identified. State the material used for each product.

 Key terms

Calendaring: a process used to manufacture thermoplastic sheet. Generally polyethylene (PE) and polyvinyl chloride (PVC) are used to create the sheet.

Activity

Identify three products produced by the calendaring process. State the materials used.

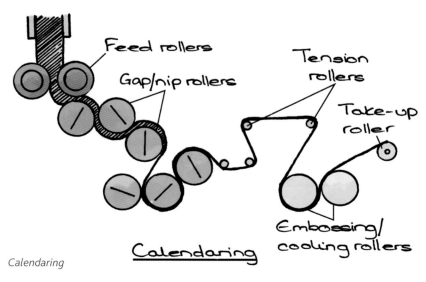

Calendaring

Line bending

Line (or strip) bending is used to form straight, small curved bends in thermoplastic sheet material.

The equipment used in this type of process is known as a 'strip heater' and comprises an electrical heater – usually a tensioned resistance wire – that is enclosed in a channel within a table. The sheet of thermoplastic material is clamped accurately over the heating element, so that the heater softens the part of the sheet that requires bending. In some line bending arrangements heating elements can be placed on both sides of the sheet, avoiding the need to turn the material over.

Once heated to the required temperature, the material can be bent. Accurate bends are achieved using bending jigs that ensure the correct angle is consistently being achieved.

Key terms

Line (or strip) bending: a method of processing sheet materials, in particular thermoplastics; limited to producing simple shapes.

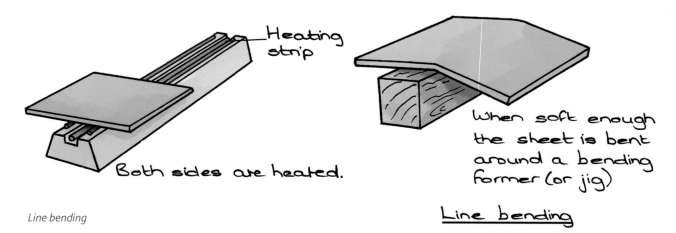

Line bending

Applications for thermosetting polymers

Unlike thermoplastics, thermosetting plastics display very little plasticity. In other words, they are very rigid. There are fewer thermosetting plastics than there are thermoplastic materials, but they have useful properties that allow them to be used in a range of applications (see p3).

For example, urea formaldehyde is a very stiff plastic that is hard and has good strength. In addition, in common with most plastics, it has very good electrical resistance properties (a good insulator) and, because it will not be softened by heat, it is a suitable material for electrical fittings.

Other applications for thermosetting plastics include the use of polyester resin for paperweights. Polyesters can also be used in combination with a **catalyst** and glass fibres to create GRP – glass-reinforced plastic.

Compression moulding

Compression moulding is probably the most important moulding process for manufacturing with thermosetting plastics. A combination of heat, pressure and time is needed to ensure all of the material's form and structure changes.

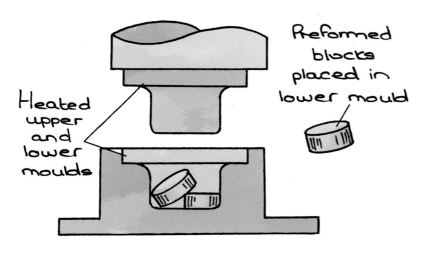

Compression moulding

Stages of the process:

Step 1 A preformed 'slug' (compressed powder) of material is placed between the two halves of the mould.

Step 2 The mould is heated to a temperature that will allow the **cross-links** to form within the material.

Step 3 The mould is closed onto the preform and the pressure used will force out any excess material. The moulds are held closed under pressure at the required temperature for a period of time that is sufficient to allow all of the material to be 'cured', i.e. all cross-links formed.

Step 4 When the mould is opened, the product can be ejected while it is still hot (it does not have to be cooled) and the process can begin again.

Advantages and disadvantages of compression moulding

Advantages

▦ Moderately complex parts can be produced over long production runs.

▦ Although there is some heavy machinery involved, start-up costs are relatively low; moulds are less expensive than those used in injection moulding.

▦ There is little waste material.

Activity

Give three applications where thermosetting plastics have been used. Identify the thermosetting plastic used and the main characteristics of the plastic that make it appropriate for the application.

Key terms

van der Waals bond: a type of atomic bonding found in thermoplastics. It is this electrostatic bond that allows the reshaping of thermoplastics when heated.

Rigid cross-link: these types of cross-links are found in thermosetting plastics and elastomers. They are a more rigid bond than the van der Waals bond found in thermoplastics, and do not react to the application of heat.

Disadvantages

■ It is necessary to manufacture a preform.

■ The process is restricted to products with low complexity.

Thermoplastic and thermosetting materials

Some materials behave in a similar way to polymers in that they demonstrate thermoplastic, thermosetting or elastomeric properties.

Plastics have a particular structure. The diagrams on p2 show the structure of the three main types.

Thermoplastics

Thermoplastics can be considered as a tangle of long-chain molecules. These molecules are held together by strong electrostatic forces, called **van der Waals bonds**. These bonds can be released with the application of heat, making it possible for the material to be reshaped.

Thermosets

Thermosetting plastics also consist of long-chain molecules but differ in that these molecules are held together by **rigid cross-links**, which in turn prevent them from being reheated and reshaped.

■ Elastomers

Elastomers have long-chain molecules that can be considered to be coils (similar to springs); when the material is distorted (compressed or stretched) the molecules distort, and when released they return to their original shape. These coiled molecules give the elastomers their elastic properties.

At rest

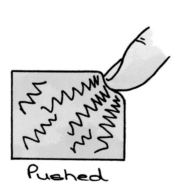

Pushed

Pulled

Elastomers

The flexibility of elastomers

Thermoplastic elastomers (TPE)

Designers and manufacturers use thermoplastic elastomers as they can be processed using conventional equipment associated with thermoplastic polymers, e.g. injection moulding and blow moulding. This has significantly reduced production cycle times compared to the use of thermosetting natural or synthetic rubbers as there is no wait for the molecular cross-links to form in the material.

An additional advantage in using TPEs is that all waste and scrap can be recycled.

There is a wide range of applications for these materials including:

- electrical components, e.g. insulating coatings for wires, cables and **fibre optics**
- overmoulding of grips or power tool bodies, kitchen utensils and pens and toothbrushes
- seals and hoses for a range of automotive and industrial applications.

Liquid silicon rubber (LSR)

This is a thermosetting elastomer made up of two components, one of which is a catalyst. To manufacture with this material the two components (in liquid form) have to be mixed together to a high degree of consistency before being processed. Processing can be completed using a slightly modified version of an injection moulding machine, the ram of which forces the liquid into a heated mould where the cross-linking can take place.

The main advantage of this material is its ability to maintain its insulating and elastomeric characteristics over a wide temperature range, typically –50°C to +250°C. It is used in a wide range of applications including seals and covers for the automotive industry; electrical connectors; products for babies and infants such as bottle teats; kitchen products such as baking trays and spatulas; and a range of medical equipment.

Other thermoplastic and thermosetting materials

Thermoplastic materials

Thermoplastic materials, once shaped, can be reshaped following the application of heat or water.

For example, a thermoplastic polymer can be reshaped by heating; heating releases the van der Waals bonds that link the long-chain molecules, allowing the material to be formed into a different shape. (A thermosetting polymer, however, has rigid cross-links, which cannot be released by heating and the material cannot therefore be reshaped.)

- Clay is a good example of a thermoplastic material. If it is still in its natural state, i.e. has not been fired, then it can be softened and reshaped when mixed with water. However, when clay has been fired, it becomes a much more rigid material that behaves as a thermosetting material, i.e. rigid cross-linking has occurred meaning that it is not affected by water.
- Paper is another example of a material that can be broken down when mixed with water. This is the basis of paper recycling.
- Metals are another group of materials that behave in a similar way to thermoplastics when heated. Due to their structure, metals can be softened through the application of heat, making reshaping easier. Indeed, most metals can be heated until they become liquid and can be cast into shape.
- Glass is a further example of a material that can be heated and reshaped, behaving in a similar way to a thermoplastic.

Thermosetting materials

As described above, there are a number of materials that once processed by heat or a chemical reaction cannot be returned to their basic components and reshaped. The most common (non-polymer) example is ceramic materials. This group of materials includes:

■ cements, concretes, refractory materials, for example, firebricks that may be used in applications such as domestic (gas) fires and industrial kilns

■ house and engineering bricks

■ products such as plant pots, paving slabs and wall tiles.

Table 2 *Examples of non-polymer thermoplastic and thermosetting materials*

Thermoplastic materials	Thermosetting materials
Clay, in the 'wet' state only – used for model making, ceramic figures and sculptures	Clay, once fired at a high temperature – used for plant pots, domestic crockery, wall and floor tiles
Paper – can be reformed once mixed with water (and some new fibres) to make recycled paper	Concrete – once the chemical reaction between the constituent parts has taken place and the product has dried out, then it cannot be remixed/reshaped
Metals – a good example is the steel used in the manufacture of cars. Once separated from other materials, it can be heated to the melting point of steel and reshaped using one of the many processes available for metals	
Glass – though very brittle materials, glasses can be heated to their melting point and reshaped	

Identifying plastics' processes

On close inspection of a product, it is possible to establish the method used to produce it.

Injection moulding

Those products that have been injection moulded usually have a complex 3-D shape that can only be produced by a moulding technique. An example of this would be the components of a computer mouse. The cover of the mouse is a very complex shape with curves and fixings for other components. In addition there are some ejector pin marks – another indicator that injection moulding has been used to produce this component.

Blow moulding

Products that are blow moulded have hollow shapes with one end sealed, while the other end remains open. This includes products such as drums for holding chemicals and liquids, bottles for spring water, etc.

In blow moulding the 'neck' of the product is usually smaller than the outside measurement of the main body.

Surface decoration can be applied. For example, raised (embossed) lettering, a product logo or a recycling symbol. Screw threads can also be incorporated into the neck of the product to secure the lid.

Other signs of blow moulding include the **sprue**, usually at the bottom of the product, and mould seam lines around the outside of the product showing where the mould halves have been joined together.

Trays made by injection moulding

■ Key terms

Sprue: a vertical channel in a mould through which plastic or molten metal is introduced or out of which it flows when the mould is filled.

Rotational moulding

All rotationally moulded products are hollow. There are no sprues, but there will be seam lines where the mould halves have been joined together. As in blow moulding and injection moulding, embossing can also be included.

Thermoforming

Products that are thermoformed (and also vacuum formed) are made from sheet materials. An amount of stretching occurs in both of these processes, making the sides of the product thinner than the base. There are no sprue marks, but there will be marks showing where the product has been cut and removed from the sheet. In addition, thermoformed products contain detail, e.g. lettering, which is sharper than vacuum-formed products.

International symbols

Look at any modern plastic product and somewhere on it will be a symbol that identifies the type of plastic material that has been used in its manufacture (see Table 3).

Table 3 *International symbols for polymers*

SPI code	Type of polymer	Common uses
♲ 1 PETE	PETE (or PET), polyethylene terephthalate	Soft drinks and water bottles; deli and baking trays; oven-safe film and food trays; carpets and fibre filling
♲ 2 HDPE	HDPE, high density polyethylene	Milk, juice, shampoo, butter and yoghurt containers; grocery, rubbish and retail bags; cereal box liners; heavy-duty pipe; bottles for laundry products, oil and car washing fluid
♲ 3 V	V (or PVC), polyvinyl chloride	Pipes, film, clear packaging and carpet backing; containers for non-food items
♲ 4 LDPE	LDPE, low density polyethylene	Bread, frozen food and dry cleaning bags; carrier bags; squeezable bottles
♲ 5 PP	PP, polypropylene	Yoghurt and margarine containers; medicine bottles; car parts, carpets, industrial fibres
♲ 6 PS	PS, polystyrene	Meat trays, cups, plates, cutlery and compact disc sleeves; video- and audio-cassette cases
♲ 7 OTHER	Other (any polymer or combination of polymers not covered by categories 1-6), includes ABS, acrylonitrile butadiene styrene	Reusable water bottles, trays for the microwave; mobile telephone outer cases, computer parts, monitors, keyboard parts

You are expected to have a good level of knowledge of a wide variety of plastics and should understand how these plastics can be applied to a wide range of products.

You should be confident to identify specific plastics used in everyday products, be able to explain how they are manufactured, and why these methods are used. The use of plastics in Product Design and manufacture brings many benefits to the manufacturer and the consumer. You should be able to understand and recall these benefits.

Detergent bottle

Refill packaging

Case study 1: Plastics

Plastics used in detergent packaging: bottled detergents

With the invention of liquid washing detergents, bottle packaging was required. The type of bottle shown in the photograph is commonly used in the storage and retail of such liquid detergents.

It is made from a tough plastic, such as polypropylene, with the top being made from high density polyethylene. Detergent bottles like these are made from durable plastics, so that they can be kept by the consumer for some time and refilled using the sachet-style packaging shown below. As HDPE and PP are thermoplastics, it is possible to recycle the bottles. They can also be made from a percentage of recycled plastics. This is an important consideration for manufacturers, as they are required by legislation to meet ecological targets.

The main body The main body of the bottle is made using blow moulding. This is a relatively fast process that is important in the manufacture of a mass-produced bottle. It is possible to mould in ergonomic features such as a comfortable handle used to carry the bottle and to pour the liquid.

The bottle top The bottle top and pouring spout are injection moulded. This process uses molten plastic injected at high pressure into precision-made dies. It enables the manufacture of accurate components such as the bottle top, complete with textured grip to help in undoing and tightening the lid, and an internal thread for joining the top to the bottle.

Advantages of using plastics The durability of HDPE and PP has obvious benefits to both the manufacturer and the consumer. The main benefit is that the bottles are less likely to burst, either in handling during warehousing and transport or in transit from the shops to home. This is an important functional aspect of bottle packaging.

As plastics are 'self-coloured' by adding a pigment to the polymer, the packaging can be coloured to meet aesthetic requirements. This is very important as colour is a key feature to brand identity.

Disadvantages of using plastics If the consumer does not refill the bottle, the plastics used would be wasted. If the consumer does not recycle the bottle, it would have to go to incineration or landfill. Polypropylene and polyethylene are not biodegradable; therefore landfill is not a particularly good option. The bottle shape is awkward to store, transport and display. This is why this type of bottle is often made with flat sides to minimise such problems.

Sachet detergent packaging This type of packaging was developed shortly after the bottle as a method of refilling bottles. The sachet is retailed at a slightly lower price than a bottle, therefore encouraging consumers to buy these instead of new bottles each time they need more detergents.

The sachets are made from a low density polyethylene film, using the calendaring process. The graphics, branding etc. are applied to the film using offset lithographic printing methods, prior to the polymer being cut and plastic welded into the bag form.

In addition to the sachets being less expensive than the bottle, they are generally much easier to transport. This is because they are lighter and, perhaps more importantly, can flex into gaps, tessellating together inside cardboard boxes or loose on display.

Packaging plays such an important part in the transport and retail of products, designers regularly need to develop new and exciting packaging methods. These can be strongly influenced by changes in consumer tastes or fashion, environmental pressures or developments in technology. Some of these influences will be examined later in the book.

Case study activity

Think of another form of packaging that uses plastics and list the benefits that the use of plastics brings. Some key words you might want to consider when doing this are:
- **function**
- **performance**
- ergonomics
- quality
- cost
- safety.

✔ Product analysis exercise 1: Thermoplastics

Plastic drinks bottle

1. Plastic drinks bottles are made from thermoplastics. Explain what is meant by the term 'thermoplastic'.
2. Name a suitable plastic for a drinks bottle.
3. Explain why this material is suitable.
4. These bottles are made using blow moulding. Use notes and diagrams to explain this process.
5. Name a suitable material for the bottle top.
6. Explain why this material is suitable.
7. Explain how the designer has considered the environment in the development of this bottle.

Key terms

Function: how a product satisfies the intended purpose.

Performance: how well a product carries out its function.

ℹ Activity

Products such as electrical plugs, saucepan handles, picnic plates and cups are also made from thermosetting plastics. Use the internet to find out which specific plastics are used and why.

Further reading

This has been just a brief look at polymers and their uses. Within each major type of polymer (e.g. polystyrenes) there are hundreds, if not thousands, of variations. To cover them all is beyond the scope of this book. If you do wish, however, to delve deeper into plastics then there is a range of publications available to help you, including:
- R. A. Higgins, *Materials for the Engineering Technician, Third Edition*, Arnold
- Norman, Cubitt, Urry and Whittaker, *A Level Design and Technology, Third Edition*, Longman.

■ Key terms

Fibre-reinforced polymers (FRP): for example, carbonfibre-reinforced polymer, Kevlar-reinforced polymer, and glass-reinforced plastic. These are composites that are made by combining a woven material, such as carbon fibre, with a polymer resin and a catalyst to make a strong, lightweight material.

Fibre-reinforced composite: a material that is made up of resins and fibres. Can also refer to materials such as reinforced concretes, where reinforcing rods (fibres) have been added to the mix.

Particle-based composites: composites that consist solely of particles of two or more different materials, e.g. cermets and concrete.

Warping: deforming in timber due to uneven drying.

AQA Examiner's tip

Composite materials are a subject area that you should become familiar with. You will need to be able to name composites and their main constituent parts. You should also be able to provide examples of where they are used.

■ Further reading

If you wish to study man-made boards in greater depth, a useful source would be:

■ *Focus CD-ROM Resistant Materials 2, Focus Educational Softward Ltd.*

■ Composite materials

Composites are produced by mixing together two (or more) different materials. The main advantage of doing this is that the properties from each of the materials can be enhanced and utilised.

For example, plastics have useful strength and rigidity with lightweight and good electrical insulation properties. These general characteristics can be enhanced by adding other materials to produce **fibre-reinforced polymers (FRP)**. Adding plasticisers to polymers makes the polymers easier to process by improving their flow properties (see p4 for more details of additives for polymers). By adding strands (fibres) of glass to polyester resins, a very tough, rigid, lightweight material can be produced, i.e. glass-reinforced plastics (GRP).

Carbon fibre composite products are manufactured in a similar way to GRP. The carbon fibres (extracted from the polymer polyacrylonitrile by heating) are mixed with a resin, then heated in a mould to produce a composite that is much stronger than GRP. Its strength makes it suitable for producing the protective components for a modern Formula One racing car, or for high performance sports or aerospace products.

Kevlar is another special composite that has good protective properties due to the materials used and the way it has been processed (see pp23–24).

Types of composite material

There are three main groups of composite materials:

■ **fibre-reinforced composites**
■ **particle-based composites**
■ sheet-based composites.

The most important of these are the fibre-reinforced composites, since these are more commonly used in the manufacture of products.

The diagram on p21 gives examples of materials found in the three composite groups:

The term 'man-made boards' refers to those sheet or moulded materials where wood or wood fibre are bonded together to form a 'new' material.

Advantages of man-made boards

■ They have increased stability against **warping**.
■ They have equal strength in all directions – unlike natural timbers.

Common fibre-reinforced composites

Here are the general characteristics of fibre-reinforced composites:

■ They have a good strength to weight ratio (i.e. light in weight with low density and strong compared to their weight).
■ They are resistant to corrosion.
■ They have a good fatigue resistance.
■ They possess a low thermal expansion.

◨ *Glass fibre*

■ Glass used in glass-reinforced plastic (GRP) is spun to produce a fibre that is then coated to aid bonding to the resin.
■ Fibres of glass are available in a variety of gauges (thicknesses) from coarse ($30\,\mu m$) to very fine ($5\,\mu m$). *(Note: $1\,\mu m = 0.001\,mm$)*

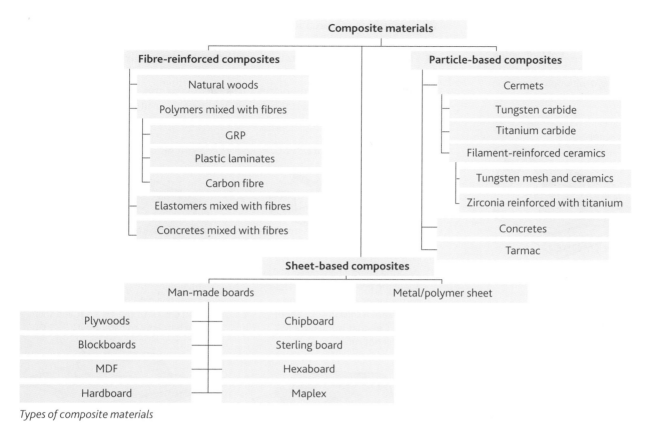

Composite materials

Fibre-reinforced composites
- Natural woods
- Polymers mixed with fibres
  - GRP
  - Plastic laminates
  - Carbon fibre
- Elastomers mixed with fibres
- Concretes mixed with fibres

Particle-based composites
- Cermets
  - Tungsten carbide
  - Titanium carbide
  - Filament-reinforced ceramics
    - Tungsten mesh and ceramics
    - Zirconia reinforced with titanium
- Concretes
- Tarmac

Sheet-based composites

Man-made boards — Metal/polymer sheet

Plywoods	Chipboard
Blockboards	Sterling board
MDF	Hexaboard
Hardboard	Maplex

Types of composite materials

Table 4 *A range of man-made boards*

Type of board		Common uses
Plywood		Backs of furniture, e.g. cabinets, bottoms of drawers, panelling; can be flexible for producing curved shapes
Block board		Generally used for tabletops and furniture carcasses
Stirling board		Flooring for sheds and workshops; also used for roofing and shuttering for casting concrete
Chipboard		Knockdown furniture, kitchen cupboards and worktops; usually veneered or laminated for furniture; also used for flooring
Medium Density Fibre board (MDF)		Furniture sides acting as a base for veneers; pattern making for castings
Hardboard		Backs of cupboards and drawer bottoms of kitchen units; can be supplied pre-coated

■ **Key terms**

Laying up: the act of laminating, for example, glass fibre matt and coating it with polyester resin.

■ A mould is required for GRP. This can be produced quite cheaply from a range of materials including woods, metals and polymers.

■ **'Laying up'** is the term used for the processes involved in manufacturing with GRP.

■ Inserts, e.g. mounting plates for securing fixtures, etc., can be included as the material is being 'laid up'.

1 Coat the mould all over with a releasing agent.

2 Wearing polythene gloves, apply the gel-coat to the mould with an even brushing action to achieve a thickness of about 1mm. Gel-coat is thixotropic and will not run.

3 Cut up the glass fibre matt into the minimum number of pieces that will cover the mould in three laminations. Add colour to the gel-coat and then the hardener to catalyse it.

4 When the gel-coat has cured, after about 30 minutes, coat it with a layer of catalysed lay-up polyester resin. On to this lay the first lamination of glass fibre matt. Stipple the matt using a stiff brush until it is thoroughly wetted and all air is driven out. Repeat with successive layers. Use surfacing tissue as the final lamination for an improved surface.

5 Leave for about 40 minutes while you clean all brushes and tools thoroughly. After this time, the edges can be carefully trimmed using a sharp knife.

Finished pond liner

6 Wait at least another 3 hours before separating the work from the mould. Full hardness is achieved after curing in approximately 24 hours, after which time it will be possible to work with wood- and metal-working tools.

Stages involved in the use of GRP

◤ *Carbon fibre matting*

This well-known material has come to the fore in recent years in its association with a variety of sports, e.g. Formula One racing cars, tennis racquets, fishing rods, etc.

The carbon fibres used in this material are produced by heating polyacrylonitrile filaments through a range of temperatures up to 2000 °C. This process effectively removes all other elements, leaving only long chains of carbon atoms ensuring a high strength, lightweight material.

Initially carbon fibre-based products were expensive to produce due to the processes required to produce the fibres. However, as these processes continue to develop, manufacturing costs continue to fall.

Processing with carbon fibres

Stages of the process

Step 1   Carbon fibres are available in the form of woven **matt**, which is cut to the shape of a pattern using ceramic scissors.

Step 2   The material is placed into a mould half, where it is impregnated with resin and forced into the shape of the mould.

Step 3   The mould halves are fixed together and everything is placed in an oven, where it is held at a temperature of 170 °C for up to 8 hours to promote the rigid cross-links in the resin.

Laying up carbon fibres in the mould

Kevlar

Kevlar is a mixture of aromatic and aramid (nylon-like) molecules. These are melted and spun into fibres. The long-chain molecules are held together by strong hydrogen bonds. These fibres are always oriented parallel to the length of the fibres giving the material its very high strength. Weight for weight, Kevlar is five times stronger than steel and about half the density of fibreglass.

How does Kevlar work?

Kevlar fibres are woven into a 'cloth', which can then be fashioned into protective equipment. It protects the wearer by operating essentially as a net – in the same way that a goal net will absorb the force of a football being kicked into it. All the horizontal and vertical fibres absorb some of the impact. Kevlar can absorb impacts that would cause serious injury to an unprotected human body. The wearer is still affected by the impact, but saved from serious injury.

Uses of Kevlar

Kevlar is used in a wide variety of applications because of its unique properties, including:

- body protection, such as bullet-proof vests where lightweight properties, comfort and flexibility are important
- sports equipment, such as skis, helmets and racquets, where lightweight properties and strength are important
- sails for windsurfing, where the material has to withstand high speeds
- run-flat tyres that will not damage the wheel rim
- gloves for use in the glass and sheet-metal industries.

Activity

GRP matting is laid up with each layer lying across the one below, rather than all the fibres running in the same direction.

Explain what the likely outcome would be if the fibres did all face the same way.

Key terms

Matt: loosely woven fibres that make up the material once resins have been added.

AQA Examiner's tip

When writing answers that include reference to high performance materials such as Kevlar and Carbon fibre you should be able to provide a range of possible applications.

Arrangement of Kevlar fibres

Kevlar body armour

General properties of Kevlar:

■ High strength to weight ratio.
■ Low electrical conductivity.
■ High chemical resistance.
■ High toughness.
■ High cut-resistance.
■ Flame-resistant and self-extinguishing.

Applications for fibre-reinforced composites

Table 5 Typical uses of fibre-reinforced composites

Composite	Common uses
Glass-reinforced plastic (GRP)	A mixture of glass fibres and polyester resins, used in: the manufacture of some vehicle bodies; the front sections of some locomotive engines and sports equipment, e.g. canoes and boat hulls
Carbon fibre	A mixture of carbon fibres and resin, used in: the manufacture of sports equipment, e.g. tennis racquets, bicycle frames, etc.; the manufacture of artificial limbs
Kevlar	A mixture of aramid and aromatic fibres interwoven into a cloth, used in body armour and sports equipment
Plastic laminates (Tufnols)	Cotton/resin composites, used in the manufacture of gears and cams giving quieter operation than metal components and greater wear resistance
Plastic laminates	Mixtures of resins and paper, used to produce worktops for kitchens

Reinforced concrete

Concrete is classed as a particle-based composite. Concretes are generally very good when subjected to compressive loads, e.g. foundations for a building, but very poor when in tension, e.g. when used as a beam that spans a distance.

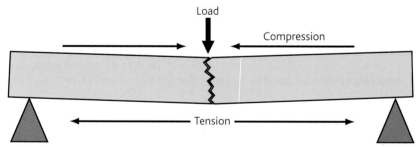

Non-reinforced concrete may crack under tension

We are looking at this material in the fibre-reinforced composites section because, in order to combat the possibility of failure under tension, reinforcing bars can be placed in the concrete shuttering prior to casting the concrete. These reinforcing bars will then become surrounded by, and gripped by, the concrete.

The inclusion of reinforcing bars has led to the design of longer spans in bridges and buildings. However, there is still some potential for cracking in places where the beam/structure is under tension, i.e. on the underside of the beam. This has led to a process where the reinforcing bars are put under tension prior to and during the casting of the concrete structure.

Once set, the tension is released on the bars having the effect of placing that part of the structure under compression. This means that the beam/structure is better able to withstand heavier loads or bridge longer spans. The diagram below shows the effect of the use of high-tensile reinforcing bars in concrete.

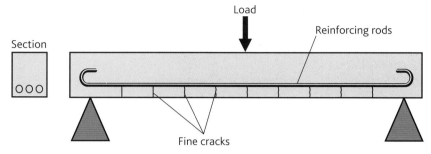

Surface cracks may still be evident with ordinary reinforced concrete

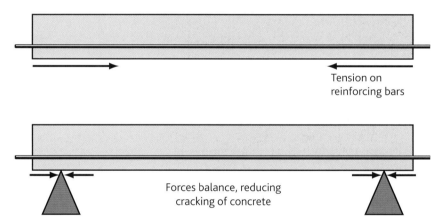

Pre-tensioned reinforcing bars greatly reduce surface cracks

Particle-based composite materials

The general characteristics of particle-based composites are:

■ They have a high strength in compression, as in the case of concretes; less so in tension.
■ They have good stability.
■ They have a uniform structure ensuring consistent strength.
■ They are generally free from surface defects.

Concrete

Concretes are made up of materials known as aggregates, as well as sand and cement. The characteristics of the final concrete material are determined by the ratio of the constituent parts.

■ **Activity**

Carry out some research into concretes and find the mixture ratio for the construction of a garden path or driveway.

Concrete is thoroughly mixed while it is dry. Water is then added. Mixing continues until every particle of aggregate and sand is coated in cement paste (this is the bonding agent). Once cast, the concrete is left to harden. During hardening, the temperature of the mix will rise; this is due to the chemical reactions that take place.

Advantages and disadvantages of concrete

Advantages

- It can be moulded into complex shapes.
- It has properties similar to stone.
- Components are more readily extracted than stone.
- It can be cast in situ (on site), whereas stone has to be quarried and cut to shape.
- It is good in compression.

Disadvantages

- It is poor in tension, making it necessary to reinforce the concrete when spanning large distances.

Cermets

Cermets are another group of particle-based composites. These are mixtures of both metal and ceramic particles. An example of a common cermet is tungsten carbide – a combination of the ceramic tungsten carbide and the metal cobalt. This material is used extensively for cutting tools, as it keeps its edge very well.

Other examples of cermets include a mixture of aluminium oxide and cobalt, used in the manufacture of components for jet engines.

Advantages and disadvantages of cermets

Advantages

- They are resistant to high temperatures.
- They are tough and shock-resistant.

Disadvantages

The very nature of the component materials of a cermet such as tungsten carbide (i.e. brittle, high melting point metal and ceramic materials) exclude processing in the same way as materials which melt at lower temperatures. Sintering, therefore, is one of the few processes suitable for cermets (see p49).

Sheet-based composites

We have touched on sheet-based composites in the introduction to this section by discussing man-made boards, such as plywood, block board, and their applications.

Metal/polymer composites

More recent developments have seen the introduction of metal/polymer composites. An example of this type of material is ALU composite. This material is a **laminate** of, generally, 0.3 mm thickness **aluminium** sheet sandwiching a polyethylene core. The overall thickness is about 3 mm. This results in a lightweight material that has excellent rigidity along with good impact resistance.

The material can be shaped by sawing, drilling or milling and cut with shears, and can be formed by rolling without distorting the polymer core.

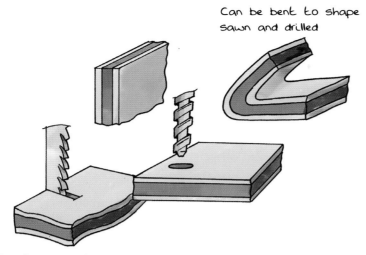

Can be bent to shape
sawn and drilled

Cross section of ALU composite

Advantages of this type of material include good sound and vibration damping qualities along with good thermal insulation characteristics combined with good strength. Applications can be found in the automotive industry where it is used for vehicle skins. This results in a much reduced level of road noise for the occupants. Other applications include partitions as well as uses in boats.

Products where traditional materials have been replaced by composites

Kitchen knives and flooring are two examples where traditional materials have been replaced by composites.

Kitchen knives

Traditionally knives for use in the kitchen have been made from a range of materials, including stainless steel. They are very tough and **corrosion**-resistant but do not keep their sharp edge very well, resulting in the need for re-sharpening.

Modern processing techniques have enabled the fusion of tungsten carbide onto the cutting edge.

Advantages and disadvantages of tungsten carbide on the cutting edge

Advantages

■ It results in a much more durable cutting edge.

■ There is a reduced necessity for re-sharpening.

Disadvantages

■ When the food is being cut, care must be taken not to cut further into materials below, e.g. the chopping board. The blade is hard enough to cut through ceramic glaze, most metals and certainly woods.

Flooring

Flooring used in the construction of modern houses is now largely chipboarding, whereas traditionally it would have been solid wooden floorboards. The edges of the chipboard sheets are also tongued and grooved in the same way that floorboards are.

i **Activity**

1 For each of the following composites, list as many applications that you can think of where they are used:

   a glass-reinforced plastic

   b concrete

   c carbon fibre

   d Kevlar

   e laminated glass.

2 Draw up a revision table for each of the composites from Activity 1 a-e. Your table should include details of the constituent parts (the ingredients) of each composite and the properties of the composite.

Practical activity

1 In pairs or small groups take a camera on a trip around your school or college. Photograph a range of (up to 10) different products that are made from composite materials. (These can be individual products or parts of the fixtures and fittings.)

   Create a collage of these in a short PowerPoint presentation. Add notes to:

   a identify a product and its function

   b name the composite material and state its component parts

   c state what non-composite materials the current material is replacing.

2 Most public buildings and large architectural structures include concrete either in foundations or in the building itself. Use the internet to:

   a find out how concrete structures are produced and,

   b give at least three examples of where concrete has played a major part in a structure.

Advantages and disadvantages of chipboard flooring

Advantages

- Large areas can be covered with one sheet.
- The cost is reduced.

Disadvantages

- Chipboard flooring would not be left on display as floorboards could, but must be covered in a flooring product such as a carpet.

Case study 2: Composite materials

Carbon fibres in bicycles

One of the most famous applications of carbon-fibre reinforced plastic is in the development and manufacture of the Lotus bicycle, designed by Mike Burrows and ridden by Chris Boardman in the 1992 Barcelona Olympics. Boardman achieved the gold medal.

Burrows, an engineer, cyclist and racer of recumbent cycling machines, had been using composites such as Kevlar, GRP and carbon fibre to make the aerodynamic body shells for his recumbent bikes. Realising the immense strength, low weight and ease of forming these materials, Burrows set about developing a new type of frame for a racing bike.

The traditional aluminium **alloy** bike frame is quite heavy when compared to composites such as carbon fibre. The aluminium alloy frame is made in a tubular construction and the tubes, being relatively wide, offer resistance to airflow (called drag). This slows the bike down.

Burrows produced a prototype monocoque (single-piece shell frame) by laminating carbon fibre over wooden moulds, producing two halves, which were then glued together with resin and reinforced with more carbon fibre. The resulting frame was very lightweight and much thinner than a traditional tubular bike frame, while still maintaining the strength of an alloy frame. This thin, almost wing-like frame, offered reduced wind resistance. In making the prototype, Burrows used the expertise of Lotus – famous for performance sports cars – in their use of advanced materials such as carbon fibre. After Burrows added the mechanical parts to the frame, Lotus conducted wind tunnel experiments with Boardman to find the riding position that would offer least wind resistance. Carbon fibre was also used to manufacture a rather striking, cone-shaped helmet that Boardman used to help the air flow over his head and down the line of his back.

The resulting design helped cut seconds off Boardman's lap time, and he comfortably took gold at the Olympics. This revolutionary bike design is now used by other bicycle racers world-wide.

Chris Boardman on a Lotus Superbike

Key terms

Alloy: a mixture of two or more metals with the aim of enhancing particular properties.

✓ Product analysis exercise 2

Glass-reinforced plastics

1 Glass-reinforced plastic is often used in products such as boats, sports equipment, water tanks and car body panels. Explain why GRP is suitable for such products.

2 Use notes and diagrams to explain how such products are manufactured using GRP.

3 An alternative to GRP might be carbon-fibre reinforced plastic. Explain the advantages of using this.

4 Materials such as FRP and GRP are known as composites. Define the term 'composite'.

5 Describe the health and safety precautions you would take when using composites such as FRP and GRP.

A yacht made from composite materials

Metals

Along with woods, metals have been in use for a thousand years or more and are seen as traditional materials. The passage of time has seen these materials develop into a wide range of metals and alloys, all with a variety of useful properties and characteristics.

You need to learn and understand the range of metals available, their general characteristics and properties along with examples of uses.

You also need a good level of understanding of how metals can be processed; this will also include the use of some basic heat treatments.

You should also be aware of corrosion processes that can affect metals.

Types of metal

The range of metals available can be classed as either **ferrous** or **non-ferrous**. Within these two groups, metals can be further separated into **alloys** or **non-alloys**. The diagram below shows how the more common metals are related.

■ Key terms

Ferrous metals: metals that contain iron (ferrite) and carbon.

Non-ferrous metals: metals that do not contain iron (ferrite).

Ferrous alloys: a mixture of two or more metals – at least one of which contains iron (ferrite) and carbon.

Non-ferrous alloys: mixtures of two or more metals – none of which contain iron (ferrite).

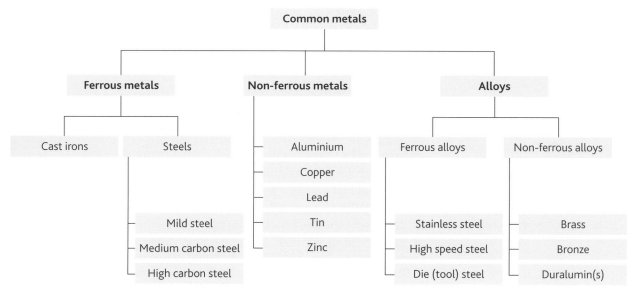

How common metals are related

Key terms

Iron: iron (ferrite) is converted from its ore by heating. The resulting impurities (slag) are removed from the furnace leaving a soft greyish metal once cooled. Iron is rarely used without combining with carbon; this gives it greater strength. The result of this combination is steel. This can be alloyed with other metals in order to enhance particular properties.

Crystal: the main building block of most, if not all, metals.

Steel: a mixture of iron and carbon. The amount of carbon present in the material determines the material's initial strength. Alloying with other metals enables specific properties such as strength, toughness and resistance to corrosion to be enhanced.

Carbon: carbon is an element found in a range of materials. Carbon is found in most organic materials; materials such as coal and diamond are made up purely of carbon. The amount of carbon in a steel has the effect of increasing strength and hardness. (See also: heat treatment.)

Sources of metals

Gold is the only metal that is found in a useable form; all other metals are found as ores. Table 6 shows the ores for individual metals.

Table 6 *Common metals and their ores*

Metal	Ore
Iron	Magnetite, haematite
Copper	Chalcopyrite
Aluminium	Bauxite
Lead	Galena
Tin	Cassiterite
Zinc	Zinc blende

Availability of metal ores

- 25 per cent of the Earth's crust is made up of metal ores.
- Aluminium is the most common ore, followed by **iron**.
- In general, the more rare the material, the more expensive it is. (However, some of the more common ores, e.g. aluminium, can be expensive to process.)

The structure of metals

All metals are made up of **crystals**. Each crystal has a boundary that is firmly bonded to the boundary of a neighbouring crystal.

The nature of the crystal depends very much on the material. For example, **steel** is made up of iron and carbon so these elements will be seen within the microstructure of the material.

Ferrous metals: iron and steel

Iron is produced directly from its ore through the use of a blast furnace. The material that is produced is called 'pig iron' and is not of a sufficiently high quality to be of any commercial use.

Pig iron is 'converted' into steel by the introduction of **carbon** into its structure. This process is carried out in a basic oxygen furnace.

An alternative steel-making process is the electric arc furnace – more often used in the production of specialist steels.

Iron and carbon

Iron is generally soft and ductile, which does not make it a very commercially useful material. When carbon (a very hard, brittle element) is mixed with the iron the characteristics (properties) of iron are greatly improved. The result is a harder and tougher material – steel (see Table 7). Increasing the carbon content has the following effects:

- The material becomes harder, i.e. the effect increasing in the direction of the arrow.
- Toughness reduces and, indeed, cast iron can be brittle under impact.
- Both medium and high carbon steel can be heat-treated to make them even stronger and harder, so producing materials that are of sufficient hardness and strength to be formed into cutting tools. Mild steel, while containing some carbon, has insufficient carbon in its structure to enable it to be heat-treated in the same way.

Further reading

If you would like to learn more about the sources and structure of metals then a useful resource would be:

- Higgins, *Engineering Metallurgy Part 1 – Applied Physical Metallurgy, Fifth Edition*, Hodder and Stoughton.

Table 7 *Types of steel*

Base material	Additional element, carbon	Type of steel	Ductility	Hardness	Toughness
Iron	<0.3%	Low carbon steel (mild steel)			
	0.3–0.6%	Medium carbon steel			
	0.6–1.7%	High carbon steel			
	3.5%	Cast iron			Brittle

Table 8 *Typical uses for steels and cast irons*

Name	Common uses
Mild steel	Nuts, bolts, washers, car bodies, panels for cookers and other white goods
Medium carbon steel	Springs, general gardening tools
High carbon steel	Hand tools, scribers, dot punches, chisels, plane blades
Cast iron	Machine parts, brake discs, engines

■ Non-ferrous metals

Non-ferrous metals do not contain iron. This group of materials includes aluminium, **copper**, lead, zinc and tin; as well as precious metals such as silver, gold and platinum. Although aluminium ore (**bauxite**) is the most abundant ore in the Earth's crust, aluminium is not the most processed metal – steel is. This is because aluminium is more difficult to process, consuming large amounts of energy. It is therefore more costly to produce aluminium.

The production of copper from chalcopyrite is a similarly expensive process requiring the ore to be crushed, followed by a number of refining processes to remove other metals from the ore. Both aluminium and copper require processing by either an electrolytic process or by re-melting; these processes are also required for materials such as tin and zinc.

Table 9 *Non-ferrous metals*

Metal	Melting temperature	Common uses and properties
Aluminium	660 °C	Kitchenware, such as saucepans; when drawn into wire, used in overhead power cables – it is an excellent conductor of electricity
Copper	1083 °C	Electrical contacts, domestic pipe work for central heating and water; in wire form, it is used for electrical cable and wire; also used in jewellery
Gold	1063 °C for fine gold	Primarily thought of as a metal for jewellery, but also has applications in electronics in the form of contacts for switches and credit/telephone SIM cards
Lead	330 °C	A very soft but heavy metal used for flashing between roofs and adjoining brickwork; very durable

■ **Key terms**

Copper: a brownish-looking metal; it can be alloyed with zinc to produce brass, or with tin to produce bronze.

Bauxite: the most common metal in the Earth's crust – can be made into aluminium using processes such as electrolysis.

AQA Examiner's tip

As with the materials we have already looked at you will need to have an understanding of the main types of metals and their overall characteristics. You should also be able to give examples of applications where metals are used.

Platinum	1755 °C	Used as a precious metal in the manufacture of jewellery; is also used in wire form to produce thermocouple cables
Silver	960 °C for fine silver	Used for many years in the manufacture of expensive cutlery and various decorative items; also used in the processing of photographic film
Tin	232 °C	Rarely used in its pure state, but applications include food wrapping (foil) and coating for steel plate in the manufacture of food cans
Titanium	1675 °C	Has a good strength/weight ratio and is a very clean material, making it suitable for surgical applications such as hip replacements; also used for spectacle frames
Zinc	419 °C	Used as a coating for steels, i.e. galvanised steels; used for the manufacture of products such as buckets, and casings for electrical units; can be die-cast to produce high detail products, such as lock mechanisms and small gears

■ **Further reading**

For those interested in jewellery and the metals used in the manufacture of jewellery, a useful resource is:

■ Sylvia Wickes, *Jewellery Making Manual*, Little, Brown and Company.

■ Alloys and alloying

In the same way that composite materials (p20) take the best from both materials for the proposed application, the alloying of metals achieves a similar result, producing materials with enhanced properties.

Individual metals have a limited range of properties that can only be enhanced by heat-treating them in some way. To obtain a better range of properties and characteristics two (or more) metals can be mixed together to produce an alloy.

For example, the addition of zinc to copper produces a much harder and stronger material than pure copper. Alloying changes other characteristics of the material. Mixing copper with zinc to make brass, for example, changes the colour of the metal to a yellow/gold making the material attractive to purchasers.

Table 10 *Common alloys*

Name	Base metal	Composition	Common use
Duralumin	Aluminium	4% copper 1% manganese 0.1% magnesium	Structural components for aircraft
Brass	Copper	35% zinc	Cast valves and taps, boat fittings and ornaments
Bronze	Copper	10% tin	Statues, coins, bearings
Nitinol	Nickel	Nickel, Titanium	Smart metal alloys for making springs and muscle wires

Benefits of alloying

In general, the benefits of alloying metals are that it:

- changes the melting point
- changes the colour
- increases strength, hardness and ductility
- enhances resistance to corrosion and **oxidation**
- changes electrical/thermal properties
- improves flow properties, producing better castings.

💡 Alloying steels

Alloying steels with elements such as chromium and nickel will produce stainless steel – a well-known group of metals with good corrosion resistance, hardness, strength and toughness.

Most metals, steel included, will become less hard and more ductile when heated. By alloying with tungsten, chromium and cobalt, a range of 'high speed steels' can be produced, which do not lose their cutting edges when working at high temperatures (Table 11).

Table 11 *The effects of alloying steels with other elements*

Alloy steel	Alloyed with	Characteristics	Common uses
Stainless steel	Chromium, nickel, magnesium	Tough and wear-resistant; corrosion-resistant	Sinks, cutlery, sanitary-ware,
High speed steel (HSS)	Tungsten, chromium, vanadium	Very hard, will cut while at red heat	Cutting tools, such as drills
Tool and die-steels	Chromium, manganese	Very hard and tough, with excellent wear-resistance	Fine press tools, extruder dies, blanking punches and dies, some hand tools
High tensile steels	Nickel	Good tensile strength and toughness, generally corrosion-resistant	Car engine components

High speed steel (HSS) in action

Work hardening and heat-treating metals

Work hardening is a phenomenon peculiar to metals. Work hardening occurs when the material is 'cold-worked' by, for example, bending, rolling, hammering and drawing.

The processes involved when the material is being worked results in the distortion of the crystals to the point where they become highly stressed, making the material 'harder' in that area.

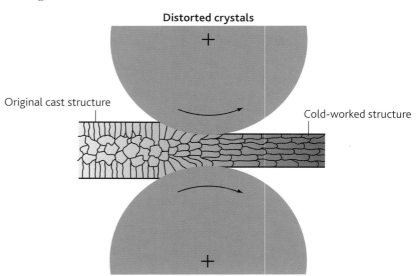

Cold rolling

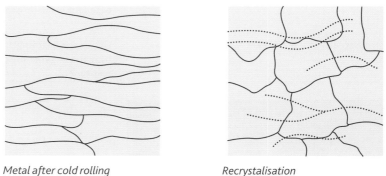

Metal after cold rolling   *Recrystalisation*

In order to return the material to its original 'soft' state the metal must be annealed. When annealing either copper or silver, both materials need to be heated to bright red then allowed to cool slowly in air.

Heat treatments

Heat treatments are those processes of heating and cooling metals in a controlled way, in order to achieve a beneficial change in the properties of the material. The more common heat treatments are:

- annealing
- hardening
- tempering
- **normalising**.

Annealing

Annealing is a heat treatment that reverses the internal stresses associated with work hardening. It is achieved by heating the material to a temperature where the crystals grow, making the material softer and more ductile. The temperature must be maintained for a sufficient amount of time for the material to 'soak' at that temperature. The material should then be allowed to cool very slowly.

Hardening

This heat treatment changes the way the carbon within the steel affects the strength and hardness of the material. When medium carbon steel, for example, is heated to a specific temperature, the carbon in the structure moves out of its normal position.

If the material is then 'quenched' the carbon does not have sufficient time to move back to its original position and so causes internal stresses, which serve to harden, and strengthen, the material.

Tempering

Tempering is the heat treatment that follows the hardening of medium and high carbon steels. If left without being tempered the product that has been hardened will, potentially, be quite brittle – so that with sufficient mechanical shock the product could well fail by cracking or shattering.

Tempering then reduces the amount of brittleness caused by hardening. The materials' internal stresses are reduced, by allowing the atoms and molecules that make up the structure of the material to 'relax' a little.

The amount of tempering given to the material depends on the use. Table 12 gives some examples.

As the tempering temperature rises:

- the material's hardness is reduced
- toughness is increased.

Table 12 *Tempering temperatures*

Colour			Temperature	Uses
Pale straw	harder	less tough	230 °C	Lathe tools
Straw			240 °C	Drills and milling cutters
Dark straw			250 °C	Taps, dies, punches, reamers
Brown			260 °C	Plane irons, lathe centres
Brown-purple			270 °C	Scissors, press tools, knives
Purple			280 °C	Cold chisels, axes, saws
Dark purple			290 °C	Screwdrivers
Blue	hard	tougher	300 °C	Springs, spanners, needles

Quenching

Quenching is the term given to the rapid cooling of heat treated components. Different **quenching** media can be used.

- Brine   Harsh
- Water
- Oil
- Air   Soft

Key terms

Annealing: a process of heating a metal that has been work hardened. 'Soaking' the metal at an appropriate annealing temperature allows the crystals to reshape, so relieving internal stresses that cause work hardening.

Annealed glass: glass is cooled very slowly in an oven called a 'lehr' to reduce internal stresses.

Hardening: hardening of steels is carried out by heating the metal (usually steel) to cherry red followed by rapid cooling (quenching). This process is usually followed by tempering to remove any brittleness.

Tempering: a heat treatment process carried out after hardening to remove any brittleness that may be present in the hardened material. The hardened material is cleaned to its natural shiny grey colour. Heat is then applied and when the correct **tempering colour** is seen the material is then rapidly cooled (quenched).

Tempered glass: another term for toughened glass.

Tempering colour: the colour seen on a piece of steel that will indicate an appropriate temperature to remove brittleness from the material.

Quenching: the term given to the rapid cooling of a metal following a heat treatment.

AQA Examiner's tip

There are a number of specialist terms associated with metals and their heat treatments. You should become familiar with these and be able to use them appropriately in your answers.

The amount of agitation given to the product in the media also determines the rate of cooling and prevents rapid local cooling, which may result in cracks.

Normalising

Normalising is a heat treatment process where the crystal structure is allowed to become uniform, i.e. the crystals become a similar size.

The process includes heating the piece of work (e.g. a forged component) to a specific temperature where the crystal structure begins to change. This temperature is maintained ('soaked') until all of the crystals have been refined. The workpiece is then cooled in air, to produce a material with additional toughness and greater ductility.

Age hardening

Age hardening is not a process in the conventional sense of the word, since no heat is applied to the metal nor is it manipulated in any way. It has been included in this section simply because it is utilised to enhance the characteristics of the material.

The phenomenon of age hardening applies generally to aluminium/copper alloys (**duralumins**). After heat treating the material is left for a period of time during which the internal structure moves slightly, making the material stronger and harder.

Case hardening

Case hardening is a method of increasing the hardness of steels that do not have sufficient carbon content to affect internal hardening. This basically refers to mild steels (i.e. those with less than 0.3 per cent carbon) and involves the addition of carbon to the outer skin of the material. This outer surface can then be hardened leaving a tough core.

Examples would include cams, where the surface needs to be resistant to the wear being imposed on it while the rest of the material needs to be tough and shock-resistant. Other applications would include gears (e.g. for vehicle gearboxes or industrial applications) where it is only necessary to harden the surface of the gear teeth leaving the remainder of the component in a less brittle state.

There are a number of techniques for achieving this, and all of them involve the component being placed into a carbon-rich atmosphere while being heated to around 950 °C. At this temperature carbon atoms are able to enter the material's structure, building up the carbon content at the surface of the material. The longer the component is left in the carbon atmosphere, the thicker the carbon layer produced.

Carburising is one such method.

Carburising

The component to be case hardened is placed in a ceramic box packed with carbon-rich material, and then heated for a predetermined length of time to produce the thickness of carbon layer required.

Following case hardening the product must be heat treated to ensure the surface is hardened. Here, the material is heated to around 760 °C, then quenched to produce the hard case.

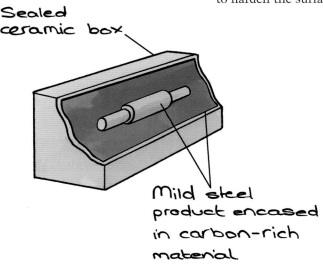

Sealed ceramic box

Mild steel product encased in carbon-rich material

Case hardening

Case hardening

Advantages and disadvantages of case hardening

Advantages

▪ Steels that do not have sufficient carbon for heat treating in the same way as steels with higher carbon contents can be given a hardened surface.

▪ This process leaves a tough inner core, making the material suitable for products such as gears, steering components and camshafts for cars: all of which take a lot of wear.

Disadvantages

▪ In the majority of cases, grain-growth occurs. This needs a machining process, such as surface grinding, to return the material to its required size.

Nitriding

Nitriding is another case-hardening technique that involves immersing the product in the hardening medium for a specified time while being heated – this time to about 500 °C. The medium in this case is nitrogen, while the materials that are case hardened in this way are special steels containing aluminium, chromium and vanadium. Products hardened in this way include components for aero-engines.

Advantages and disadvantages of nitriding

Advantages

▪ No additional hardening is necessary.
▪ It removes the chance of cracking on the surface.
▪ It increases resistance to corrosion.
▪ It's a clean process
▪ It's economical for large numbers.

Disadvantages

▪ Initial set-up costs are high.
▪ If over-heated there is a permanent loss of hardness.

Other hardening methods

Other methods of hardening the surface of a component include flame hardening and induction hardening. Both of these techniques rely on the material used having a carbon content of 0.4 per cent or more, and involve heating the surface only, followed by rapid cooling by a jet of water. Both of these processes can be mechanised and are used for the surface hardness of gears and camshafts.

Advantages of flame and induction hardening

▪ Localised areas of the product can be hardened, leaving those areas unaffected where toughness is required.
▪ Grain growth does not occur with this method of hardening; so additional machining is not required following hardening.

Processing metals

There are numerous processes available for manufacturing products from metals. A number of these processes and techniques can be carried out by hand and are sometimes referred to as 'smithing'. For example, the precision cutting and forming of precious and semi-precious metals by a metal smith or jewellery maker fit into this category.

▪ **Further reading**

A useful resource of information about traditional heat treating methods is:

▪ Tubal Cain, *Hardening, Tempering and Heat Treatment*, Argus Books.

These processes can be divided into three main areas:

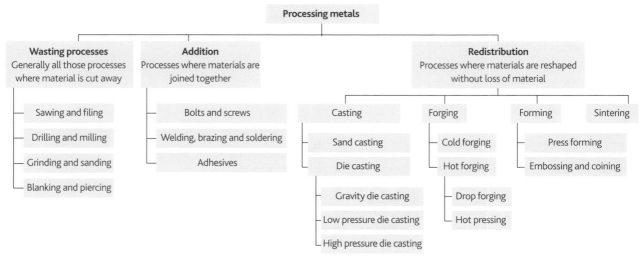

Processing metals

It is clear that a number of processes relate equally well to a number of different types of material. For example, wasting processes like sawing and filing apply equally to woods as they do to plastics as well as to metals. In this section, we will only look at those processes that relate to metals.

Wasting processes (relating to metals)

Blanking and piercing

Sheet metals can be cut to a required shape using punches. These cut through the material using a shearing action, much in the same way that scissors cut through paper.

A guillotine is usually used to cut sheet metal off a roll into useable sheet sizes. These sheets are then passed into either manually operated or automatic machines that will cut the material to shape and/or punch holes into it.

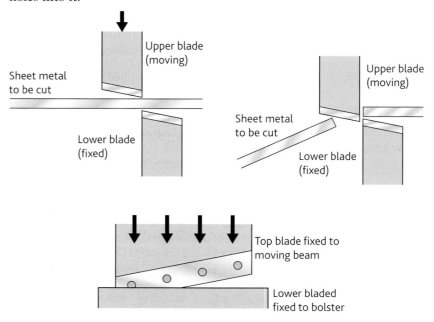

Shear action

When a sheet of metal has a hole punched into it, it has been pierced. When the piece that has been punched out of the sheet is to be used, it is called a 'blank'.

Products, such as soft drinks cans, are made by punching disc-shaped blanks from the sheet material. The process is set up to maximise efficiency with as little waste metal left as possible.

Some products require both blanking and piercing, e.g. casings for desktop computers.

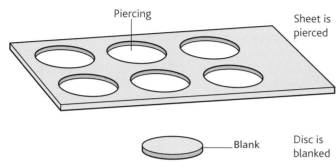

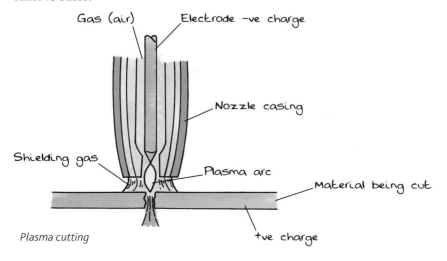

Blanking and piercing

Other cutting processes

Heavyweight products such as armoured tanks, earthmovers and diggers, have components cut from steel sheets that are between 8 mm and 12 mm thick. The normal action of a guillotine or hydraulic punch is inadequate in this case, so other cutting processes are used.

Profile cutting using oxy-acetylene torches has been used for a number of years in, for example, the shipbuilding industry, for cutting large thick sheets of steel to shape prior to **welding** into position in the construction of a ship.

More modern techniques include plasma cutting and the use of lasers to produce sufficient energy to cut through the thick sections required for diggers and earthmovers, for example.

Plasma cutting

Plasma cutting uses an electric arc to generate the heat energy required, plus the energy of either compressed air or an inert gas such as argon to blast through the material. This process produces very little waste material. A fine cut is achieved with little or no **finishing** required to remove burrs.

Plasma cutting

AQA Examiner's tip

Manufacturing with metals covers a broad range of processes. You should become familiar with the main types of processing and be able to provide examples of where they are used in the manufacture of products.

Key terms

Welding: the general term given to joining primarily metals, and some polymers, by heat fusing the component materials together.

Finishing: refers to the removal of burrs or other blemishes in a material following processing.

Did you know?

Polymers can be 'welded' in one of three ways:

1 with the use of heat to soften the components being joined, followed by the inclusion of a filler material

2 with the use of solvents to melt the polymer chemically at the edges being joined

3 with the use of ultrasound (very high frequency vibrations that agitate the atoms and molecules so they become heated). The material then softens, aiding joining.

Laser cutting

Laser cutting can produce profiles of much finer detail. The width of cut is much narrower than that of plasma cutting, resulting in even less waste material. Laser cutting, as well as plasma cutting, can be automated using fully controlled **CNC** machines resulting in components of consistent quality.

There is a much broader range of materials that can be laser cut compared to those for plasma cutting. Plasma cutting is restricted largely to metals because of their electrical conductive properties whereas laser cutting can be carried out on materials such as paper and card, plywoods and MDF that have been formulated for this type of cutting, as well as plastics such as acrylics, making it an ideal process for jewellery products. Laser cutting can also be used for engraving. The amount of energy emitted by the laser is variable by controlling the power output, but a finer control can be achieved by altering the speed at which the laser travels over the material. Altering the speed and power settings determines whether the material is to be cut or engraved.

The results of laser and plasma cutting

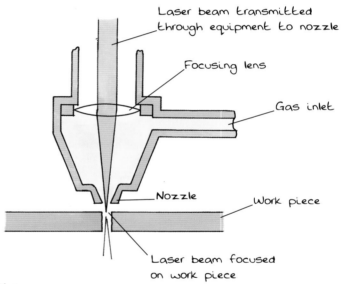

Laser cutting

Processing by redistribution

Forming materials to shape can be achieved by a number of processes, the use of which depends on the type of product being produced and the nature of the material being used.

Processes associated with redistribution techniques include:

■ press-forming
■ forging
■ casting
■ moulding.

These processes include hot- and cold-working techniques. The term 'redistribution' refers to the shaping of the material either cold, heated or as molten material. Examples include the sheet metal forming of a drinks can or car body, the forging of heated metals into shape to produce coins, tools or axles for vehicles, and the casting of molten metals to produce such varied products as sculptures or disc brakes for cars.

Press-forming

Press-forming is carried out with the material at room temperature. The process relies heavily on the ductility of the material being pressed. If insufficiently ductile, the material may have to be annealed to increase its ductility.

Press-forming is carried out using a punch and a die which are both manufactured from toughened die-steel; this makes them resistant to impacting loads, and wear from contacting the material being pressed.

Car body panels are pressed from mild steel sheet to produce the vehicle's overall shape once assembled. The complex shapes produced require the generation of very high stresses to overcome the resistance of the material being pressed.

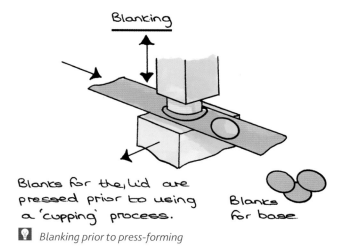

Blanking

Blanks for the lid are pressed prior to using a 'cupping' process.

Blanks for base.

💡 *Blanking prior to press-forming*

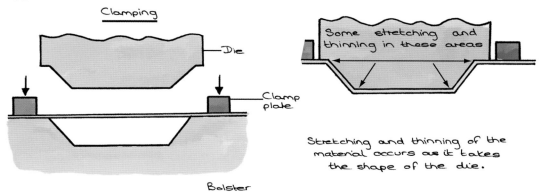

Clamping

Die

Clamp plate

Bolster

Some stretching and thinning in these areas

Stretching and thinning of the material occurs as it takes the shape of the die.

Sheet metals being pressed

There are advantages of pressing a sheet material to a more 3-D shape, including that of greatly increased stiffness. This, in effect, has the benefit of reducing the amount of material necessary to build the vehicle to a good safety standard.

In addition to forming to shape, press tools can also incorporate shears to cut sections away. If we look again at the completed car body panel, we can see the holes have been cut to form door pillars and windows.

Other examples of press-formed sheet materials include domestic radiator panels, kitchen products such as meat trays, and cooker tops.

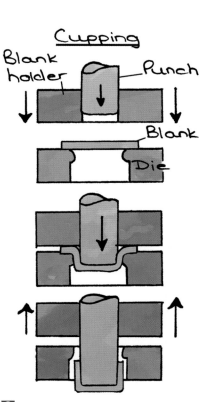

Cupping

Blank holder

Punch

Blank

Die

Press-formed car body panel

💡 *Cupping*

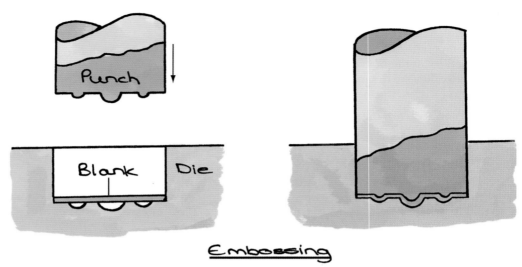

Embossing

Embossing

Embossing

This process is similar to press-forming in that it is used to change the 3-D shape of the sheet material. The main difference is that embossing is used to create decorative features with some quite intricate detail.

Examples of embossing include jewellery, confectionery tins, paper and card products such as letter-headed paper and greetings cards.

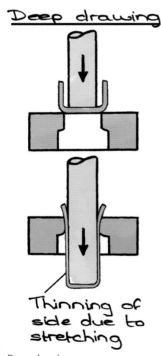

Deep drawing

Deep drawing

Forming sheet metals into the required shape means the material undergoes a number of processes. Exactly which processes are used will be determined by the product being made.

Continuing with the example of the soft drinks can (see p39), the blanked discs are formed into a cup shape using, as the name suggests, the 'cupping process'.

In order to obtain the elongated shape of the can, the cupped shape is then deep-drawn. This requires the material to be pushed through a series of forming rings, which employs the material's property of ductility allowing the material to be drawn out without fracture.

■ A phenomenon of deep drawing is reduction in the wall thickness of the can. It is quite possible that the wall thickness has been reduced to a third of the thickness of the base, to accommodate the elongation of the side.

■ During deep drawing, the base of the can is formed by press-forming.

■ Other processes are used to shape the neck of the can prior to filling and sealing the top to the can body.

Benefits of forming

Car bodies are good examples of products manufactured by forming, in this case using press-forming.

Spinning is a traditional process used for forming 3-D hollow objects from flat sheet metals. The process involves a measured circular sheet of material (this can be aluminium, brass, copper, mild steel or stainless steel) which is gripped in a machine similar to a lathe.

Activity

Create a series of sketches showing how a stainless steel kitchen sink may be produced. Use the stages shown above as a guide.

One of the supports for the material is the former around which the material is to be forced to 'flow' as the diagram shows.

Products manufactured in this way include saucepans and woks, prior to having a handle fitted. The tell-tale signs of spinning are the concentric lines around the outside of the product, denoting the path of the tool.

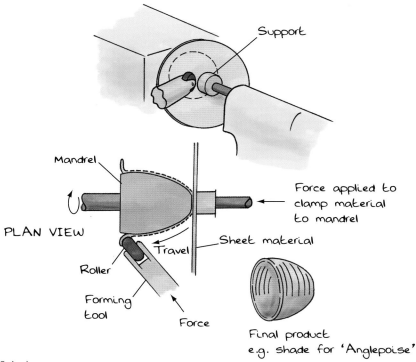

Spinning

Advantages of press-forming

▪ Sheet metal: for most car bodies this is mild steel formed to shape using dies. This gives the material a more 3-D shape, either through simple punching and folding or by stretching into a curved shape.

▪ The act of folding a material gives that material greater stiffness and rigidity (see the activity below). A similar phenomenon is seen when a sheet of mild steel is forced into a 'cup' shape, which again is capable of supporting its own shape as well as additional forces.

▪ The material has been stretched, requiring good ductility in the material. By being stretched, the worked material hardens (see section on heat treating metals, p34–37); since hardness is a by-product of strength, the material's structural strength increases.

So a car body achieves its strength and rigidity by the joining together of a large number of press-formed mild steel components to form a monocoque shape, which does not require an additional chassis. At the same time, weight is kept to a minimum.

Casting processes

Like polymers, metals can be heated to known melting temperatures. When molten, the liquid metal can then be poured (or forced under pressure) into a mould. Moulds can be created from sand, alloy steel or ceramics, depending on the metals being cast.

Activity

Try this for yourself. Take a sheet of paper. On its own it is quite flimsy; now either roll it into a tube or crease it into a fold (or folds). What has happened?

◤ *Sand casting*

In this process, sand is used for the moulds. The sand is especially prepared to contain oils that act as binders to help it hold its shape while the hot metal is being cast into it.

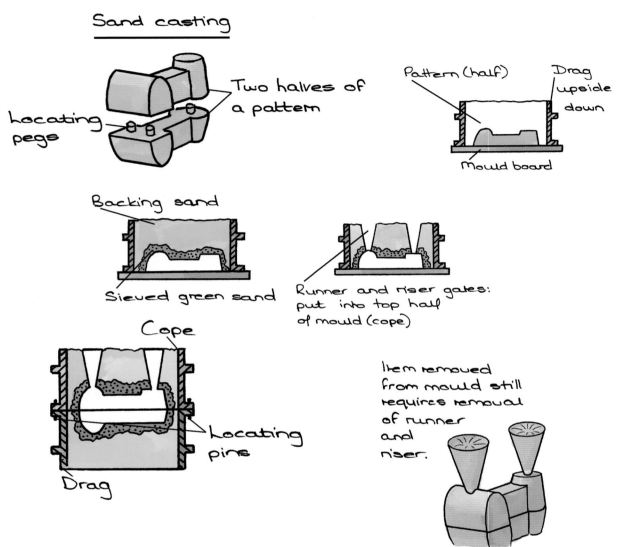

Stages of the sand casting process

Stages of the process:

Step 1   A 'pattern' is made: this could be made from a range of materials such as woods (like yellow pine, jelutong); metals (such as aluminium); polymers (like polystyrene). Patterns can be split for more complex shapes.

Step 2   Each half of the pattern is placed on a baseboard. A mould box half is placed over it.

Step 3   Green sand is 'tamped' around the pattern forcing it into contact with the pattern. This is followed by backing sand (usually recycled sand).

Step 4   The pattern is removed from the mould half. The runner and riser gates are then cut into the top half of the sand mould.

Step 5 The mould halves are fitted together with locating pins, ensuring correct alignment.

Step 6 The molten metal is poured into the running gate. The riser is used to indicate when the mould is full. De-gassing tablets may be necessary to reduce the risk of a porous casting.

Step 7 Once the metal has solidified, the sand mould is broken open leaving the product with runner and riser gates attached. These will be removed either by using a band saw or by some other means, depending on the material being cast.

Advantages and disadvantages of sand casting

Advantages

- Complex 3-D shapes can be produced.
- Cores can be used to produce hollow sections.
- It's appropriate for small runs.
- Automated processes are suitable for longer production runs.

Disadvantages

- Due to the poor surface finish, some machining will be necessary.
- It's not as accurate as die or investment casting.
- It has a low rate of output and is therefore suitable only for small production runs.

Die casting

Die casting is the term used for the processes of casting metals with a low melting point into alloy steel dies (or moulds). It is known as a permanent mould process, and the molten metal either enters the mould under the action of gravity or it is forced into the mould under pressure.

The alloys cast in this way are generally zinc, aluminium and magnesium based alloys. Their low melting temperatures make them particularly useful for large-scale production. (See Table 13.)

The processes involved in die casting vary due to the amount of pressure/ force applied to the molten metal as it enters the mould. In general, the higher the force applied, the quicker the process and the finer the detail being produced.

Gravity die casting

In this process the molten metal is poured into the dies through runners, in a similar way to that seen in sand casting. The process uses the force of gravity to ensure the molten metal reaches all parts of the metal mould.

- The dies are made from alloy steel and are split to allow for removal of the completed product.
- Gas rings around the outside of the die keep the mould heated, ensuring even cooling of the cast metal.
- **Fluxes** are also used to prevent oxidation of the metal as it is being cast.

 Activity

Give at least three examples of sand cast products.

State the material used to manufacture each of the products. Identify further manufacturing processes that the products have undergone.

Table 13 *Metals used in die casting*

Metal used	Melting temperature
Aluminium	660 °C
Magnesium	650 °C
Zinc	850 °C

 Key terms

Flux: a chemical used to prevent oxidation of the material at the joint area just prior to joining.

Did you know?

Borax is used as a flux when joining by brazing. It is known as an 'active flux'; when heated it will clean the joint as well as keep it clean during the joining process.

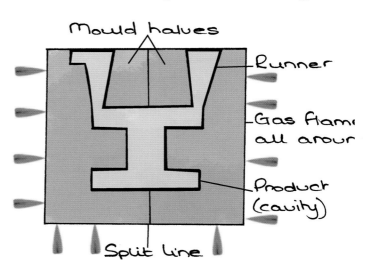

Gravity die casting

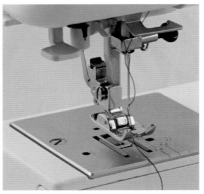

Product made by high pressure die casting

As the name implies, gravity is the only force applied to the molten metal as it enters the die and makes contact with all parts of the die. Therefore products manufactured in this way tend to be large with simple shapes. Examples of products include car and motorbike wheels.

💡 ⬛ *Pressure die casting*

Die casting processes can also use high or low pressures to force the molten material into the die. The additional pressure is required to ensure that the molten metal reaches all parts of the more intricate dies.

High pressure die casting uses a hydraulic ram to force the material into the die.

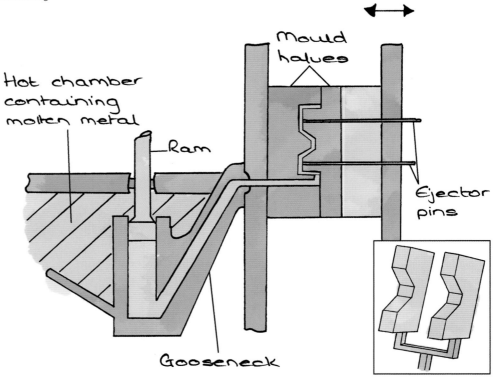

Hot chamber high pressure die casting

Further reading

A useful website with examples of die casting products and the processes involved is: **www.dynacast.com**.

In this process molten metal is poured into a cylinder, either from a crucible or from a ladle. The hydraulic ram then forces the molten metal into the closed dies.

The dies are water cooled, resulting in rapid cooling of the product. As the dies open, ejector pins push the product out of the die.

In the hot chamber high pressure die casting process the molten metal is also forced into the dies by the use of a hydraulic ram but, in this case, the ram is fed directly from the reservoir of molten metal.

Typical products of high pressure die casting include small, highly detailed components. Examples include components for lock mechanisms for uPVC sliding doors.

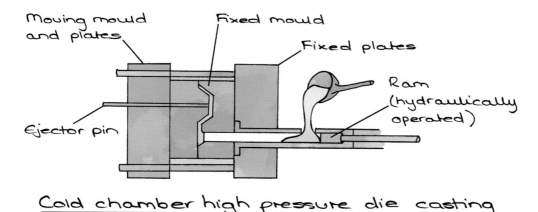

Cold chamber high pressure die casting

🔆 *Cold chamber high pressure die casting*

Industrial die casting

A development of hot chamber die casting is the multi-slide die casting process. Traditional die casting processes use just two halves of a die to form the shape, making it difficult to produce components with very complex 3-D shapes.

By using four (or more) slides, complex 3-D shapes can be achieved. Each of the components of the die is secured to one of the slides and contains either a cavity (external) or core (internal) shape which, when closed together with the other dies, will form the correct shape for the product. Each of the slides moves independently of the other for opening and closing; this is controlled by a computer and operated by pneumatics. Mechanical locking mechanisms hold the dies together while the material is being injected.

Multi-slide die casting is used for the rapid manufacture of small zinc and magnesium components. Products include door locks and sensor casings for cars and the internal components of domestic electrical sockets.

Advantages of die casting

From the products' point of view there are a number of advantages of die casting over sand casting.

- ▣ *Finish* The surface finish of a die cast product is superior to that of sand casting; it's as smooth as the finish of the die surface.
- ▣ *Accuracy* The shape of the die determines the shape of the product, therefore the accuracy of size and detail are as required.
- ▣ *Quality of the material* Die cast products tend to be better from the material's point of view due to the effects on the material structure of rapid cooling.
- ▣ *Scale of production* Rapid cooling of the components (<1 second per cycle) makes high pressure die casting suitable for large-scale production; this is necessary to cover the cost of dies and for the manufacturer to make a profit.
- ▣ *Energy* Alloys with a low melting point require less heat to melt, resulting in lower energy costs.

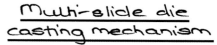

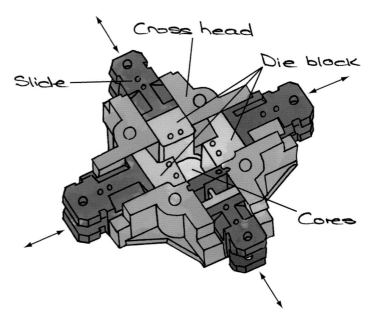

Multi-slide die casting mechanism

Investment casting

Although investment casting is still used for the production of casting
materials with a high melting point, it is an extremely old process.

Stages of the process

Step 1   A wax pattern is produced to a high degree of accuracy.

Step 2   This is then coated in a high temperature ceramic material, by
dipping the wax pattern into the ceramic slip. When a sufficient
thickness of ceramic material is achieved, it is left to dry.

Step 3   Once dry it can be fired in a kiln. This will of course cause the
wax pattern to melt (hence the alternative term for this process
'lost wax casting') leaving the cavity to be cast into.

Step 4   When the ceramic mould has cooled, the molten metal is poured
in. This is generally done using gravity to help fill the mould.

Step 5   When the cast has cooled, the ceramic mould is broken open
thereby destroying it and leaving only the cast product.

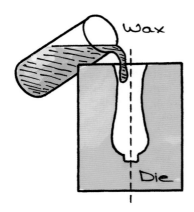

1. Wax pattern is
moulded.

2. Wax runner and
riser attached.
Sprayed with clay.

3. Fired in kiln. This
bakes the clay
hard and removes
the wax.

4. Molten metal
poured in until it
appears at the
riser.

5. After cooling,
the clay mould is
smashed to
remove casting.

6. Heat-treat to
obtain desired
mechanical
properties.

Runner and riser
removed.

The stages of investment casting

Typical products of investment casting are:

- turbine blades for jet engines
- tools and dies for a variety of applications
- motorcycle steering head components
- valves and controls for the food industry.

Advantages and disadvantages of investment casting

Advantages

- Good finishes can be obtained along with a fair degree of accuracy.
- Complicated shapes that cannot be produced by other casting processes can be made.
- Complicated shapes can be produced in materials that cannot be machined.
- There is no split line showing on the product.

Disadvantages

- The cost is very high.
- The size of components is limited by weight.

Sintering

Sintering is the process used in the manufacture of materials that are difficult to process in any other way.

The process of sintering relies on the materials being crushed into a powder. The powder is compacted into a die, which will eventually give the product its final shape. The compacted shape is then heated to promote bonding between the particles of material.

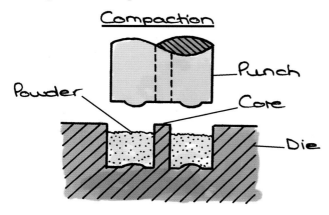

Product being pre-formed by compaction prior to sintering

Typical products manufactured in this way are cutting tool tips and hard magnetic products made from cobalt.

Sintering (or **powder processing** as it is sometimes known) is also used in the ceramics industry. The process is exactly the same as for cermets and metals.

> ### Key terms
>
> **Sintering:** a process whereby powder particles are fused together at their contact points between other particles.
>
> **Powder processing:** the range of manufacturing processes for metal or ceramic powders.

Clay powder with low moisture content is pressed into shape in a hydraulic press. The clay is still in the green state, but can support its own shape until fired in the kiln where the particles of clay powder become bonded together.

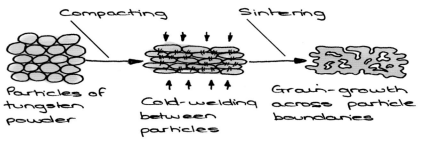

Sintering

Advantage of sintering

■ Sintering is an appropriate process for materials that are difficult to process in any other way.

Forging

Forging processes can be carried out either by hand or machine. Most forging processes are carried out while the metal is hot; this avoids the risk of work hardening and also requires less energy to achieve the required result.

Basic hand processes are carried out with the use of hammers, swages and anvils. Larger forces can be achieved by the use of mechanical hammers. Processes include: bending; drawing down; punching and drifting; twisting and scrolling; and drop forging.

Bending

A bend is produced in the piece being worked; the bend can be either sharp or gradual. A more gradual bend can be achieved with the material cold, while a sharp bend will require the metal to be hot.

Drawing down

This process reduces the thickness of the material but, unlike the drawing process, which stretches the material by putting it under tension, the metal is hammered into a thinner section. This usually results in increasing the length of the piece being worked.

Punching and drifting

Punching is achieved by hammering a spiked tool into the piece being worked, while a drift is used in a similar manner to tidy up the hole that has been produced. Holes can be produced in any shape; it depends on the shape of the punches and drifts.

Twisting and scrolling

These two processes can be carried out with the metal cold or hot – the result will depend on the metal being forged.

All of these processes require manual labour and a high degree of skill, resulting in its suitability for relatively small numbers only.

Products made in this way include wrought iron gates, horseshoes, and stirrup irons for riding.

Activity

Identify three products where manufacturing has involved sintering. Explain why sintering is appropriate in each case.

A horseshoe being shaped by forging

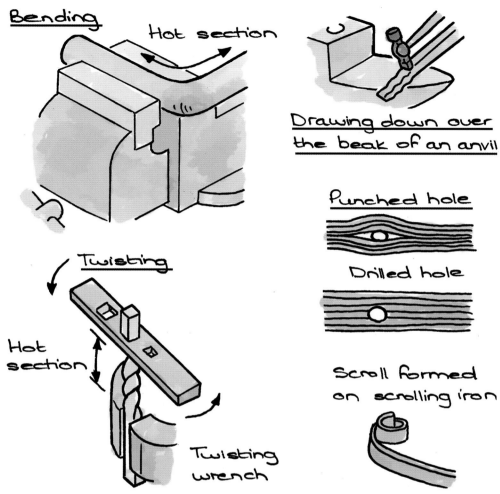

Bending

Hot section

Drawing down over the beak of an anvil

Punched hole

Drilled hole

Twisting

Hot section

Twisting wrench

Scroll formed on scrolling iron

Hand-forging processes

Drop forging

Drop forging is used where larger numbers of similarly shaped objects are required, for example, spanners and hip replacement joints. Drop forging is a refining process. For example, a piece that has been drawn down to a rough shape will be placed between a pair of drop forging dies.

One half (the upper half) is attached to a vertical sliding hammer. Very large forces are exerted onto the metal blank between the die halves, forcing it into the shape of the dies. It is usual that the component being produced will pass through a number of dies before the final shape is achieved.

Products manufactured in this way vary but for the automotive industry cam shafts, stub axles and gears are examples of drop forged products.

Advantages of drop forging

To highlight the advantages of drop forging over casting and cutting to manufacture a product we can use an engineer's spanner as an example. These advantages also apply to other products where large forces may be applied and where it is essential that the product does not fail, e.g. g-clamps, engine pistons and crankshafts.

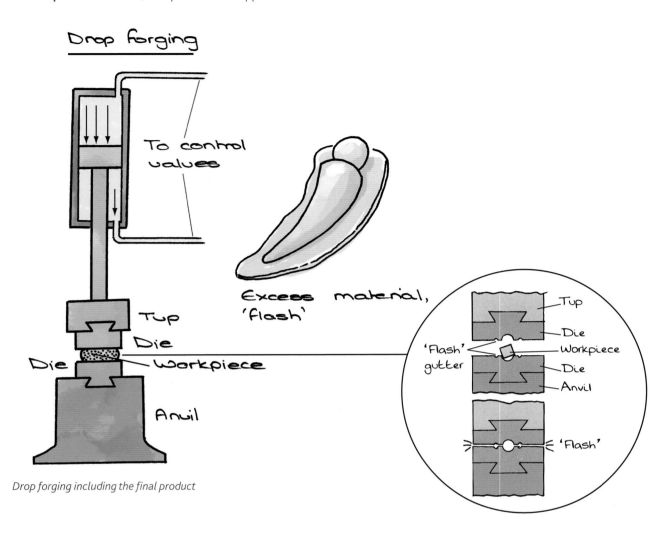

Drop forging including the final product

Further reading

For information on a full range of manufacturing processes, including milling, turning, casting, pressing and several high-tech machining processes, visit: **www.ee.washington.edu**

The function of a spanner is to fit over a nut or bolt head in order for the user to use its leverage to tighten or loosen the nut or bolt. Any failure in the material would render the spanner useless.

Looking at the material structure of a cast iron spanner, it is clear to see that there is no overall direction to the grain. This means that if sufficient force is exerted then there is a good probability that the jaw or handle will fracture.

Materials that have been cut from sheet, on the other hand, have a parallel grain orientation due to the rolling process forming the sheet. Therefore, a rolled steel spanner will be stronger than a cast iron spanner. However, if sufficiently high forces are applied then fracture (or at best distortion) will occur at the points shown.

A spanner that has been drop forged, however, will have its grain refined and orientated to the shape of the die resulting in a tough, strong, durable product.

Cast iron spanner

Possible fracture points

Weakness in these areas will allow spanner jaws to spread when force is applied

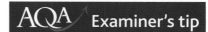
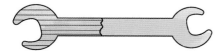

Rolled steel spanner

Where the grain flow follows the shape of the spanner there is greater strength

Forged spanner

 Product analysis exercise 3: Alloys

Pipe fittings, taps and valves

1 Alloys are materials made up of a mixture of two or more metals. For the garden tap shown, name the alloy and list its constituent parts.

2 Explain why the alloy named above is suitable for such products.

3 The garden tap shown has been pressure die cast. Use notes and diagrams to describe this process.

4 Explain why casting is used to make such products.

5 Explain the quality control checks manufacturers would make on such products.

✓ Product analysis exercise 4: Non-ferrous metals

Aluminium drinks can

1 Drinks cans are made from aluminium. Explain why aluminium is a suitable material for drinks cans.

2 The main body of the drinks can has been deep drawn. Use notes and diagrams to explain how this process works.

3 The base of the can is concave. Explain why drinks cans are designed and manufactured this way.

4 Some drinks cans may be made with a steel body and an aluminium top. Give reasons why manufacturers would do this.

Wood

Wood has been used as both a structural material and as a decorative material for thousands of years, to provide shelter, furniture and personal decoration. Wood is probably the oldest known natural material used by humans. Today wood is still used extensively for a variety of applications: from outdoor shelters to fine pieces of furniture, not forgetting, of course, paper making. However, there is a major challenge to preserve resources, in particular the slower growing **hardwood** trees.

You should become familiar with the two main types of this naturally occurring material, and gain an understanding of the material's main properties and characteristics. A good knowledge of the different species together with examples of typical uses should be developed, as should an understanding of the role of man-made boards in the manufacture of timber-based products.

Sources of wood

Wood is a natural material and can be found all over the world with different species found in different areas. Approximately 80 per cent of UK wood needs are supplied by other countries.

Types of wood

There are two basic types of tree, namely hardwoods and **softwoods** (see diagram below). The difference between the two types is botanical, in as much as hardwoods are generally **deciduous** broad-leaved species while softwoods are generally **evergreen.**

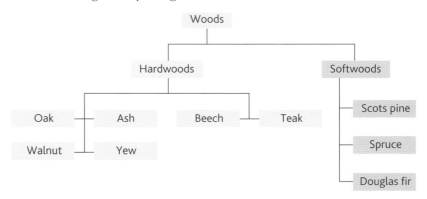

Types of wood

Examples of hardwoods grown in the UK include oak, ash, beech, sycamore and willow; while examples of imported tropical hardwoods include teak, cedar and mahogany.

There are a smaller number of useable softwoods than there are useable hardwoods. Softwoods such as larch, spruce, Scots pine and Douglas fir are grown in forests and plantations in the UK, but approximately 90 per cent of the UK softwood needs are supplied by countries such as Norway and Sweden.

The structure of wood

- All woods are fibrous with the fibres (or **grain**) growing along the length of the trunk or branch.
- These fibres consist of cells (**tracheids**) of, mainly, cellulose supported by **lignin** resin.

■ Approximately 55 per cent of the tree is cellulose, while 28 per cent lignin resin holds it all together. The remainder is made up of carbohydrates, like sugars. Wood can therefore be thought of as a natural composite.

Strength in wood

Being fibrous, wood has its greatest strength in the direction of the fibres. In other words, if a length of timber were to be put under tension along the grain it would be able to support a far greater load than if it were put under tension across the grain, which would result in the timber splitting at a much lower loading.

Defects in wood

Wood is a natural material and therefore is not as consistent in structure as, for example, polymers.

Knots

The main difficulty with woods is that they can contain defects such as **knots**; these are where branches have begun to grow out of the trunk of the tree. Knots can weaken the structure of the material as well as produce an irregular grain.

Conversion

Conversion is the term used when sawing a tree trunk into useable pieces of timber. There are two basic forms of conversion, namely (i) **slab sawn** and (ii) **quarter sawn** (of which there are a variety of methods).

As well as cutting the timber into useable shapes, the choice of conversion method can also enhance the grain and help make the materials more stable.

Slab sawing

Different methods of quarter sawing

Different methods of sawing

Splits in timber

Splits

Other defects include **splits** that occur when the material is drying, or from natural events such as lightning strikes, producing hairline cracks across the grain (more often found in imported hardwoods from Africa).

1. Along the grain

2. Across the grain

Resulting split

The effects of putting timber under tension

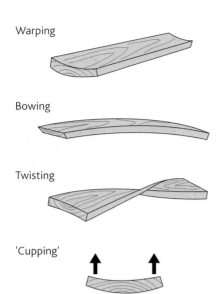

Warping

Bowing

Twisting

'Cupping'

Defects due to drying

Key terms

Shrinkage: all timbers shrink due to moisture lost in seasoning.

Moisture content: the amount of 'water' in the timber. Usually shown as a percentage of volume.

Twisting: a form of warping that is due to a combination of a method of conversion (sawing the trunk of the tree) and uneven seasoning.

Rot: the breaking down of the lignin resins in woods that hold the tracheids (cells) together.

Deathwatch beetle: insect responsible for the destruction of mainly hardwoods, e.g. oak-frame buildings; churches and barns can be affected by the deathwatch beetle.

Kiln drying: a form of seasoning that uses steam in a controlled way to reduce the content of moisture in timber.

Decay: the deterioration of woods. (See dry and wet rot.)

Aesthetics: the features in a product that make it visually appealing, e.g. colour, texture, shaping, styling features.

Shrinkage

Shrinkage occurs as the material is dried out and loses moisture during seasoning. Moisture plays a large part in the use of timbers. For example, if a timber product is to be used outside, then if it were dried to a 5 per cent **moisture content** it would very quickly absorb moisture resulting in the material being more prone to rotting. Conversely, a timber product with a higher than 5 per cent moisture content for indoor use would quite quickly dry out leaving it with unsightly splits and evidence of shrinkage. Warping, bowing, **twisting** and 'cupping' are deformations of the material due to uneven shrinkage.

Dry and wet rot; insect attack

Other defects found in woods include attacks by fungus (dry **rot**), wet rot and attack by insects.

Dry rot reduces the wood to a dry, powdery consistency resulting in little strength.

Wet rot occurs where there are both damp and dry conditions. This alternating cycle breaks the material down by decomposing it.

Insects in the form of, for example, woodworm (seen in softwoods) and **deathwatch beetle** (seen in hardwoods) attack the material by laying their eggs in the pores or in crevices. These eggs hatch into larvae that then proceed to tunnel their way through the cellulose structure of the material, until they emerge through flight holes as beetles.

Seasoning woods

Seasoning is, in effect, a controlled drying of timber. This can be achieved either through natural seasoning or by **kiln drying**. Whichever method is used, the moisture content of the material must be below 20 per cent. The ideal is that the moisture content of the timber is the same as that of its surroundings. This is known as the Equilibrium Moisture Content (EMC).

The benefits of seasoning

- It increases the strength and stability of the timber.
- The reduced moisture content reduces the risk of the timber causing corrosion to the surrounding metalwork.
- It makes the timber less prone to rot and **decay**.

Green timber Not all timbers are seasoned thoroughly. The term 'green timber' refers to woods that have been cut down, converted and stored for up to 12 months. An example of the use of green timber is in the construction of timber-framed houses. These are usually architect-designed one-off structures. Using green timber in this way has the benefits of the **aesthetics** of the grain of the wood, along with drying cracks that give the material character.

Green timbers have traditionally been used in the craft industry. Products such as chairs, spoons, baskets, hurdles for gardens and fencing, have been made using this material and traditional techniques such as cleaving (a method of splitting the timber to obtain the shape required).

 Veneers, laminates and composites

Veneers

Veneer is the term given to a thin layer of wood that has been shaved off the trunk of a tree. Hardwoods are the usual materials to make up veneers, because they tend to be more decorative and durable than softwoods.

Veneers are used in sheet form to provide a more decorative surface to inferior quality woods. For example, a veneer of yew could be applied to a piece of chipboard that would be used in the manufacture of a hi-fi or television cabinet (see Table 14).

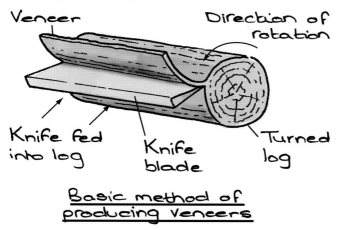

Basic method of producing veneers

Paper backed veneers

These are very thin, typically 0.8 mm, natural wood veneers supported, as the name suggests, on a paper backing. The advantage of the paper backing is to avoid the veneer splitting due to its delicate nature. The paper backing also helps prevent glue seeping to the surface of the material.

A very small radius of curvature, around 25 mm is possible due to its thin section and paper support making it ideal for covering the fairly detailed mouldings found on kitchen cabinets and other items of furniture and decoration, e.g. jewellery boxes.

The use of veneers can reduce the cost of a product by enabling the manufacturer to use lower-cost materials for the main structure, and then finishing in a veneer. This reduces the need to purchase solid timber, which would be too expensive for mass-market products.

💡 Laminates

A laminate is a material that has been placed in layers with the same or other materials. Examples of laminates include surfaces for kitchen worktops and laminate flooring products.

Kitchen work surfaces

Kitchen worktops are made up of layers of paper in a melamine resin; the top layer of paper gives the required decorative finish while a layer of hardwearing, heat-resistant polymer is the final layer. The base material for the whole worktop would be a particle board such as chipboard.

AQA Examiner's tip

As with other materials there are specialist terms associated with woods. You should be able to use these appropriately in your answers to exam questions.

A greenwood product

Table 14 *Veneers and base materials*

Suitable veneers	Suitable base materials
Beech	
Oak	Medium Density Fibre board (MDF)
Ash	Chipboard
Walnut (including burr walnut)	Block board Plywood
Yew	

Product finished with a wood veneer

Laminate flooring being laid

Laminate flooring

Laminate flooring is made up of layers of printed materials in a resin on a supporting material, such as MDF. The final top layer of the flooring is a very hardwearing thermosetting polymer.

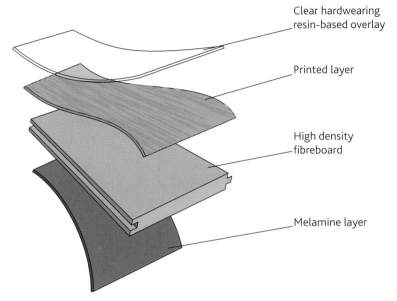

Clear hardwearing resin-based overlay

Printed layer

High density fibreboard

Melamine layer

Construction of laminate flooring

Plywood

The previous two examples show how polymer-based laminates can be used with **wood products**. Plywood, on the other hand, is a good example of the use of laminated veneers to produce large sheets of stable material with a natural wood finish.

Layers of hardwood veneer are bonded together. The grain direction in each additional layer is laid at 90° to the previous layer. The result is a sheet material that is very stable against warping.

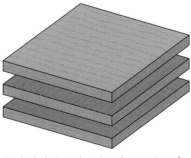

Exploded view showing that grains of subsequent layers of veneer are laid at 90° to each other

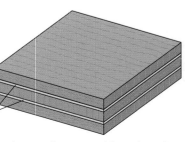

Veneers held together by layers of resin

There is always an odd number of layers, ensuring the grain on the outside layers is in the same direction

How plywood is constructed

Steam bending

Most woods can be steam bent including laminates like plywood. The process involves moistening the timber in a steam chest to a point where the material is more pliable. Care should be taken when working with plywoods though since prolonged immersion in the steam chest may de-laminate the material. The wood material is then held in shape around a former until dried after which it will retain its shape. This technique can be used on a small scale to produce items of wooden jewellery and on a larger scale for producing ribs in a traditionally made boat hull.

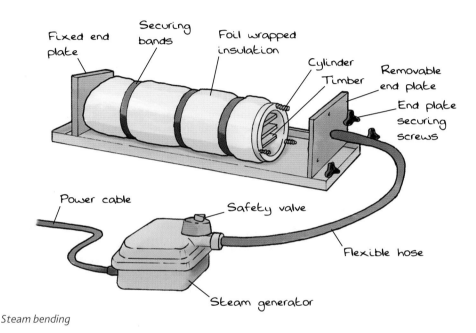

Steam bending

💡 Laminated wood products

As we have seen, a laminate is made up of layers of material bonded together. The advantage of this is that it produces a very stable material.

The range of laminated wood products includes CD racks and furniture, along with structural items such as moulded beam trusses for sports venues.

Wood-based composites (man-made boards)

We have discussed composites earlier in this book (pp20-29) but another look, particularly at wood-based composites, is appropriate here. In fact, timber can be thought of as a natural composite due to the structure of the material containing cells that are supported by natural resins.

In the same way a number of wood products (the term given to those materials made from wood residues or smaller pieces) are also composites. See Table 15 on the following page.

𝑖 Activity

Investigate how man-made boards have been used in the construction of a house and in the manufacture of furniture in various rooms of a house. Identify the types of man-made board used and give reasons for their use, including details of any finishes that have been applied.

■ Further reading

Two useful websites covering a range of aspects of working with woods are:

- **www.woodmachining.com** for articles on wood machining, software, cutting tools and safety
- **www.woodweb.com** for an extensive collection of articles from the wood industry, including materials and components, machining, joining and finishing.

Table 15 *Wood products*

Man-made board	Made up of:
Plywood	Layers of veneers and resins; always an odd number of veneers
Block board	Strips of wood bonded together with a veneered surface
Chipboard	Fine chips of woods mixed with resins
MDF	Very fine wood fibres mixed with resins
Hardboard	As MDF – can be impregnated with oil
Sterling board	Shavings of wood compressed into resins

■ Case study 3: Wood

Natural timber and manufactured boards

Natural timber and manufactured boards are extremely popular materials with designers and manufacturers. Such materials not only have excellent functional and aesthetic properties, but are also more sustainable than other materials. One company that uses timber and manufactured boards extensively is IKEA.

IKEA prides itself on making good quality contemporary products at an affordable price, with minimum impact on the environment. As IKEA and its licensed suppliers make huge numbers of wooden products, it is very important that the timber they use is from sustainable sources.

Where IKEA uses natural timbers such as pine or birch, it will ensure that the timber is harvested from managed forests. In such woodland, as one tree is felled, it is replaced with several saplings to ensure that timber is available for future generations. In addition to this, IKEA generally uses timbers that are fast growing, maturing at, say, 30–40 years (as opposed to some hardwoods, such as oak, that take over 80 years to grow to maturity). Therefore the timber it uses can be replaced in a relatively short time period.

IKEA television bench made from aspen

One product that is made from timbers is the aspen television bench. Aspen is a timber that grows rather like a weed. It is widespread, grows rapidly and, until recently, has not had any particular commercial value. IKEA makes veneers from aspen to laminate into products such as the television bench pictured on the left.

Some designers choose to use timber for its aesthetic properties. The garden designer Diarmuid Gavin, famous for his contemporary garden structures, often uses hardwoods such as oak for its aesthetic effect in, for example, a garden building such as a summerhouse or gazebo. Green oak is easy to use, as it is soft when wet, and the timber tends to split as it dries out which can add to the overall aesthetic effect and give the timber product a more natural appearance. Oak has the added advantage that it does not need to be finished in order to preserve it. However, finishes such as combined stains and preservatives may be added to give the timber a colour.

Product analysis exercise 5: Wood and manufactured boards

Laminated dining chair

1 Study the photo of the dining chair.

a The chair is made from laminated beech veneers. Explain why beech is suitable, making reference to the following requirements:

- aesthetic
- functional
- manufacturing.

b Use notes and diagrams to sketch how the veneers are laminated into the shape of the seat.

c Sketch how the seat could be joined to the legs.

d The seat is finished with a polyurethane varnish. Explain why this is suitable and how it would be applied.

2 The table top pictured is made from MDF. Explain why this material is often used in such furniture.

3 The table top is finished with a melamine formaldehyde laminate. Explain why this is used.

Glass

Glass as a material

There is a wide range of materials that can be classed as glass, but for the purposes of this book glass is essentially the material used for glazing windows, manufacturing bottles and so on.

Manufacturing with glass

Lime-soda glass is made from a mixture of sand, lime and sodium carbonate that is heated to 1500 °C in a large furnace. The resulting molten material is tapped off to form a continuous flow that can then be '**floated**' on a tank of molten tin to form a glass sheet called **plate glass**. During the process the glass sheet is annealed to reduce any stresses that might have built up in the material, while at the end of the process the material is cut to the required size using diamond wheel cutters.

Glass made in this way is a mixture of new materials and recycled materials called '**cullet**' obtained from recycling centres. Up to 90 per cent of cullet can be included in the furnace.

Glass blowing

Glass **blowing** is used to manufacture hollow objects such as bottles. Mouth blowing is restricted to the more expensive pieces of glassware. For everyday products, a more automated process is used where a 'gob' of glass is formed by a cycle of pressing and blowing into a mould.

Slumping

Slumping is the process where glass is heated until it becomes sufficiently soft, allowing it to take the shape of a mould. Special curved glass for windows is produced in this way, as are car windscreens.

A variation of the use of slumping involves filling a ceramic mould with a mixture of clear and coloured glass fragments (cullet). This is then placed into a furnace. The glass becomes molten, taking up the shape of the mould. The result of this process is a block of glass patterned by the way the coloured glass has flowed into the clear material.

Key terms

Lime-soda glass: used for windowpanes, storage jars and bottles.

Float glass: sheet glass is produced by floating molten glass on a bath of molten tin. The flat surface of the molten metal gives the glass its flat, smooth surface.

Plate glass: a high-quality glass of few impurities that has been rolled and polished. Uses include mirrors and large windows.

Cullet: glass that has been crushed into very small particles ready for re-melting and recycling.

Blowing: used to produce an air bubble in the first gather of glass, then to enlarge the 'bubble' to produce the final object. Traditionally glass is blown by a glass blower, but some manufacturing processes, e.g. bottle manufacture, include blowing the material into a mould.

AQA Examiner's tip

Glass is not listed in the materials and components section of the AQA spec. but in exams you might be asked to name a traditional material as an alternative to plastics.

Slumping: a process where sheet glass is heated to a temperature where it softens, and is allowed to take the shape of the mould.

Lehr: a furnace in which hot glass (about 500 °C) is placed after working, enabling it to be brought down to room temperature very slowly.

Toughened glass: glass is heated uniformly and then rapidly cooled by air jets. This causes the outside surfaces to be under compressive stress, while the inside of the material is in tension. External forces must overcome these stresses to shatter the glass.

Fired clay or plaster of Paris mould ready for slumping

A piece of glass of the required size is placed over the mould

During heating in the kiln the glass softens to the point where it will take the shape of the mould

Slumping into a mould

Annealing glass

Glass, like most other materials, contracts on cooling and in doing so internal stresses can develop between the more rapidly cooled outer surfaces and the core of the material. To remove these stresses, and so reduce the risk of the material cracking, the glass product is cooled very slowly in an oven called a **'lehr'**.

General properties of glass

Glass is extremely brittle. Mechanical shock will cause the material to break, e.g.:

Glass blower at work

- impacts such as dropping
- a cricket ball, for example, hitting a pane of glass
- thermal shock, e.g. placing an already hot glass into ice or cold water (or vice versa).

Glass is much stronger in compression than in tension and has a good chemical resistance.

Toughened glass

As in most groups of materials, the properties of glass can be modified. Glass used in the construction industry, for example, can be toughened by heating it to 400 °C followed by rapid cooling with air blasts. This produces compressive forces on the two outer surfaces on the glass, while the internal core of the material remains in tension. In order for this glass to break, an external force must overcome the internal stresses. No further processing of **toughened glass** is possible, since any cutting or damage to the outer surface will cause the glass to shatter. Glass that has been processed in this way is used for vehicle windows and glass doors.

Coloured glass

Glass can be coloured by adding oxides of metals such as iron, copper and nickel. Examples of coloured glass products are stained glass windows, wine and beer bottles and tinted windscreens for cars.

Artists and designers who use glass in their work may simply add coloured 'cullet' to the plain glass they are working with to create patterns in the piece they are creating. This will simplify the equipment they need to use as only one furnace is required to melt the plain glass in.

Lead crystal and Pyrex

Adding lead oxide increases the way the material reflects light and is used in the manufacture of 'cut glass' wine glasses, decanters and vases. **'Pyrex'** is the manufacturer's name for a range of heat-resistant products made from **boro-silicate glass**. In this material, boron oxide is added to the glass mixture. Its resistance to high temperatures makes Pyrex ideal for cookware applications and for laboratory equipment. Other oxides can be added to produce specialised glasses for specialist applications, such as the windows used in spacecraft.

Laminated glass

Laminated glass is a very tough composite material made up of two thin sheets of plate glass between which is sandwiched a sheet of tough clear polymer. If the glass is broken, the polymer holds the fragments together. This makes the material suitable for security applications.

Glass as a thermal insulator

Pilkingtons are probably the largest manufacturer of glass in the UK. The company has developed a glass that acts as an insulator to heat. This is known as 'K' glass and allows heat (via sunlight) into a building while reducing the amount of heat that escapes.

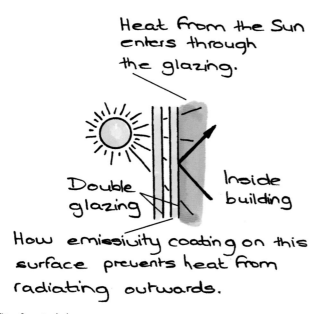

Heat from the Sun enters through the glazing.

Double glazing

Inside building

How emissivity coating on this surface prevents heat from radiating outwards.

The benefits of coated glass

Self-cleaning glass

Self-cleaning windows are a new development from the glass industry. A special coating is applied to the outer glass surface, which is virtually invisible. The coating:

■ prevents droplets settling on the surface by forcing the water to spread out into a sheet, thereby reducing the formation of spot marks

Key terms

Lead glass: when lead is added to glass, it improves clarity and the ability to reflect light (refraction). Products include optical products such as prisms and lenses. Expensive 'crystal' tableware is made with this material.

Pyrex: a well-known heat-resistant glass containing boron.

Boro-silicate glass: glass containing boron and used generally for kitchenware and laboratory equipment, due to its heat resistance and good resistance to chemicals.

interacts with ultraviolet light to break down organic dirt (e.g. finger marks, dust, pollen) into simpler compounds that can then be washed away by rain.

This new type of glass is ideal for inaccessible windows, e.g. windows high up in tower blocks.

Glass versus polymers

If you think about all the products that are or have been produced from glass, it is more than likely that polymers have been, or could be, used to replace it. The exception comes when the products used involve high temperatures, i.e. above 200°C.

Having said that, some ready-made meals available from supermarkets can be placed in a conventional oven at up to 200°C while the contents are being cooked. These containers are usually made from a thermoplastic polymer, such as PET, or a food quality PVC. This is possible due to developments in polymer technology.

A further example of where polymers have replaced glass is in the manufacture of bottles. Think about all those products that could be contained in a glass bottle. Examples include: foodstuffs like jams and sauces, wines and spirits, medicines, cleaning fluids, etc. A large range of these is now contained in plastic bottles.

Advantages of using polymers instead of glass
- They are lightweight (for transportation).
- They have a low melting point (recycling).
- They can be impervious to gases (carbonated drinks in PET).
- They can be squashed without breaking.
- Screw tops can be used.

Advantages and disadvantages of using glass instead of plastics
Advantages

- Glass is a more rigid material than a polymer, especially thermoplastic polymers.
- Glass is more scratch-resistant than most polymers.
- Generally, glass has a greater clarity where transparency is required.
- Glass is not affected by heat as most polymers are.
- Glass can be used where heat resistance is required, e.g. in kitchenware.
- Glass gives a sense of quality to a product due to its weight, texture and light-handling qualities.

Disadvantages

- Glass is heavy (increased transportation costs).
- Glass has a high melting point (more energy needed for recycling).

Ceramics

Introduction to ceramics

We tend to think of ceramics as those materials used to produce crockery (cups, saucers, plates, etc.) and ornamental and decorative products (vases, figurines, tiles, etc.). There is, however, a wide range of ceramic materials that include engineering applications, such as the tiles for the NASA space shuttle.

A NASA space shuttle

Most of the more common, everyday ceramics products are clay-based materials. These include a range of clays with different additives, providing products with a range of different finishes. Some clays can be gritty in nature, others can provide high-strength products for use in hotels, or cheap earthenware for everyday domestic use.

At the top end of the market is **fine bone china**. This type of clay contains finely ground animal bone giving the fired material its translucent quality.

Engineering ceramics

Most ceramic products are made from clay. Engineering products include house bricks, engineering bricks (once used in the construction of sewers – not yet superseded by concretes or plastics), electrical insulators for pylons, etc. There are an increasing number of high-temperature applications where metal-oxide based ceramics are being used. Table 16 shows the materials used, their maximum working temperature and potential applications.

Table 16 *Metal-oxide based ceramics*

Substance	Melting point	Common use
Alumina	2050 °C	Spark plugs, crucibles, cutting tools
Beryllia	2350 °C	Crucibles for high-temperature nuclear reactors
Magnesia	2800 °C	Furnace linings
Zirconia	2690 °C	Liners for rockets, wall insulation for high-temperature furnaces

Useful features of engineering ceramics

- Ability to withstand high temperatures without distortion.
- Strength and rigidity at high temperatures.
- Freedom from 'creep' (essentially grain growth that increases the size of the product).
- Hardness and resistance to wear.

Manufacturing ceramic products

The manufacture of ceramic products has changed significantly over the past 15–20 years. Very much a traditional industry, the approach was often craft-based – this approach being continued by studio potters creating their own brand of ceramic ware. For example, hollow objects such as pots and jugs would be thrown on a wheel and shaped by adding water to the clay to make the material more pliable.

In more industrial practices hollow objects are cast using a method called **slip casting**. This involves pouring liquid clay (**slip**) into plaster of Paris moulds which in turn act as a sponge to extract moisture from the surface of the pot. After a given amount of time the excess slip is poured away and the mould is allowed to dry further. After another 24 hours or so the pot can be removed from the mould ready for firing.

Flatware such as dinner plates and saucers have been produced from a slab of clay which has been turned using a method called '**jiggering**'. As the clay rotates, an arm with the profile of the underside of the plate is pulled down onto the clay until it is the desired thickness. The plate is left on its mould until sufficiently dry to be removed and then sent for firing.

Fine bone china

A potter at a potter's wheel

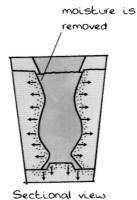

Large rubber bands

Skin forms as moisture is removed

Product

Plaster mould filled with slip (liquid clay). Large rubber bands hold the mould halves together

Sectional view

Plaster-of-Paris mould absorbs moisture from clay forming a skin

When required thickness of skin is reached the mould is emptied. Excess slip is returned for recycling and the product is removed

Slip casting

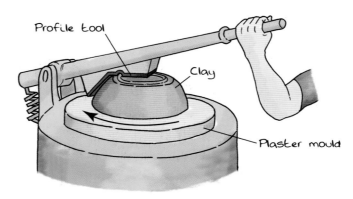

Profile tool

Clay

Plaster mould

Jiggering

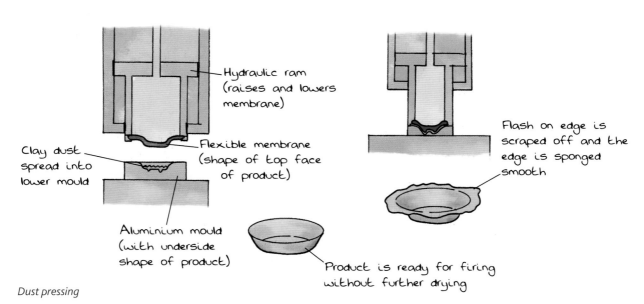

Hydraulic ram (raises and lowers membrane)

Clay dust spread into lower mould

Flexible membrane (shape of top face of product)

Aluminium mould (with underside shape of product)

Flash on edge is scraped off and the edge is sponged smooth

Product is ready for firing without further drying

Dust pressing

Developments in the ceramics industry have seen the introduction of automated equipment which will shape, turn and fix a handle to a cup without human intervention. Slip casting is still used although this is also completed, including drying, on automatic equipment.

The production of flatware has taken a slightly different route. Modern processes use a clay powder which is fed in between two moulds that contain the profile of the product. This is known as dust pressing. The clay dust is then squeezed between the two moulds under very high pressures to ensure the clay particles stay together. Once removed from the moulds the product is sponged to remove any flash and then sent straight for firing without the need for further drying.

A further development in slip casting uses a piece of equipment similar to an injection moulding machine. The main difference lies in the moulds which as well as being of the profile of the product are made from a porous end plastic material. The purpose of this porosity is so that a vacuum can be applied to the mould to remove moisture from the clay slip in the mould thereby making it possible to speed up the drying time of the product. This effectively reduces the cycle time of the machine.

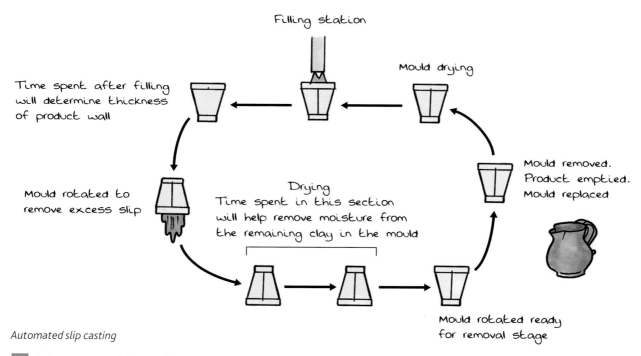

Automated slip casting

Papers and boards

You should develop an understanding of the range of papers and boards available and how appropriate these materials are for different purposes.

Types of paper

Designers must have a mechanism by which to demonstrate ideas or final products to clients and so receive feedback as to the potential success of proposed solutions. Some papers are more appropriate for specific media and drawing techniques.

Cartridge papers, for example, provide a good surface for sketching and using coloured pencils for **rendering**. There are a variety of qualities but the heavier papers are generally more versatile, being less prone to yellowing with age and likely to be acid-free.

> ### Key terms
>
> **Renderings:** colour drawings using tones of colour and texture to produce a realistic artist impression of designs. These can be done using CAD.

Watercolours can be used with cartridge papers, but to prevent 'cockling', the papers must first of all be stretched, hence special watercolour papers are available. These provide a good surface texture that will accept acrylics, gouache and pastel, as well as watercolour.

There are three main textures available in watercolour papers:

1 Hot-pressed papers have a hard, smooth surface.
2 Cold-pressed papers have a rougher surface, which enhances the finished image by allowing more of the colour to be absorbed.
3 A third type is rougher than cold-pressed paper, having more peaks and hollows (known as tooth) on its surface.

Bleed proof (or marker) paper is similar to cartridge paper but a protective layer applied to the reverse of the sheet prevents the marker ink from bleeding through to the next sheet.

Layout paper is another type of paper used by designers, particularly in advertising. Its partial translucency allows it to be used as a tracing paper.

The designer builds up an advertising **layout** from a number of elements. As each of these elements is approved by the client/agency then they are added to the layout until the layout is complete.

Ingress papers are available for use with pastels, while bleed proof papers are useful for working with markers. Pastels can also be used with coloured sugar papers giving a more textured surface than ingress paper.

Other papers are available to the designer for more formal, engineering drawings, showing details such as dimensions and construction details.

💡 Paper properties and uses

Optical properties

The most important optical properties for papers are brightness, colour, opacity and gloss. (Brightness is the degree to which white or near-white papers and cards reflect light.)

Opacity

An opaque paper will allow little or no 'show through' of the image from the other side of the paper. This is one of the most desirable properties of writing and printing papers.

Gloss, glare, finish and smoothness

These terms are used to describe the surface characteristics of paper.

■ Gloss refers to surface lustre.
■ Glare refers to the way the paper reflects light.
■ Finish refers to the general surface characteristics of the paper.
■ Smoothness refers to the absence of surface irregularities.

Strength and durability

The strength of paper is determined by the following factors:

■ strength of individual fibres
■ average length of fibre
■ strength of bonds between fibres
■ structure of the paper.

Strength falls away rapidly with the increase in moisture, due to the breakdown of inter-fibre bonding.

Tensile strength

Most papers require a certain minimum strength to withstand the production processes: including printing, embossing and folding, as well as handling.

Bending strength

The thinner the sheet, the more flexible and light it is; conversely the thicker and heavier a paper is, the more stiff it is.

Porosity

Porosity is reduced with the addition of size to the paper. Greaseproof paper is made by beating the paper, resulting in a dense sheet with very little porosity.

Manufacturing with papers and boards

Papers and boards are used widely in the manufacture of products such as packaging for flat-pack products, flowers and electrical goods, as well as products such as paper cups, newspapers and magazines. All of these products require materials that meet the functional requirements. Heavy papers can be stiff, while papers with specific finishes such as pearlescent, holographic, mirrored or having metal effects such as brushed or galvanised steel, simulated anodised aluminium applied to them make them useful for model making. Certain techniques of printing have allowed development in printing holograms onto high security items such as bank notes (which are a form of high grade plastic paper that have been treated with specific techniques such as watermarks and metalised strips) and credit/debit cards.

Cards and boards

The term 'carton board' covers a range of packaging materials from single layer card for products such as cereal packages or soft drinks cartons (with a sealing layer of polymer) through to multi-layer corrugated cardboard in a variety of weights and thicknesses, for shoe boxes to packaging for electrical goods. Carton board is produced from recycled carton board and paper as well as some new wood fibres. The material can be bleached or unbleached and has a surface that can be readily printed on. The thinner carton boards usually have one printable white surface, the reverse remaining self-coloured.

Packaging made from carton board consists of folded and glued shapes – the shape giving the packaging its strength and rigidity.

Foam boards

Foam boards are a multi-layer board made up of two outer layers of card.

- ■ The outer surfaces have a high gloss finish.
- ■ The middle layer is foam.

Foam board has a number of uses in the design process, from **mood** and **presentation boards** to use as a modelling material. It is generally light in weight, easily cut, but difficult to bend.

Correx boards

These boards are produced by extruding a thermoplastic to produce a sheet material that is useful for the manufacture of simple products. This material is lightweight and durable and can be bent easily in one direction only. Special fasteners can be used with correx, making it possible to manufacture products.

Holograms can be printed onto high-security items such as bank notes and credit/debit cards

■ **Key terms**

Mood boards: collection of images, colours, fabric/material samples, etc. used to guide designs towards a style.

Presentation boards: boards usually used to present designs to a client or others. These may have rendered drawings, dimensioned orthographic views, and so on.

A selection of foam boards

Printing

There are a large number of products available that contain graphics to identify and promote the company and product, provide information regarding contents of food products, weight and warnings as to whether a product is hot or heavy, **copyright** information and barcodes. Examples include packaging for breakfast cereals or fast-food outlets. Other products can contain graphics that are purely decorative, for example, decorated china tableware.

These products are printed using a commercial printing process. The diagram below gives an overview of printing processes available.

Printing processes

Commercial printing processes include:

- lithography
- letterpress
- flexography
- gravure
- screen printing.

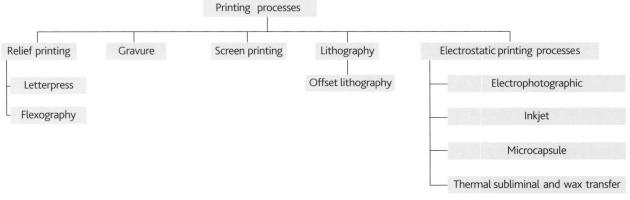

Printing processes

Processes such as letterpress can only print one colour at a time; screen printing can only use solid colours: for a multi-colour image a number of screens must be used.

For processes such as lithography, flexography and gravure, multiple colours can be printed in one pass through a press. This is known as **process colour** printing and uses four transparent inks:

- cyan (blue-green)
- magenta (red)
- yellow
- black.

The four colours are printed one on top of another in varying amounts to produce the density and tone of colour required. Colour photographs and other artwork can be faithfully reproduced in this way. Spot colours, on the other hand, use custom-mixed inks (or **Pantone colours**) and are widely used in package printing, where large areas of uniform colour are common.

Letterpress

Letterpress is one of the earliest methods of printing. This process involves the use of raised letters onto which a coating of ink is deposited. By pressing the plate holding all of the letters onto the material being printed, e.g. paper, the ink will be left behind, producing the printed document. Letterpress is still used today for specialist printing, e.g. personalised wedding invitations.

Offset lithography

Offset lithography is probably the most versatile and economic of the commercial printing processes. The process uses the same four colours: **c**yan, **m**agenta, **y**ellow and blac**k** (CMYK). One-, two-, three-, four- or five-colour presses can be used, depending on the number of colours being printed. For example, black text on white paper would use a single press, whereas a modern newspaper with colour photographs would be printed using the four colours (CMYK). Five-station printing presses can be used where the fifth station prints a spot colour (a single colour other than the CMYK colours) or a varnish.

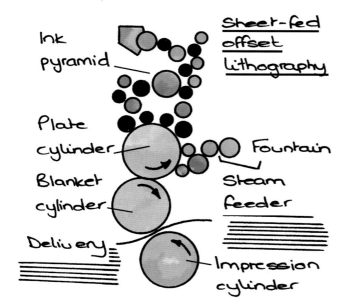

Roller arrangement for sheet-fed offset lithography

Stages of the process

Step 1   Printing materials can be fed into the machine as a sheet (as in carton printing) or **web-fed** (from a roll, as in newspaper printing). This process is suitable for batches of 1,000 items or more at speeds of 4,000 to 12000 impressions per hour.

Step 2   Printing plates are produced from photosensitive aluminium, the image being etched onto the plate using lasers. The plates will then be fitted to the machine and a test run will be carried out to ensure all **registration marks** line up and that the colour is the correct density.

Step 3   The printing process itself relies on the plate being wetted with a damping roller, while the grease-based inks will only go into those regions where required. The plate cylinder rotates onto a blanket roller, which then becomes coated with the ink, which, in turn, is transferred onto the paper.

> **Key terms**
>
> **Web-fed:** printing onto a continuous roll of paper, rather than onto individual sheets (sheet-fed).
>
> **Registration marks:** marks printed with each colour in a two-, three- or four-colour printing process that should line up to create a sharp, clear image.

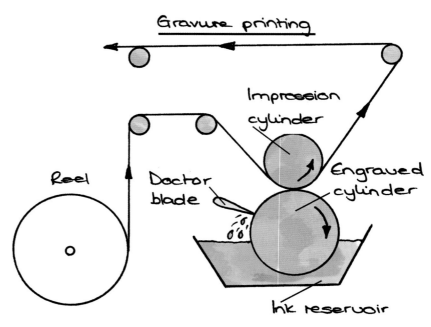

Roller arrangement for gravure printing

Electrostatic printing processes

Digital printing

Digital printing processes include electro-photographic and inkjet printing.

■ Electro-photographic printing involves the depositing of toner onto the substrate (e.g. paper, card). The amount of toner being deposited is controlled by varying its electrostatic properties. Dry or liquid toners can be used. These are fixed by absorption, heat or chemical reactions.

■ Inkjet printing involves spraying electrostatically charged ink droplets directly onto the substrate, relying on absorption or heat to fix the inks.

Advantages of digital printing

It has a much reduced make-ready time, therefore:

■ It's economical for short **print runs** of up to 1,000 copies.
■ It's ideal for 'on-demand' printing.

Thermal transfer printing

Thermal transfer printers apply the process colours (cyan, magenta, yellow and black) one at a time by heating the wax to leave droplets of colour on the substrate (i.e. paper or acetate sheet).

Dye sublimation printing

Dye sublimation printing is a form of thermal transfer printing, but works in a quite different way. The dyes used change from solid to gas without becoming liquid at any point. The thermal printing head varies the temperature of the dye, and so controls the amount of dye being printed onto the substrate (e.g. paper). This means that the image is continuous and is not made up of dots of colour (called dithering) as in electrostatic and thermal (wax) transfer methods.

Die cutting, creasing and folding

Products such as cardboard 'vases' used by florists are produced from a flat sheet of corrugated cardboard. The product is supplied to the florist in the form of a flat sheet, pre-cut to the required shape with fold lines already creased.

One side of the cardboard sheet has been printed with one colour only. The shape has been cut using a die cutter. The die cutter comprises two types of blade, one of which is the cutter while the other blade has a rounded edge that will produce a crease in the cardboard ready for folding.

Die cutting is used in the production of a variety of paper and card products. Specialist machines can do folding of papers and cards automatically. These machines are programmable, giving great flexibility in the combination of folds that can be achieved.

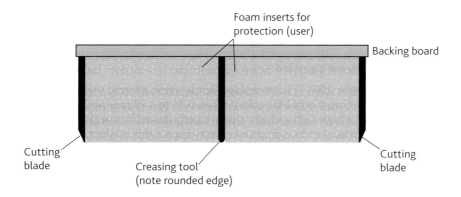

Foam inserts for protection (user)

Backing board

Cutting blade

Creasing tool (note rounded edge)

Cutting blade

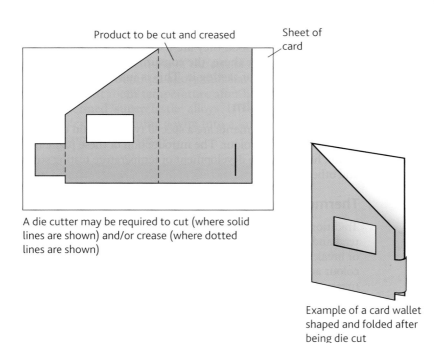

Product to be cut and creased

Sheet of card

A die cutter may be required to cut (where solid lines are shown) and/or crease (where dotted lines are shown)

Example of a card wallet shaped and folded after being die cut

A die cutter

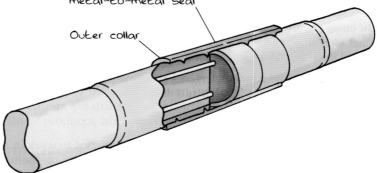

SMART metal shrinks when heated. This forces the outer collar to cut (or swage) grooves in the connector therefore creating a good metal-to-metal seal

Outer collar

Secure electrical connector

Water valves in coffee pots can be controlled using muscle wires made from shape memory alloys. Again it is the material's contraction when heated that is utilised ensuring the water is at the correct temperature. As the water boils, heat from the steam produced heats the wire causing it to contract. Corrosion is not a problem since these alloys have very high corrosion resistance.

Piezoelectric devices

The piezoelectric effect is achieved by applying an input to a quartz crystal or a polycrystalline material called PZT, causing a desired output to be seen. If a quartz crystal is put under strain, e.g. compressed, a small electrical charge is produced, although the amount of movement in the material is extremely small due to its high stiffness. Piezoelectric devices come in two forms. They can be made into sensors which give an electrical signal from the force or pressure applied or they can be actuators which react physically by changing shape or size due to an electrical signal being applied to them.

Piezoelectric sensors

The charge is proportional to the amount of force being applied, so when conditioned by instrumentation to give a useable signal, the sensor will give a direct indication of the load being applied. Applications for this type of sensor range from large structures, such as bridges, to sensor mats used in burglar alarm systems.

Piezoelectric actuators

Piezoelectric actuators, on the other hand, work the opposite way round. When a voltage is applied to quartz crystal, a small displacement is produced in the material. The displacement is very small but produces a high mechanical force. A stack actuator – literally a stack of PZT (a common piezoelectric material) – can be used for micro-positioning applications and for fast-acting valves and nozzles.

Smart grease

Smart grease is a viscous material used for applications where controlled release of energy is important. Where 'normal' greases and oils work to allow two components to slide over each other freely, smart grease is used to control the rate at which the two components move.

For example, in a spring loaded application such as a pen click mechanism, the speed at which the mechanism operates is normally determined by the strength of the spring. By placing smart grease between the moving parts the speed at which the mechanism operates is controlled to a more uniform rate.

Applications include glove compartments, ashtray lids and retractable cup-holders on car dashboards, vehicle steering mechanisms where the damping properties of the grease help reduce vibration through to the steering wheel. Domestic applications include anti-vibration and noise control in washing machines, control knobs and switches on a range of devices from kitchen equipment to Hi-Fi controllers. Personal electronics also benefit from these greases where a mechanism such as that found in a flip or slide phone is found. Controlling the motion of a pen nib can be achieved with these greases to give the user a perception of quality from the smooth motion of the mechanism.

Smart fluids

In a similar vein to smart grease, smart fluids have a **rheological** effect on components. In the case of smart fluids this is taken a stage further. A smart fluid starts life as a liquid. If it is stirred or shaken vigorously it immediately changes to a solid (or near solid). When rapid movement has stopped it immediately turns back to a liquid. This makes it useful in applications where damping is required (controlled movement, e.g. shock absorber on a car suspension) or where sudden impacts occur. Products could include personal equipment for climbing such as lightweight soft hats that become rigid when knocked.

Electroluminescent wires

An electroluminescent wire is a cable that glows. It is made up of a number of wires comprising a central conductor and a number of outer conductors. The outer conductors are coated in phosphor while the inner conductor is coated in a **semi-conductor material**.

The luminescent glow is achieved when an alternating current is applied across the inner and outer wires. This means that, in effect, to get the wires to glow an a.c. voltage is connected between the wires at one end of the cable. An inverter is used to provide the appropriate voltages and frequencies. It is the frequency of the alternating current that determines the intensity of glow, i.e. the higher the frequency, the brighter the light levels.

Electroluminescent cables can produce a variety of colours determined by the colour of the outer polymer coating. They are small enough to be woven into textiles for use in costumes. Other uses include lighting for walkways and steps in theatres and cinemas or simply as a decorative interior light.

Glowsticks

Glowsticks, once activated, can provide temporary lighting whether it is for parties and concerts, or camping, diving or when emergency light sources are required. These products rely on a chemical reaction that releases energy. Electrons become excited to a very high level initially, however, when the level of excitation reduces to a 'normal' level then light energy is produced. The colour of glow is determined by choice of fluorescent dye added to the mixture.

The sticks can be activated by bending the outer plastic tube. This breaks the inner glass tube releasing a liquid, such as hydrogen peroxide, into the main tube. The hydrogen peroxide mixes with the outer liquid in the tube to produce a glow.

Activity

Working in teams, create a mind map for a range of products that you think would benefit from the application of smart greases.

Key terms

Rheological: refers to the deformation and flow of matter. In this case the way greases and fluids react to movement between adjacent components.

Semi-conductor material: a material that will conduct electricity only under special circumstances, e.g. when it has reached a specific temperature or when a particular voltage has been applied. By doping the material with small amounts of 'impurities' (i.e. other elements) the temperature and/or voltage can be more closely controlled.

Electroluminescent cables

The length of time the glow lasts for depends on the liquids used. Temperature also affects intensity of glow with warmer temperatures producing higher illumination levels.

Once used, glowsticks cannot be recharged since the chemical reactions are non-reversible.

Smart textiles

Just like other 'smart' materials, smart textiles and fabrics react to their environments. For example, thermochromic or photochromic dyes can be used in textiles where they will change colour in response to heat or sunlight. Fabrics with thermochromic dyes incorporated in them could be used for medical applications, e.g. to indicate a patient's temperature. Clothes made from fabrics containing photochromic dyes might be used to warn of high levels of UV radiation. Fabrics that contain quantum tunnelling composites (QTCs) enable the use of electronics within a garment.

Quantum tunnelling composites

Quantum tunnelling composites are, in essence, metal-filled polymers which have the unique characteristic of changing from an insulator to a conductor when deformed by some deliberate force or pressure. In other words, when the QTC is squeezed, its electrical resistance drops. The term Quantum Tunnelling refers to the way the metallic particles allow electrons to pass between them.

QTCs are used to create touch-sensitive fabrics. Particles of metal are combined in a fabric made from an elastic polymer. When the material is squeezed, the particles move closer together and the material can become a conductor. This means that these fabrics can be used as pressure sensors or switches that respond to touch providing connectivity between garment and electronic device.

The main advantage of this technology is that the sensing and switching devices are more reliable than traditional mechanical switches. Fabrics do not resist movement and can be cleaned in the usual way.

Further benefits include fabric keypads that can be placed on the outside of garments avoiding the necessity for direct handling of the device they are controlling.

Technologies such as SOFTswitch (**www.softswitch.co.uk**) enable the control of the output from heating devices integrated into the clothing by gently stroking fabric up or down. This clearly has the benefit to the wearer of being able to control their own temperature in otherwise hostile environments.

LEDs can also be incorporated into the fabric to give a visual indication of temperature, or volume in the case of controlling the output from a digital device such as an iPod.

Electronic smart glass

Electronic smart glasses fall into one of three distinct types while essentially carrying out the same function, i.e. to change from transparent to dark when a voltage is applied. In addition to controlling the amount of light that passes through the glass they also help control heat loss. These products have applications in industrial and commercial space as well as for glazing. This type of glass is employed in the rear view mirrors of cars. When the sensor detects bright light the mirror glass darkens.

Liquid crystal glass is a laminated material comprising a liquid crystal display (**LCD**) core sandwiched between two layers of glass. From being in the 'off' state to having a voltage applied changes the glass from a 'milky white' appearance to a partially clear one. Applications for this technology are limited to interior products such as internal partitioning and screens.

Electrochromic smart glass – this is a microscopically thin electrochromatic layer on the glass surface. When a low voltage is applied via a switch or sensor to these layers it has the effect of changing the glass from dark to clear.

SPD (suspended particle device) glass works in a slightly different way. Again the glass is a laminate, but between the two outer layers of glass is suspended a conductive film made up of light absorbing particles. When there is no voltage applied to the film the particles absorb light, therefore the glass remains dark. When a voltage is applied the particles allow light to pass through. The amount of light passing through can be varied by varying the voltage.

Modern materials

Modern materials are considered to be those that have only been available in their present form since the 1960s/70s onwards. In fact, some of them may have been experimental materials for many years before this. These materials cannot be considered smart since they do not react in any way to the environment in which they are used.

Fibre optics

Although considered a new technology, fibre optics were first discovered as long ago as 1870. The first commercial application was around 1966, transmitting information using glass fibres. A good deal of development into reducing the losses found in fibre-optic cables has been carried out since then, enabling data to be transmitted over long distances.

Fibre-optic cables work by transmitting light as a series of pulses, i.e. '0s' and '1s'. An example of how light travels through glass fibres can often be seen in decorative lamps.

Significantly greater quantities of data can be transmitted than when using copper wires. Each glass fibre in a fibre-optic cable can carry data and, when multiplexing is employed, one fibre alone could replace hundreds of copper cables.

A transmitted television signal is converted from an electronic signal to a light signal by the transmitting modulator, which changes the signal from its analogue source to a digital format where the signal is either on or off ('1s' or '0s'). At the receiving end of the fibre-optic cable (a digital TV for example) the signal is once again converted to electronic data.

Key terms

Liquid Crystal Displays (LCD): liquid crystals are carbon-based compounds that can be made to move in response to a small voltage. When they are in their 'natural state', they allow light to pass through. When charged, the crystals align with the flow of electrons, making a pattern or block of colour.

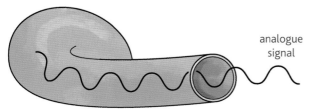

Copper cable
Could be a single cable or multi-stranded, yet only one signal

Copper cable

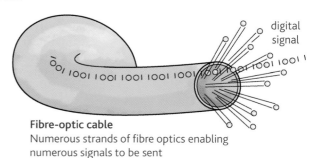

Fibre-optic cable
Numerous strands of fibre optics enabling numerous signals to be sent

Fibre-optic cable

Liquid crystal displays

Liquid crystal displays (LCDs) have been around for a number of years; they can be found in a variety of electronic products, including:

- the alpha-numeric displays in calculators and electronic dictionaries
- mobile telephones
- PDAs and laptop computers.

Liquid crystals are carbon-based compounds, which when aligned in their 'natural' form will allow light to pass through. If, however, a small voltage is applied to the crystals, then their orientation is changed to match the path of the electron flow, so blocking light. This is what makes them appear black on the display.

LCDs can be reflective or backlit. Reflective displays reflect the light entering the display back out again. Calculators generally have reflective displays. Mobile telephones and laptop computer displays are usually backlit, making them useable in poor light conditions.

Engineering timbers

Glulam is the term given to the process of lamination particularly for large span beams used in the construction industry. The benefits associated with this technique of producing beams are that they can be made to the customer's requirements so are not restricted to simply straight profiles. Curved and arched beams are also possible with the same high strength to weight ratio seen in laminated products. Depending on the required shape very large spans, up to 160 metres or more, can be economically manufactured then transported to site for assembly.

Glued laminated timbers are constructed by bonding together pieces of timber of known quality, i.e. where defects such as knots and splits have been removed. These pieces are around 50 mm thick with each piece being end-glued together to make long lengths. To construct a useful beam a number of long lengths are glued together. The woods that are used can vary and, depending on use, can vary within an individual beam. Engineering timbers are often a good way of using small sections of timber off-cuts that would normally go to waste. This therefore has some positive environmental benefits.

Kevlar

Kevlar has five times the strength to weight ratio of steel. The fibres cannot be twisted so they are woven flat and it is this that makes it such a useful material for protection as bullet- and knife-proof vests. Effective protection is achieved by applying a number of layers to the garment. Although very structured it remains flexible.

A derivative of Kevlar – Nomex – can provide further protection against heat. This is the material that racing drivers wear to protect them against any fires that might break out in the case of accidents. Firefighters will also wear garments of Nomex and Kevlar in order to protect them in their jobs.

As well as its use in protective clothing Kevlar has uses in the aerospace industry where it can be found as a lining in jet-engine casings. When mixed with a polymer, it can be formed to produce armour plating in helicopters, vehicles and helmets.

Carbon fibre

This material is made up of just that, carbon fibres. To enable them to become useful the fibres are woven into a cloth. To make them useful in a range of applications the fibres are impregnated with a resin which bonds them together. This can be epoxy, polyester or phenolic resin depending on the intended application.

To manufacture a product from carbon fibres the resin-impregnated material is forced into the shape of a mould. The material is then cured in an autoclave – a large steam heated oven which cures (sets) the material. Depending on the resin and application the material is cured at an appropriate temperature for a predetermined period of time. The whole process can take a number of days. The size of autoclave can limit the number of products being produced at any one time.

A carbon fibre laptop

Carbon fibre finds applications in Formula One racing where its light weight coupled with high strength gives the cars their ability to travel at high speeds. Other applications in sports include helmets and other safety equipment, tennis racquets, high jump poles and so on. Military applications include helicopter rotor blades, while paramedics would use carbon fibre boards to transport casualties.

Metals

Numerous developments in metals have been achieved over the last few years including coated metals, more widespread use of titanium and metal foams.

Coated metals

Coatings for both protection and decoration are now applied to sheet metals. These include polymer coated mild steel sheets and aluminiums. The polymer (PET or PP) can be applied as a transparent material or in a range of colours. These materials are of food quality so do not taint the contents and have good chemical resistance and so will not react with the contents. There is usually more than one polymer layer but the coating materials are defined by the nature of the application. The top layer is usually printable.

Applications in packaging include examples of food cans, soft drinks cans and containers for paints and varnishes.

Nickel coated steels are used where a non-corrosive surface is required. Originally electroplated nickel can also be deposited on the steel component more evenly by a chemical process, making the final product much cheaper to use than stainless steel. Nickel coated steels have a variety of uses including moulds for injection moulding, vehicle suspension parts and brake pipes.

Metal foams

Developments in metal processing have resulted in foamed metals. Examples include metals such as aluminium which can be foamed in much the same way as polymers, e.g. polystyrene. This results in a lightweight rigid material that can be sandwiched between solid sheets of the same material.

The advantage of foaming a material lies in its potential application, i.e. impact resistance. Impacts into solid sheets will transmit the majority of the impact, whereas foams slow down or absorb the impact by dispersing the energy amongst the thousands of cell walls. This clearly has implications in vehicle design or even military applications where blast protection is required.

Other applications of foamed metals are in filtration where high temperatures occur.

■ Did you know?

In the packaging industry the correct term for an internal polymer layer is a 'lacquer' while the term for an external polymer layer is a 'coating'.

■ Key terms

Plastic coating: the process of heating a metal (usually mild steel) product to around 230 °C and then dipping it into a fluidised bath of thermoplastic plastic granules, which stick to the product. A smooth plastic finish is achieved.

■ Did you know?

Along with iron ore and bauxite (aluminium ore), titanium ore is one of the most common in the earth's crust. It is only recently that processing has made it more economical to extract and use.

Titanium artificial leg

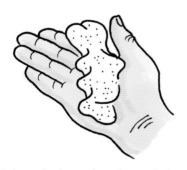

Reheated polymorph can be manipulated to create the desired shape

Further reading

- Sarah E. Braddock and Marie O'Mahoney, *Techno Textiles*, Thames and Hudson
- Matilda McQuaid, *Extreme Textiles*, Thames and Hudson.

Titanium

It may seem strange that this material is included here but it is only recently that changes in the extraction of the material from its ore have enabled this material to become more widely available.

The main characteristic of titanium is its high strength to weight ratio. This makes it appropriate for use primarily in the aerospace and medical industries. Applications include jet engine components, medical implants, and surgical instruments, military equipment and equipment for chemical plants. Other applications include jewellery (watches, body piercings, frames for glasses), sporting equipment (cycle frames, golf club heads) and colours for paints.

Other characteristics of titanium are that it is corrosion resistant, it can be coloured easily and it does not react with body fluids.

Polymorph

Polymorph is a low melting point polymer that finds useful applications in prototyping. It softens at 60 °C making it possible to fuse the grains of material together followed by manipulation of the material to create the desired shape. Reheating in hot water will allow further work to be carried out. Students often use polymorph to make prototype handle grips or even to simulate an injection moulded plastic product.

Precious metal clays

Precious metal clay (PMC) is an innovation primarily for jewellery makers. This material enables shapes to be formed in much the same way as when using 'ordinary' pottery clay. It is made up of 99.9 per cent silver (or gold) with a clay binder and water and feels like, and works the same way, as clay. As such, simple modelling tools can be used to create the desired shape. This is often much quicker than preparing patterns and moulds for casting. PMC is commonly used to make bespoke jewellery.

Work is air dried, after which it is fired by heating to near melting point temperatures so that the precious metal particles fuse together to make a solid metallic object. After firing, the object can be soldered, enamelled and polished as necessary.

Microfibres

Microfibres are very fine polymer-based fibres, usually made from polyamide or polyester, that have been designed to mimic the microstructures found in nature. The main advantage of these fibres is their fineness (up to 60 times less than the thickness of a human hair) which allows fabrics to be woven so densely that they are waterproof and breathable as well as being lightweight. This means that they will prevent water droplets from entering the fabric while allowing perspiration, in the form of water vapour, to pass through the fabric to the outside. For the wearer this means that an even body temperature can be maintained in hot or cold conditions.

Modern fabrics made from microfibres have applications in sport and leisure as well as in all other areas of fashion.

Micro-encapsulation

Further developments in microfibres have meant that chemicals can be incorporated into fabrics. These chemicals are held in tiny capsules that have been attached to the fibres. During wear the capsules gradually break releasing chemicals such as scents/perfumes, antiseptics and other medical preparations such as antibacterial products.

These fabrics can then be manufactured into clothing or applications such as bedding which can be impregnated with natural remedies for insomniacs, for example. There are medical applications such as tights that contain medication which will be released over a period of time to give relief to patients.

Phase change materials (PCMs)

When these materials are microencapsulated in a polymer-based outer shell and incorporated into fabrics they take on the role of temperature control. Incorporated into clothing the PCMs interact with the skin's temperature in such a way as to control temperature swings by absorbing, storing and releasing heat while, at the same time, changing from solid to liquid and back again. So in simple terms, this material absorbs body heat while exercising and then as the body cools in rest conditions, the material releases the heat, keeping the user warm.

The microencapsulation polymer enables the phase change material to be held securely within a fabric and is robust enough to withstand manufacturing processes such as spinning, weaving and knitting.

Examples of applications include clothing and sleeping equipment for extreme conditions, e.g. Arctic expeditions and medical kit where the control of body heat is important.

Dichroic glass

This material was originally developed by NASA for applications in space including reflective visors on helmets, coatings for space craft windows and reflective surfaces on satellites. Other applications include coatings for mirrors used in medical lasers in order to refine the quality of reflected light. More recently though dichroic glass has been used in the manufacture of jewellery items.

The term 'dichroic' means two colours. Glass is coated with very thin layers of metal oxides and quartz crystal. Light is both transmitted and reflected by the glass. The colours that are reflected are determined by the types of oxide used. The unique quality of the material means that the colours that are reflected appear to move when viewed from different angles.

Man-made boards

Developments in man-made boards have seen the introduction of flexible sheet materials such as MDF and plywood and very precise forms of plywood called aeroply.

Flexible MDF

MDF board is generally a rigid material. However, flexible MDF is now available and is used to form curved shapes. This is achieved by grooves in the material which allow the material to bend slightly at each cut due to the thinner section at that point. The grooved surface is usually applied to the inside of the product so as not to be seen while the width of the grooves determines the amount of curve achieved. The direction of curvature is decided by the direction of the cut.

Grooves can also be cut along the sheet enabling the user to curve the length of the material.

PMC product before and after firing

■ **Did you know?**

Glass has been around since Roman times but it is only since the 19th century that glass has been successfully produced in volume for windows.

Flexible MDF

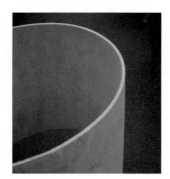

Flexible plywood

Furniture product using Maplex

The material will need to be supported by a framework to make it secure. Two or more layers of flexible MDF can be put together to produce a more rigid curve. Veneers and laminates can be applied to the material to provide a more decorative finish.

Applications include profiled kitchen drawer fronts, items of furniture and exhibition display boards.

Flexible plywood

Flexible plywood is produced in a similar way to standard plywood but there are subtle differences that make this product bendable. As with ordinary plywoods there are an odd number of layers. In this case there are only three layers since any more would restrict the movement of the material. The two outer layers are of an open grained timber and are much thicker than the inner core. The direction of the grain on the outer layer determines the direction of curvature, in a similar way to the cuts in flexible MDF.

Although thin standard plywood can be made to bend, the advantage of flexible plywood is the much tighter curves that can be produced.

Flexible plywood needs to be supported so that the shape can be maintained. Applications include furniture manufacture and other applications where a curved surface is required.

Aeroply

As the name implies this material has its roots in the aircraft industry where it was used to provide the outer skin of aircraft, being glued to a timber frame. It is still used in the construction of gliders. Aeroply is a thin section plywood of very high quality. Its thin section makes it very lightweight while it retains good strength. It is bendable and can be formed around a supporting framework.

This material can be used for more decorative purposes such as in the manufacture of wooden jewellery. It can be laser cut and formed using steam bending techniques.

Maplex

Maplex is a relatively new material designed to replace MDF since although made from wood fibres it does not contain the potentially toxic resins that bind the fibres in MDF. This material generally has good strength and rigidity although there are grades that can be bent.

The material is worked in a similar way to MDF. Applications for this material lie in the furniture industry as well as being useful in the manufacture of interior fittings.

Hexaboard

Hexaboard is an exterior quality birch plywood with a hard phenolic resin laminated surface. The hard, durable phenolic surface has been embossed with a hexagonal pattern to make it safer to walk on; this makes it particularly suited to flooring applications. Applications include flooring for commercial vehicles and aircraft, factory floors, stages and so on – anywhere that good impact resistance and wear characteristics are needed.

✓ Product analysis exercise 6

Tefal 'red spot' pans

1 The Tefal 'red spot' range of pans uses a smart material to make a red dot in the centre of the pan. Explain what type of smart material is used and how it functions.

2 Explain what function the red dot has.

3 Describe how similar smart materials are used in other products that you are familiar with.

Tefal 'red spot' pan

✓ Examination-style questions

1
a Explain in detail what is meant by the term 'smart material'   *(2 marks)*
b Name a smart material and a product that it is used in.   *(1 mark)*
c Briefly explain what the term 'alloy' means.   *(1 mark)*
d Name an alloy and a product that it is used in, and state one advantage of using the alloy in this product.   *(2 marks)*

2
a For each of the following materials, explain why they are suitable for the product listed. Your answers should make reference to the function, aesthetics or manufacture of the product.   *(4 × 4 marks)*

	Material	Product
i	Mild steel sheet	Car body panel
ii	Carbon fibre composite	Racing bicycle frame
iii	Aeroply	Cantilever styled chair
iv	Foamboard	Architectural models

b Name an alternative material that might be used to make a racing bicycle frame. Briefly explain the benefits or drawbacks of using this material.   *(4 marks)*

> **AQA Examiner's tip**
>
> In Section 1, for 1 or 2 marks, you will only need to write a short sentence answer.

> **AQA Examiner's tip**
>
> Glass is not listed in the materials and components section of the AQA specification but in exams you might be asked to name a traditional material as an alternative to plastics.

✓ *After studying this chapter it is hoped you will:*

■ be familiar with a range of materials, and types of material, such as woods, metals, plastics, composites, glass and ceramics

■ appreciate where these materials are used and why

■ understand how materials can be combined to form alloys and composites to provide advantages for their use in products

■ be familiar with a range of commercial and industrial processes used in the manufacture of a variety of products

■ be aware of the range of 'smart' and 'modern' materials available to the product designer.

Hand and commercial processing

Through the study of this chapter it
is hoped that you will:

- understand how materials and components are processed to create the product from the design.

- understand further processes relating to joining, the deterioration of materials, finishes and finishing processes, and testing materials

- understand the general nature of manufacturing systems used to produce commercial products.

Link

As in Chapter 1, you will need to use other resources – books, CD-ROMs, the internet, etc., to give you all the information you need for success as a product designer. Some references for further reading are provided.

Key terms

Filler rod: a material that is used to help create the joint between two materials. For example, a solder filler rod is used when joining copper pipe together.

Temporary: a temporary joining method is one where the components can be joined and separated without damage to the material. An example would be a nut and bolt assembly.

Permanent: a joining method where separation of the component parts results in damage to the materials. An example is a welded joint.

Many of the processes you need to know about relating to particular materials and components have already been covered in Chapter 1.

Joining processes

Introduction

We will be taking a look at appropriate joining processes available for use with a range of materials.

Products such as mobile telephones have components that are manufactured using a variety of processes from a range of materials. All these components need to be assembled to create a single functioning product. To achieve this, a variety of joining processes will have been used.

For example, removing the battery cover from a mobile telephone simply requires it to be pushed out of its locations to release it. The battery cover can be replaced by reversing this procedure. This is achieved by integrating the joining method into the two components to be joined.

Other joining processes require the inclusion of an extra component or material. Examples include nuts and bolts being used to clamp two or more components together or the use of **filler rods** when soldering or welding components together.

You will need to be aware of the general types of joining process and whether the processes are **temporary** or **permanent**. You should begin to know and understand the differences between soldering, brazing and welding, and how they are carried out. You should also understand the basic types of **wood joints**, including knock-down joints, and how these might be used. Knowledge of joints that are created with the use of screw threads in their many forms (nuts, bolts, **self-tapping screws**, captive nuts) is also desirable, as is an understanding of a range of **adhesives** and appropriate applications.

Choosing a joining method

Before we can say exactly which joining method we are going to use, there are a number of important factors that must be considered.

- The most important, of course, is the material – a wood cannot be welded, for example.
- Temporary or permanent: will the joint need to be dismantled at all?
- Joint strength required: how strong does the joint have to be? Will it be under high levels of stress?
- Stiffness needed: does the joint need to be flexible in any way, or should it be rigid as in a frame structure for a piece of furniture?
- Effect of joining method on materials being joined: will materials being joined be adversely affected by heat from welding, soldering or brazing for example?
- Appearance around the joint: will the joining process affect the surface finish? Will extra processes be required to 'clean' the joint?

Once these factors have been considered, then an appropriate choice of joining method can be made. Joining methods fall into two broad categories – those that are temporary and those that are permanent.

Temporary joining methods

Temporary joining methods are those that do not damage the materials being joined when the joint is undone. The most common example of this is the nut and bolt arrangement.

There is a large range of different types of standard components that carry out a similar function. These include **wood screws** and self-tapping screws, which cut their own threads as they are screwed into a material. If a metal, such as steel, is thick enough, a thread can be formed in an appropriately sized hole, removing the need for a nut.

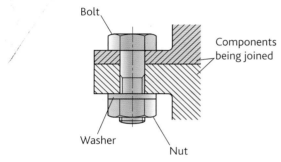

Nut and bolt assembly

For sheet material, specially shaped spring steel nuts are used with self-tapping screws, whereas with woods a range of different nuts made from plastics or metals for use with bolts and screws are available. Collectively, these are called 'captive nuts', because they are held in position in, or on, the material.

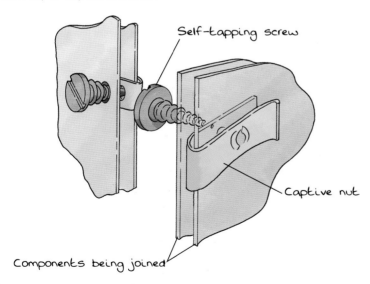

Self-tapping screw in spring steel captive nut

Knock-down joints make extensive use of captive nuts. These products are so called because they were originally designed for use with flat-pack furniture. A range of **knock-down (KD) fittings** is shown on p100. Notice that they make use of a range of threads and cams depending on their intended use.

Key terms

Spot welding: a form of **resistance welding** where the metal components being joined are clamped between two electrodes. An electric current is passed between the electrodes causing a build-up of heat at the centre of the joint, fusing the two components together. Used extensively in the assembly of car body panels.

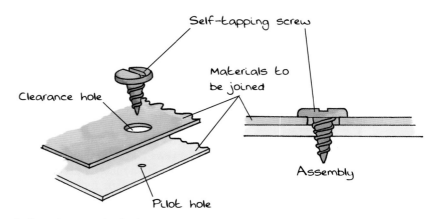

Self-tapping screw in plastic

Permanent joining methods

Permanent joining methods are those where dismantling them will damage the materials being joined. Good examples of this type of joint are the **spot welded** joints found on car body panels, which are intended to be extremely rigid and last for the lifetime of the car.

Summary of joining process

The diagram below shows a range of joining processes.

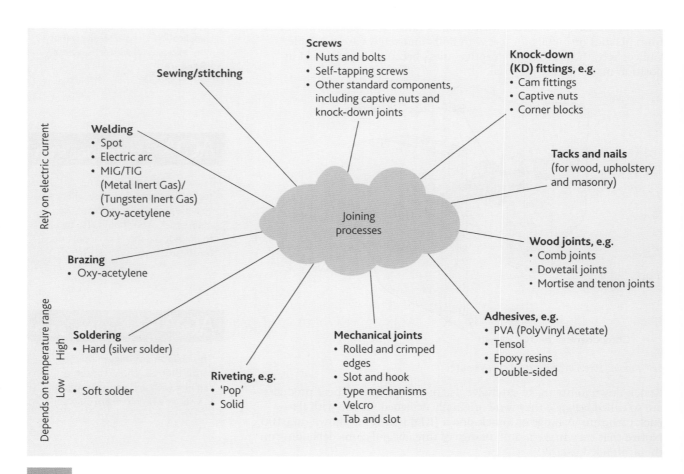

Joining metals

Metals can be joined in a number of different ways. We have already discussed nuts, bolts and screws. Other methods, such as folding and **crimping**, involve the forming of the metal to provide a joint; while others, such as **soldering**, **brazing** and welding, require the application of heat and, in some cases, the inclusion of a filler rod.

Processes involving forming

Some very simple joints can be made in sheet metals by folding the materials together. An example of this can be found in the sweet tin shown. The seam down the length of the container is produced by 'hooking' the two edges together.

The base of the container is secured by crimping the folded edge on the base to the bottom edge of the container. This is the same method used to secure the aluminium top of a soft drinks can to the main body.

Seam joint

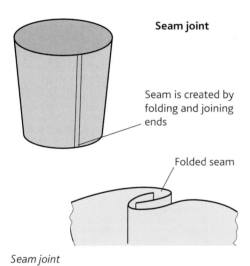

Seam is created by folding and joining ends

Folded seam

Seam joint

Crimped joint

Base is 'crimped' to the container by folding edges together.

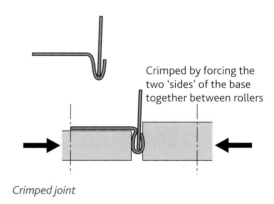

Crimped by forcing the two 'sides' of the base together between rollers

Crimped joint

Processes involving heat

The range of processes covered by this section includes:

- soldering
- brazing
- welding.

They all involve the fusion of the materials being joined by a filler material.

Soldering

- Soldering requires the lowest temperature of the three joining processes above.
- There are a range of solders available from soft solders to **hard solders**.
- Soft solders are used for joining electronic components to circuit boards, or for small copper or brass components.
- Hard solders are used for products requiring additional strength and in the construction of products requiring the soldering of a number of mating components.

- Soft solder melts at around 200 °C.
- Hard (silver) solders are so called because they contain a small amount of silver that is alloyed with copper and zinc. The amount of each material differs to produce a range of hard solders that melt at temperatures between 600 °C and 800 °C. These solders can be used in the manufacture of hand- and machine-crafted jewellery.
- Traditionally, solders have contained lead in the ratio 60 per cent tin and 40 per cent lead. Nowadays solders are available that are lead-free, containing 96 per cent tin, 3.5 per cent silver and 0.5 per cent copper. These are more expensive than traditional solders.

Making a soldered joint

Whichever type of solder is to be used to make a joint, the process remains basically the same.

Stages of the process

Step 1 Materials to be joined must be cleaned to remove grease and dust. The surfaces to be joined should be kept clean with the use of a flux.

Step 2 The mating surfaces must fit together without there being large gaps, but must be held together securely while being heated up.

Step 3 A blowtorch is used to heat the material around the joint, ensuring both pieces are heated evenly. The solder filler rod is rested on the joint; the heated material will melt the solder and capillary action will allow the solder to run between the joint.

Step 4 As soon as the joint is completely filled, it should be allowed to cool.

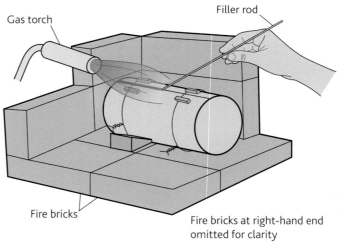

Soldering

Soldering precious metals

In order to join precious metals such as silver, a solder of known silver content is required. This is so that the materials being joined, (e.g. two components both of 925 sterling silver), can be hallmarked by the maker.

Particular care should be taken when soldering silver so as not to discolour the material by heating too much; this discoloration is called 'firestain' and is difficult to remove. Care should also be taken to use as little solder as necessary so as not to make the solder evident on the piece and also to avoid having to remove excess solder.

Silver piece showing hallmarks

The pieces to be joined should be cleaned and smoothed by using successively finer grades of wet and dry paper, then pickling in an acid bath containing 2 per cent solution hydrochloric acid. This will remove any grease marks.

When inserting and removing objects from the acid bath, care should be taken not to get any on the skin or in the eyes. To this end, safety glasses and gloves should be worn and the piece should be handled using plastic tweezers. When removed from the acid bath rinse off with clean water; if necessary dry with tissue.

Mix some Easy-flo flux with water so that it is a milky colour and apply it to the area being soldered with a soft artist's paint brush. This will ensure the solder only runs where the flux lies so be careful how much you put on the piece.

There are two ways to apply solder to a piece of silver. Both involve cutting the solder strip into small pieces (approx. 1mm square) called 'pallions'. These help the solder to melt more easily.

The pallions are placed either against the edge of the joint or in between the two pieces being joined. *Note:* when joining two surfaces together it is advantageous to use the latter method to avoid the force from the blowtorch moving the pallions out of position. The diagrams show both of these techniques.

A blow torch is used to heat the components and the solder until the solder melts and runs between the two pieces using capillary action. The material will become bright red at this stage. Once all the solder has melted the heat should be removed and the piece allowed to cool.

Borax cone
Water
Fine paint brush
Ceramic dish

Apply flux to components only in the region of the joint.

Pallions of silver solder placed around components to be joined

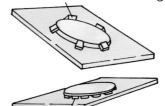

Pallions placed between components

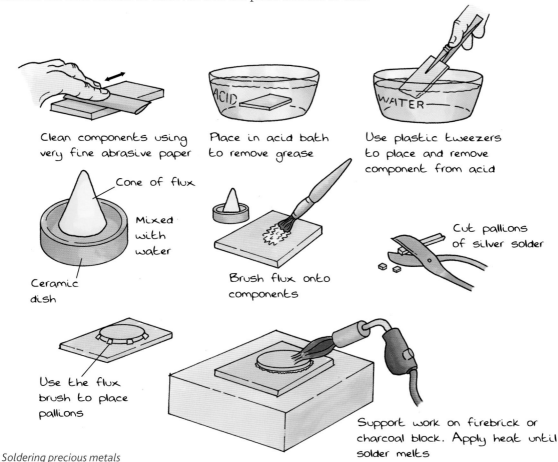

Clean components using very fine abrasive paper

Place in acid bath to remove grease

Use plastic tweezers to place and remove component from acid

Cone of flux
Mixed with water
Ceramic dish

Brush flux onto components

Cut pallions of silver solder

Use the flux brush to place pallions

Support work on firebrick or charcoal block. Apply heat until solder melts

Soldering precious metals

Final silver piece

When sufficiently cool the pieces should be cooled further in cold water. The assembled piece should then be cleaned again with wet and dry and placed in the pickle bath to remove any stubborn stains. This should then be followed by a final polishing.

Aluminium welding

Aluminium is a notoriously difficult material to join by fusing and it takes a tremendous amount of skill to achieve a good joint.

However, there are kits on the market that enable aluminium to be soldered effectively. The materials used for filler rods have a low melting point (in the case of TechnoWeld® around 380°C). This ensures that the aluminium being joined doesn't reach its melting temperature and effectively destroy the job.

The techniques used for joining aluminium in this way differ from other methods of soldering and brazing in that there is no flux involved. The joint produced is fusion-welded but at a much lower temperature than the melting point of the material being joined.

Stages of the process

Step 1 Clean the components to be joined by abrading the surface with a stainless steel wire brush.

Step 2 Each component will need to be coated with the filler rod material. For each component heat around the area to be joined. Keep the flame moving to avoid the risk of melting the component. Allow the heat from the component to melt the filler rod.

Step 3 When a pool of filler metal has formed on the component, the material should be abraded with the abrader tool to allow the filler rod material to fuse properly with the component material, i.e. to get below the protective oxide layer.

Step 4 Repeat for the second component.

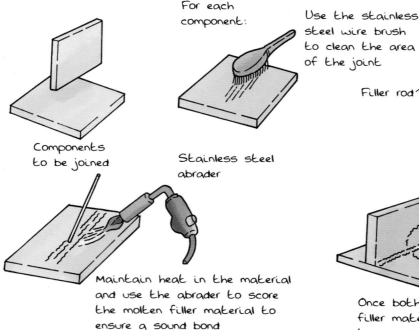

Components to be joined

For each component:

Stainless steel abrader

Use the stainless steel wire brush to clean the area of the joint

Filler rod

Scored area

Heat the area around the joint. Allow heat from the material to melt filler rod

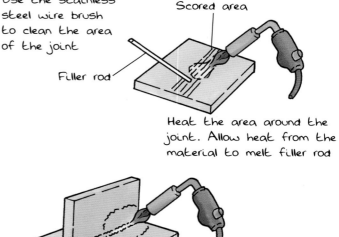

Maintain heat in the material and use the abrader to score the molten filler material to ensure a sound bond

Once both components have been coated in filler material use the heat from the torch to provide sufficient heat to fuse the two pieces together

Aluminium welding

Step 5 Place components together in the position in which they need to be joined, then apply direct heat to the joint area. Keep the flame moving, until the joint material melts and the components are joined.

Step 6 Allow to cool slowly to ensure an effective joint.

It is important to note that this joining technique differs from other methods of joining aluminium, in particular **MIG** and **TIG welding**. Refer to p97 for details of these processes.

Brazing

- Brazing takes place at a higher temperature than soldering.
- The filler rod in this case is a brass alloy, called brazing 'spelter' and melts at around 880 °C.
- The materials that can be joined using this process include copper and steel (in particular mild steel).
- The process is essentially the same as soldering, with the materials being joined, cleaned and kept clean using a flux – in this case Borax is used. Components are held together while being heated.
- When the correct temperature is reached, the brazing rod melts at the joint, filling the joint by capillary action. Again the material is allowed to cool before having excess flux and braze removed.

Welding

Welding differs from soldering and brazing, in that the materials being joined must be the same. If a filler rod is being used then it should be the same material as that being joined.

Methods of welding

There are a number of different methods of welding, including the use of oxy-acetylene or an electric arc to generate the heat required. Other techniques use an electric current passing through the materials to fuse them together.

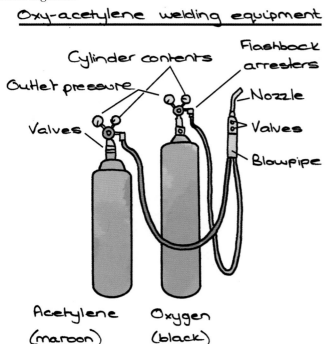

Oxy-acetylene welding equipment

Cylinder contents

Flashback arresters

Outlet pressure

Nozzle

Valves

Valves

Blowpipe

Acetylene (maroon)

Oxygen (black)

Oxy-acetylene welding This uses a mixture of oxygen and acetylene to create a flame that will burn at a temperature of around 2500 °C at the hottest point. This will clearly be sufficient to melt mild steel at the joint, allowing the melting of a filler rod to fuse the joint edges together.

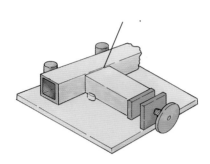

1. Set the components to be joined so that there is a small gap between them, e.g. 1 mm

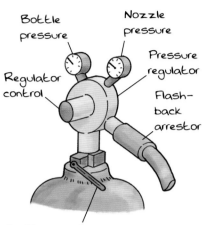

2. Release the valve on each gas bottle using the key

3. Adjust the nozzle pressure as required using the regulator control knob

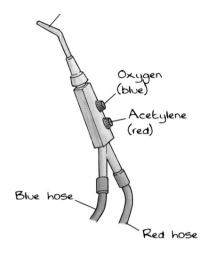

4. Open the acetylene (red) and ignite using flint gun

Note: ensure the extractor is switched on

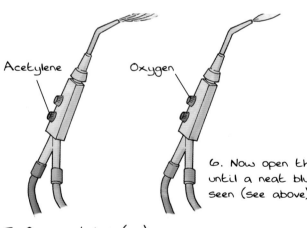

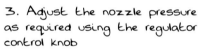

5. Open acetylene (red) until soot disappears

6. Now open the oxygen (blue) until a neat blue flame shape is seen (see above)

7. Heat the area around the joint so that the metals at the joint and the filler rod melts together

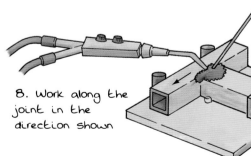

8. Work along the joint in the direction shown

Oxy-acetylene welding

Electric arc welding This generates sufficient heat to melt the joint edges by creating an electric current through a gap (arc) between the materials being joined and the filler rod (electrode). The electrode is coated in a flux which, when melted, prevents the joint area becoming oxidised.

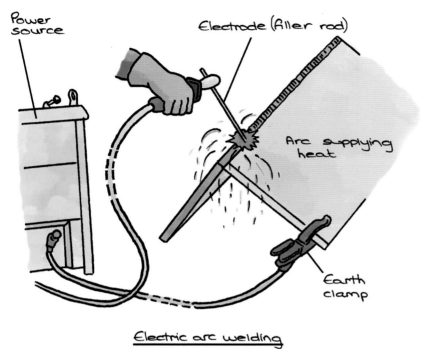

Electric arc welding

MIG and TIG welding These are more refined forms of electric arc welding which can be used to join thin sheet material. MIG (Metal Inert Gas) and TIG (Tungsten Inert Gas) welding use a gas jet around the filler wire to prevent oxidation of the material. Different gases are used with different materials, e.g. argon is used with aluminium.

TIG welding   *MIG welding*

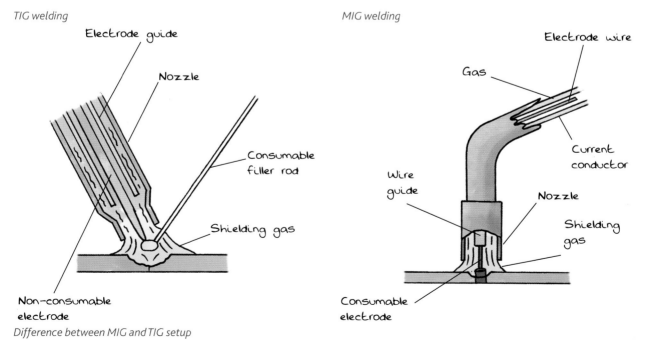

Difference between MIG and TIG setup

Using spot welding
to join sheet metals

Using spot welding to join sheet metals

Spot and seam welding Both spot welding and **seam welding** use an electric current as the **heat source**. Spot welding, as the name suggests, provides a spot of heat to fuse the metals together. It is usual to find a series of spot welds in a structure like a car body shell. Seam welding, on the other hand, passes an electric current through the material as it passes under rollers. A typical application for this type of joining method is tin-coated mild steel for food and drinks cans.

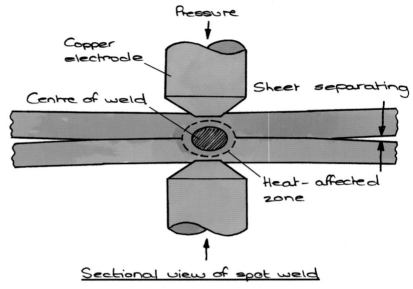

Sectional view of spot weld

■ Key terms

Seam welding: a form of resistance welding used for joining seams in fabricated tubes and in food cans.

Heat source: any piece of equipment that applies heat in an appropriate manner for the purposes of joining materials. For example, oxy-acetylene equipment is used as a heat source for gas welding and brazing.

i Activity

Identify the safety precautions that must be observed when joining metal components by (a) oxy-acetylene welding and (b) electric arc welding.

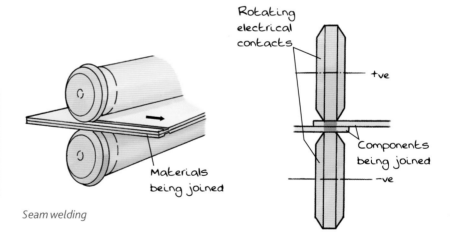

Seam welding

Joining wood

A variety of both temporary and permanent joining methods can be used with woods, depending on the intended application.

When large sections of timber are used – for example, the oak framework for a house – the beams and posts can be joined together by a combination of **traditional wood joints** and pegs.

When large section beams are used for temporary support, a more temporary joining arrangement may be used. In the case shown above, a barn wall is being supported by a framework that is bolted together.

A modern roof truss is produced in a different way, i.e. without the use of traditional joints. Each of the timbers is cut to the correct size and shape and, once set up in a jig, plates with spikes (effectively nails) are forced into both sides of the joints.

For traditional household furniture, more traditional wood joints would be used. The type of wood joint again depends on the application.

Note: All of these joints would be secured with an adhesive, such as PVA (Poly Vinyl Acetate), making them permanent.

Wood joining methods

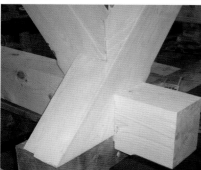
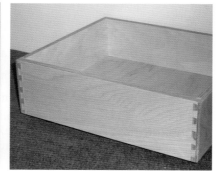

Examples of different wood joining methods

Self-assembly furniture

Self-assembly furniture is produced in high volume, being supplied to the consumer as a flat-pack of component parts. In order to accommodate self-assembly, a range of fixings has been developed specifically for use with this type of furniture. With every flat-pack there

Key terms

Traditional wood joints: wood joints that require machining to make interlocking parts and often combined with adhesive.

AQA Examiner's tip

You should develop an understanding of the traditional wood joining techniques and be able to give examples of where they would be used.

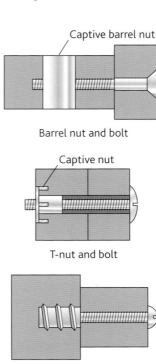

Barrel nut and bolt

T-nut and bolt

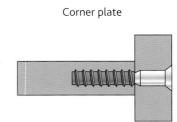

Cam fitting

Corner plate

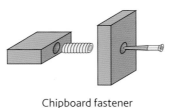

Screw socket

Chipboard fastener

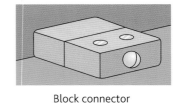

Screw connector

Block connector

💡 *A range of knock-down fittings*

is a pack of **knock-down (KD) fittings** included. The joining methods used may comprise any or all of the following: captive nuts, cam fittings and corner blocks, depending on the materials used in the manufacture of the furniture. (Kitchen units are generally made from laminated chipboard, while bedroom furniture may be made from solid pine.) Examples of these joining methods are shown above.

Along with these fixings there will be:

■ hinges that have been especially made to fit into the pre-drilled holes

■ a range of screws developed specifically for use with self-assembly furniture (different screws will be used for chipboard products from the standard screws used with natural woods).

All of the joining components, including hinges and handles, are manufactured in large numbers by specialist companies and, although originally designed for the specialist application of self-assembly furniture, are very common. These are standard components and can be readily purchased from local suppliers.

Wood adhesives

Where a joint is to be permanent – whether it is a traditional wood joint in natural timber or wood products assembled with knock-down fittings – an adhesive can be used to aid the integrity of the joint.

The adhesive used would generally be PVA. This would be spread on the two halves of the joint that have already been cleaned, and the whole joint clamped together until the adhesive is dry. Any excess can be wiped away with a damp cloth before it has a chance to dry.

Joining polymers

Mechanical means

Polymers can be joined together by mechanical means, i.e. nuts and bolts. The choice of material from which nuts and bolts are made depends on:

- the application
- the type of polymer to be joined
- the amount of load the joint is to carry
- whether or not the joint will be affected by the environment.

Standard fixings can be obtained in mild steel, stainless steel, brass and nylon; used appropriately, these will produce a durable joint.

Adhesives

Adhesives can be used to join polymers but, in general, are not wholly successful. Tensol is an adhesive in liquid form that is used especially with acrylics. It acts as a **solvent**, by dissolving the components together at the joint.

The use of adhesives in packaging is more successful. When heat is applied directly to the film lid of a pre-cooked food package, a layer of adhesive is melted on the rim of the container allowing the film lid to adhere to the container. This also creates a seal between the two components making the packaging hygienic.

Ultrasonic welding

The use of very high frequency sound waves is an excellent method of joining plastic materials, especially sheet materials. The two parts being joined are firmly clamped together. Very high frequency (ultrasonic) vibrations are then introduced to the materials through the clamp. This has the effect of generating heat, which is produced by the vibration of the atoms and molecules of the materials being joined.

Ultrasonic welding is generally used on consumer products, children's toys and automotive products such as instrument housings and glove compartments, as well as a range of other plastic products found on vehicles.

Metals are also ultrasonically welded. In this case, welds are formed not by heating the materials to a melting point but by the application of pressure and very high frequency mechanical vibrations. Different metals can be joined using this process. During the process, particles of each material will penetrate the other creating a fusion between the metals. This type of process is used in electrical and electronic industries for fusing components together for products such as electrical leads to terminal connectors for the automotive industry, or sensors for the heating market.

AQA Examiner's tip

Polymers require specific joining techniques. You should develop an understanding of these and be able to give examples of where and how these would be used.

Key terms

Solvent: any chemical that will dissolve a material. For example, a thermoplastic produced from crude oil will begin to deteriorate in the presence of oil or its vapour.

Ultrasonic welding: the use of very high frequency vibrations to generate heat within the area to be joined, thereby allowing the materials to fuse together. Plastics and some metals can be joined in this way.

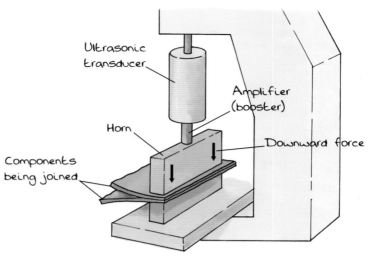

Ultrasonic welding

Plastic welding

Thermoplastics can be welded using similar principles to those for welding metals, in that the application of heat is used to fuse a filler rod to the components being joined. A powerful heat gun is used to provide the heat necessary to melt the material. An attachment ensures that it softens the components and the filler rod at the point where it is to be joined.

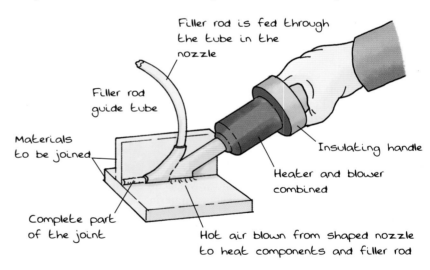

Plastic welding gun

This method of joining plastics is particularly applicable to producing one-off products such as containers from thermoplastic sheet and for the repair of damaged products where the inclusion of a filler rod will not be detrimental to its function.

Integral fixings

Polymers can be used to manufacture complex 3-D shapes needed to produce modern products. The advantage of this is that fixings, such as posts for screws, captive nuts, locating and securing clips, can all be made integral to the component being joined.

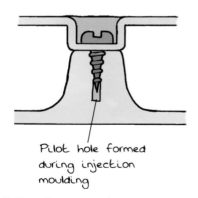

Self-tapping screw and screw post

Click fixings

Examples include the battery cover, 'express-on' covers for mobile telephones, and the clips that hold a CD into its case. These types of fixings rely on the elastic properties, as well as the strength and durability, of the polymers used to make the components.

■ Joining ceramics

Ceramic products, such as teapots and cups, are manufactured from the same material throughout, whether it is an earthenware body or a fine bone china. The handles on these products will have been stuck on while the clay material was in its 'green' state, i.e. before firing. The 'adhesive' used in this instance would be a liquid clay (called slip) – a much watered-down version of the clay used for the product. Once the handle is fixed on the body of the teapot or cup, then the whole thing is fired to produce a single piece.

Adhesives

The main advantage of using adhesives as a joining technique over any other method of joining, is that it is essentially invisible. Adhesives do not damage or change the shape of the components being joined, whereas nuts and bolts are visible and spot welds can cause indents in the metals being joined.

There are two main groups of adhesives:

■ *natural adhesives* include any of the animal- and vegetable-based glues, and naturally occurring resins such as gum arabic

■ *synthetic adhesives* include manufactured adhesives, such as **epoxy resins**, phenolic and formaldehyde resins, anaerobic adhesives and the silicon-based adhesives.

■ Key terms

Epoxy resin: a thermosetting plastic material made up of two parts – resin and hardener.

Table 17 *Examples of adhesives and where they might be used*

	Type	Examples	Uses
Natural adhesives	Animal glues	Animal hide, bones, hooves	Used to glue woods, fabrics and leathers
	Natural resins	Gum arabic	Used for papers and fabrics, and binders in watercolour paints
	Inorganic cements	Portland cement	Used in the building industry for bonding bricks and blocks
Synthetic adhesives	Synthetic resins	Cascamite (powder mixed with water)	For bonding woods; is waterproof and can fill slight gaps
	Epoxy resins	Araldite Two (part adhesive, hardener and resin)	Joins most materials
	PVA	Poly Vinyl Acetate (water-based)	Used for gluing woods; generally not waterproof
	Contact adhesives	Evo-Stik (works by evaporation of solvent)	Used for bonding sheet materials on contact
	Hot glue sticks	(Work on application of heat)	For rapid bonding of papers and cards
	Acrylic cement	Tensol	For gluing acrylics only

Using adhesives to join materials together requires good surface preparation, i.e. surfaces should be thoroughly cleaned of dust, grease and any previous coatings. The adhesive should then be applied to the components, either one or both depending on the type of adhesive being used. The components being joined will then have to be held together until the adhesive has dried.

Advantages of using adhesives

■ They are able to join dissimilar materials.

■ The insulating properties of adhesives help prevent corrosion through electrochemical action of dissimilar metals while some adhesives, particularly the silicon-based varieties, act as sealants as well as bonding agents. Examples of this can be seen on vehicle windscreens, where the old rubber seal has been replaced by a silicon-based adhesive which also acts as a sealant around the windscreen.

■ Case study: The Dyson DC24 vacuum cleaner

The DC24 Dyson Ball vacuum cleaner is a good product to study as it shows a range of temporary joints that are used throughout the casing and the functional parts of the cleaner.

If the underside of the vacuum cleaner is examined, we can see that the cover that fits over the brush is fixed using self-tapping screws. These screws enable the cover to be removed so that blockages can be cleared and, in the event of the drive belt breaking, it can be replaced easily. As the screws have standard Philips heads, they can be removed with a common screwdriver. No specialist tools are needed.

The DC24 features a number of parts that use 'click' fittings. Two parts in particular are the handle and the dust canister. The handle on the DC24 is removed from the vacuum cleaner as it forms a 'wand' that can have tools inserted into it to enable vacuuming of stairs and other inaccessible parts. The handle features a squeezable part that disengages a click **fastening** from the main body of the vacuum cleaner. The dust canister uses a spring-loaded fastening to attach the canister to the main body of the machine.

Within the motor housing, and other sections that contain electrical parts, the manufacturer may use temporary fastenings such as machine screws but they may have torx heads which require a torx driver to undo them. This helps to prevent unqualified consumers tampering with parts of the cleaner that could lead to electrical shock. However, temporary fixings are still required to allow for maintenance of such parts.

The casing of the DC24 is made from recyclable plastics. Dyson has a facility that enables owners to return their cleaner at the end of its useful life, so that the plastic parts can be shredded and later recycled. The use of temporary fastenings such as self-tapping screws and machine screws enables all of the parts to be disassembled relatively easily.

Very few, if any, permanent joints are used in the manufacture of the DC24. The casing is injection moulded and therefore fewer joints are necessary. Basically, the more joining that has to be done in the manufacture, the longer it takes to make, increasing cost. Where it is necessary to join plastic parts together, they are normally joined with temporary joints such as those described above.

> **Key terms**
>
> **Fastening:** any product that is designed to hold materials together. Examples include spring clips, self-tapping screws, and nuts and bolts.

Dyson Ball vacuum cleaner

Product analysis exercise 1: Joining processes

Aluminium bicycle frame

1 Study the photograph of this aluminium bicycle.

a The aluminium bicycle frame has been fabricated together. Use notes and diagrams to explain how this is done.

b If the bicycle frame had been made from a mild steel tube, what joining method would have been used? Explain why the same joining method cannot be used as for aluminium.

c The bicycle seat is adjusted using a temporary joint. Use notes and diagrams to show how this temporary joint functions.

 Product analysis exercise 2: Joining processes

Stainless steel saucepan

1 The saucepan shown is made from stainless steel.

a Explain why stainless steel is a suitable material for manufacturing a saucepan.

b Name the process for manufacturing the body of the pan.

c The handle has been spot welded on. Explain why this process is appropriate.

d Use notes and diagrams to explain how the spot welding process works.

Corrosion, decay and degradation

Over time and under varying conditions materials will eventually begin to break down. In this section we will concentrate on what happens to metals, woods and plastics under these conditions.

You need to become aware of these processes and use the correct terms when discussing them in your answers to examination questions. For example, metals are said to corrode, woods decay and plastics degrade.

Corrosion of metals

Most metals have an oxide layer on the surface of the material. This is always present and is the result of the way oxygen in the atmosphere reacts with the material at its surface. Generally, this oxide layer is helpful to the material by being sufficiently dense and impermeable to prevent further oxidation. If we take a non-corroding material, such as brass, and purposely scratch the surface, exposing 'new' metal, the oxide layer closes up immediately and helps protect the material.

Rust

Ferrous metals, with the exception of stainless steel, are the only group of materials that **rust**. This type of corrosion is caused by the material's oxide layer being porous, allowing moisture to make contact with the surface of the material. This in turn causes the surface of the material to rust, i.e. to become the familiar red-brown colour. Moisture will penetrate the initial layer of rust, which, in turn, will oxidise a further layer lifting up the previous layer.

Electrochemical corrosion

In this type of corrosion, a very small electrical current is produced when two different metals are joined together. All metals have a natural

 AQA Examiner's tip

You should be able to show an understanding of how materials breakdown. You should be able to use terms correctly when discussing particular types of materials.

Key terms

Rust: the oxidation of steels (not stainless steel) due to contact with the air that may well contain moisture. The oxide layer of steels is porous so further oxidation can take place. This results in a thicker oxide layer as the material breaks down.

Key terms

Electrochemical cell: the term given to the conditions necessary to promote corrosion between two different metals. The additional component is an electrolyte. An example of an electrolyte is rainwater containing salts and acids.

Activity

Clean a piece of mild steel sheet so that it shines. Hold your thumb or finger on the cleaned area for a few moments. Leave it on a shelf for 24 hours. When you come back to it, what do you see? Probably a rusty brown fingerprint. How has this happened?

Did you know?

If you study physics or chemistry you may know that when two materials, especially metals, are put together there will be a tiny electrical charge between them. You can experience this yourself if you chew on aluminium foil or catch a fork or spoon on your tooth. It is the electrical difference between the two materials that gives you that very small electric shock.

Key terms

Wet rot: decay in woods that is a direct result of alternating cycles of the timber being wet followed by drying, i.e. an accumulation of moisture that breaks down the cellular structure of the timber.

Dry rot: a fungal attack causing a breakdown of lignin resins that hold the cellular structure of the material together. The fungus is *Merulius lacrymans* and is usually present in dry, unventilated areas. The strands of the fungus can also penetrate brickwork, enabling it to travel quickly through a building.

voltage. When two different metals are joined together in the presence of rainwater (and the acids it might contain), then an **electrochemical cell** is produced and one of the materials will begin to corrode. The diagram below helps to explain this.

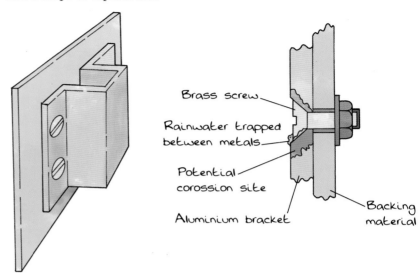

Electrochemical corrosion

Electrochemical corrosion can be very slow because of the very small voltages and currents involved, but over time corrosion will eventually occur. For example, if brass screws are used to hold aluminium sheets together, there will be the basis for an electrochemical cell. If rainwater comes into contact with this join, then an electronic circuit is produced because of the voltage difference between the two materials. Aluminium is the material that will begin to break down at the junction of the two materials. The brass itself will remain generally unharmed, though it may be difficult to separate from the aluminium.

Surprisingly enough, soft drinks may contain some potent acids, though these are not generally harmful to the consumer. Pour cola, or a similar drink, into a clear plastic container followed by a few old copper coins. Leave for 24 hours or more before removing them from the liquid. What has happened to them? Identify the chemicals in the liquid that might be responsible for the change.

There will, of course, be repercussions for the material used for the container. Glass and plastics, like PET (polyethylene terephthalate), are resistant to acids. However, aluminium cans have to be protected so that the liquid does not corrode the container thus contaminating the drink. This is achieved through coating the aluminium with a thin layer of polymer.

Corrosion through chemical attack

Acids have a corrosive effect on most metals and can rapidly destroy a metal component. This is often associated with extremely dangerous forms such as hydrochloric acid. These types of liquids are generally held in plastic containers, since polymers in general have a high resistance to them.

Decay of woods

Being a natural material, wood is open to attack from a number of fronts:

- wet rot
- dry rot
- attack by insects.

Wet rot

Wet rot occurs where timber endures alternating wetness and dryness and begins to decompose. Moisture is absorbed into the timber where it will partially dry out, followed by more moisture absorption. This results in the resins and fibres breaking down. A protective barrier must be applied to prevent the ingress of moisture.

Dry rot

Dry rot is a fungus that spreads its strands very quickly through woods, e.g. in a building. It is called 'dry rot' because of the way it converts the timber into a dry, soft, powdery state. The fungus thrives where the conditions are damp and unventilated, with little circulating air. Increased ventilation will help prevent dry rot in the first instance, but where it has already attacked timbers they should be replaced.

Insect attack

The furniture beetle (or **woodworm** as it is more commonly known) can be responsible for attacking softwoods and hardwoods in floorboards and furniture. The deathwatch beetle will generally only attack hardwoods, e.g. the structural timbers of old buildings.

Insects lay their eggs in a crack or crevice in the timber. The larvae that hatch eat their way into the fibrous structure of the wood creating tunnels. When the time comes for the grub to pupate, it returns to a cavity that is near to the surface. When the beetle finally forms, it eats its way out through a flight hole.

Moderate attacks by woodworm or deathwatch beetle can be treated with chemicals, but where the damage is severe, the affected timbers should be removed and burned to prevent further contamination.

Degradation of plastics

Many plastics degenerate in the environment. To some degree this is simple oxidation, but is more seriously caused by ultraviolet radiation.

Stability of plastics

Many plastics are relatively inert and will resist chemical attack. For example, although polythene is unaffected by prolonged contact with concentrated acids, including hydrofluoric acid, it is less stable when exposed to outdoor environments. In this case it will tend to become more brittle and opaque.

Some rubbers used in hoses and seals can perish, becoming brittle and useless if not stabilised.

Weathering of plastic materials

Unless stabilised, almost all polymers (in particular thermoplastics) will deteriorate in appearance. This seems to be due mainly to the combined effects of oxygen and ultraviolet light.

Most polymers absorb UV light causing the chemical bonds in the molecular chains to break, thus shortening them. At the same time, the oxygen in the atmosphere leads to the formation of chemical groups and possible cross-links. Both of these events cause the material to become weaker and less flexible.

A stabilising substance that will shield the material from UV radiation, by making it opaque, is added during manufacture. Pigments such as

> **Activity**
>
> Review the section on joining processes. What method of joining aluminium sheets is preferable to the use of screws? Explain the reason for your choice.

> **Key terms**
>
> **Woodworm:** an insect that attacks both hardwood and softwood by laying eggs in crevices in the material. The larvae eat away at the timber then emerge through flight holes – the tell-tale signs of woodworm infestation.

'carbon black' (used in the tyre industry) will absorb UV radiation and thereby act as an effective screen.

Example of weathering

Take, for example, the effect of weathering in the material being used for glazing a greenhouse. The 'glazing' can be made from thin sheets of LDPE (low density polyethylene). This will last for a couple of seasons, before it will start to degrade due to exposure to very strong UV light from the Sun. The overall cost of replacing the LDPE is lower than using glass as the glazing medium, which would also require a stronger frame to take the heavier material.

 Product analysis exercise 3: Corrosion, decay and degradation

1 Study the photograph of the wrought iron gates.

   a Explain why the wrought iron would corrode if the gates were not given a protective finish.

   b Describe a suitable protective finish and explain in detail how it would be applied.

2 Study the photograph of this wooden gate.

   a Explain why wood generally decays if it is not given a protective finish.

   b Describe a method that could be used to prevent the wood from decaying.

3 Study the photograph of the plastic playhouse.

   a Describe how some plastics degrade.

   b What methods would the manufacturer use to ensure that the plastic used in the playhouse does not degrade?

Key terms

Self-finishing: the term given to a material that has an acceptable finish after processing. Generally applied to plastics that do not need any further processing to produce the required finish; they can be given a very high-quality finish by being produced in moulds that themselves have a high-quality finish. The term can also be applied to metals, such as stainless steel; copper; brass; and woods, such as oak and teak which, depending on application, may not require further processing to produce the required finish.

Self-coloured: the term given to a material that has an acceptable colour after processing. Plastics are said to be self-coloured when they have their colour added prior to processing and, therefore, appear as the desired colour.

Finishes and finishing processes

Introduction

You need to be aware of the range of finishes that can be applied to products and the reasons why these processes are necessary. The difference between finishes and finishing processes must be defined, along with an understanding of terms such as **self-finishing** and **self-coloured**.

Why include a finishing process?

The **applied finish** of a product significantly affects its aesthetic qualities, giving it a greater sense of quality and value and therefore adding to its appeal. There are a variety of reasons, as well as aesthetics, why a finish should be applied to a product, including:

- protecting the material against corrosion
- making the product water repellent
- improving its resistance to wear and fatigue
- improving its ability to reflect or absorb heat
- improving its ability to insulate against heat or electricity.

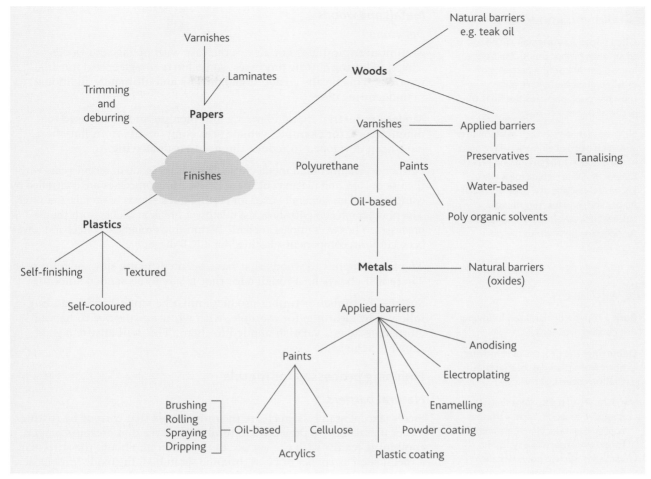

Finishes

Finishing materials

Plastics

Self-finishing

Plastics are known as self-finishing materials. This means that the quality of the mould must be very high to ensure that any trimming of flash or excess material is kept to a minimum.

Self-coloured

One of the advantages of using plastics to manufacture products is that it can be self-coloured. By including pigments with the powders or granules in the hopper of the moulding equipment, a product component, e.g. casing for a CD or mobile telephone, can be produced in the desired colour.

Textures

Textures can be added to polymers by applying the texture to the surface of the mould. This is directly transferable to the polymer because of the way the softened material is forced under pressure into every part of the mould. Conversely for a smooth finish, the surface of the mould would have a correspondingly smooth finish. These processes will clearly add expense in the production of the mould.

> **Key terms**
>
> **Applied finish:** refers to coatings that are applied to the surface of the material for protection and/or decoration.

Key terms

Burr: a rough edge created following a cutting process.

Deburring: the process of removing burrs from the edge of material that has been cut.

Varnish: a hard transparent finish that is applied to wood. Yacht varnish is applied to products that are intended for external use; while synthetic varnishes, such as polyurethane varnish, are used internally.

Natural barriers: protective layers close to the surface of a material that protect the material from corrosion, decay or degradation. An example is the oxide layer that is present on non-corrosive metals, such as stainless steel or copper.

Blueing: a method of finishing steel products that involves heating the product to around 300 °C followed by quenching in oil. It is the oil that gives the material a characteristic 'blue' finish.

AQA Examiner's tip

In exams, always refer to specific finishes, e.g. polyurethane varnish rather than simply varnish.

Metals and woods

Deburring

Minimum trimming is not always the case with metals and woods where, following cutting processes, some **burrs** (rough edges) must be removed. This means an additional process and ultimately additional manufacturing costs.

Modern industrial metal blanking and piercing processes used to manufacture, for example, vehicle seat components from flat sheet, have been developed to reduce the need for **deburring**.

Further developments in metal cutting have been made in recent years with the use of laser and plasma cutting. These cutting processes are controlled by computer and are generally used for cutting thick sheets of metals accurately. The photographs on p40 show the quality of finish available from these processes. The two samples are both 12 mm thick toughened steel and have been cut from components destined for a JCB digger.

The same applies to woods that have been cut using saws or routers. There will always be a rough edge that needs to be sanded smooth.

Surfaces of timber or timber products must be smoothed by sanding followed by cleaning, for example, with white spirit prior to having a finish such as a **varnish** applied to them. This will ensure a good finish is achieved.

Finishing processes for metals

Natural barriers

Steels (except stainless steel) are the only metals that corrode by rusting. Other metals have a protective natural oxide layer that prevents oxygen combining readily with the surface of the material. Should the surface of a metal such as copper or brass, become scratched, the oxide layer closes up very quickly and continues to protect the metal though the scratch will still be clearly seen.

Stainless steels have such a protective oxide layer. This is provided by chromium, a material which is used to protect steel components by being electroplated onto them.

Blueing is a technique for producing a protective surface for steels – though it has limited success. Blueing is achieved by heating the steel component to around 300 °C and then quenching in oil. The result is a fine oxide layer that will help protect the material from environmental effects.

Applied barriers

As we have seen, steels in particular need protecting from corrosion. There is a large range of materials that can be applied to metals, by:

- electroplating
- dipping
- spraying
- brushing
- rolling.

Electroplating

Other metals can be used to coat a base metal. The method used is **electroplating**, which is an electrochemical process that allows ions from the coating material to form on the base material, giving it the finish of the coating metal. An example of this is chromium plating that is used to enhance the properties of bathroom taps, kitchen equipment and vehicle components.

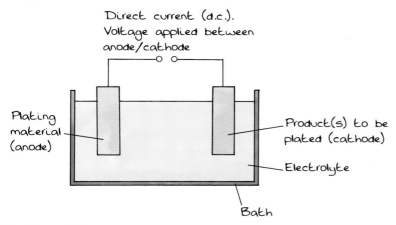

The electroplating process

Metals that can be used as coating materials in this way include:

- gold
- silver
- tin
- zinc
- copper
- chromium.

Anodising

Natural barriers can be enhanced. Aluminium, for example, can be **anodised**. This process makes the surface of the aluminium more durable and resistant to scratches. Anodising is produced in an electrochemical cell (in a similar way to electroplating) where a sulphuric acid solution is the electrolyte, with the aluminium product as the anode and lead as the cathode. Passing an electric current through the electrolyte solution effectively builds up a tough oxide layer that will accept dyes. It is finally sealed with a lacquer.

Dipping and spraying

Metals can be coated with other metals by dipping or spraying in conjunction with some kind of heating system. The materials need to be cleaned, then fluxed prior to applying the coating material. Examples include:

Zinc plating A galvanising process achieved by dipping steel in molten zinc heated to 450–60 °C, and is usually the first layer of protection for car bodies.

Tin plating Tin is applied by passing the sheets of steel through baths of molten tin at 315–20 °C. This is used in the manufacture of food cans.

Enamelling

Vitreous enamelling is a process where finely ground glass, formed into a water-based slurry, is sprayed onto a metal product, e.g. components for cookers or for pressed steel baths. It is then fired, so that the coating becomes a continuous layer of heat- and scratch-resistant material.

Enamels can be used to decorate items of jewellery or other precious metalwork. Very fine glass powders in a wide variety of colours are available to the jeweller. These are applied to the surface in layers then

Anodised bicycle wheel rims

Key terms

Electroplating: the use of the process of electrolysis to coat a base metal with a second, more decorative metal. For example, silver-plated cutlery.

Anodising: an electrochemical process that is used to make the surface of aluminium more durable. In addition, coloured dyes can be added for a decorative finish.

heated sufficiently to fuse the glass particles together and to the metal base. Between each layer the enamelled surface is smoothed under running water with a *water-of-Ayr* stone. This provides the key for the next layer.

In order to prevent the metal base distorting due to the number of heating and cooling cycles a counter enamel layer is applied to the underside of the base material.

Enamelled jewellery

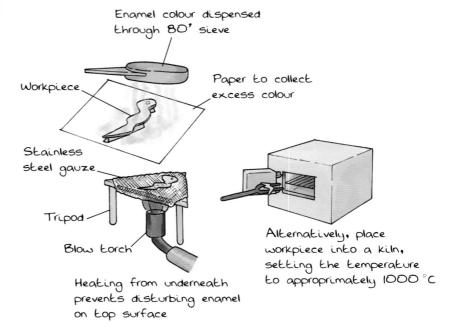

Enamelling jewellery

Titanium coatings

Titanium is an extremely hardwearing material. It is therefore advantageous to coat products such as cutting tools and some kitchen equipment with this material to preserve the cutting edge.

The coating can be applied in one of two ways:

1   *Physical vapour deposition* is explained fully on p116. It can be used in low temperature applications such as in coating spectacle lenses.

2   *Plasma spraying* uses a super heated inert gas (formed by applying a high energy electric arc to it, to melt the fine titanium powder being fed into it. This rapidly expands and accelerates the material so that it adheres well to the product.

Not all of the product is treated in this way. For example, in the case of a knife edge, one side only is coated. This ensures that if any wear takes place then the edge is always being regenerated.

Painting

For a paint finish to be applied successfully, the metal surface must be thoroughly cleaned and degreased using a paraffin-based liquid. This ensures that the primer (the first layer of paint) keys into the material's surface. The second layer will be an undercoat. This helps give a professional finish to the topcoat. Paints can be brushed on, rolled on or sprayed.

Car bodies are generally made from mild steel. Nowadays they last a lot longer before corrosion takes over, primarily because of all the layers of protection that have been applied to them. Following the galvanising layer (described above) numerous layers of primer, undercoat and topcoats of acrylic or cellulose paints are sprayed onto the car body. A layer of a hard, clear lacquer could well follow this.

Special paints such as 'Hammerite' have been developed especially for metals. These paints do not require a primer or undercoat and can be applied directly to the metal surface. The finish achieved can be a smooth or hammered effect.

Electrostatic spray painting is a development that relies on an electrostatic charge between the paint and the metal object being painted. The paint material will have a positive charge applied to it while the object being sprayed will have a negative charge applied. The electrostatic attraction between the two ensures a secure bond between material and coating.

Powder coating

Powder coating is a method of applying paints to a product that has been statically charged. This is a dry process where a powder is used instead of paint. The powder is sprayed through an airgun. The powder is positively charged while the product is negatively charged, resulting in a very strong attraction between the coating material and the product. Once coated, the product is baked in an oven where the heat melts the powder over the product producing a harder and tougher finish than is obtainable with conventional paints.

Examples of products coated in this way include domestic white goods such as fridges and washing machines, gates and fencing.

Since this is a dry process, it is environmentally sound – no solvents or propellants are used – and any excess coating materials can be recovered.

Plastic coating

Plastic dip coating can be used on a range of products., for example, a die-cast bottle opener.

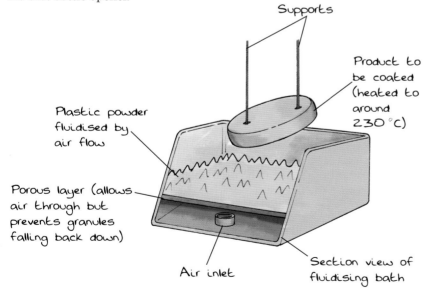

Plastic dip coating

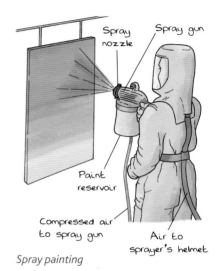

Spray painting

> ### ■ Key terms
>
> **Electrostatic spray painting:** an electrostatic charge is set up between the object to be painted and the paint particles, making a secure bond between paint material and product surface.

> ### ■ Key terms
>
> **Powder coating:** this process uses an electrostatic charge to coat the metal product. Once coated, the product is baked in an oven to produce a smooth, high-gloss finish.
>
> **Plastic dip coating:** a method of finishing a metal-based component. The component is heated to above the softening point of the polymer, which is in the form of a fine powder, then dipped into the polymer. The polymer adheres to the heated metal, which begins to cool, and so the polymer solidifies into a protective layer.

Activity

Suggest at least two different applied barriers that could be applied to a child's swing, (produced from mild steel) to protect it from the weather. Explain, using diagrams where appropriate, how these barriers would be applied.

The process involves heating the metal component to around 230°C. The fine plastic granules are fluidised by passing air through them. This helps provide an even coating of material over the component being coated. The product is dipped into the fluidised polymer and removed. Heat from the product melts the plastic material, which cools in air providing an even coating over the product.

Finishing processes for woods

Unprotected wood expands because it can absorb water, especially in outdoor applications. This causes the resins that bind the cells together to break down, rendering the material very weak. Bacteria and fungi can also attack wood.

Woods do not have the same natural protection against the environment as metals, and are prone to decay over a period of time. Hardwoods have a greater resistance to the environment than softwoods, due to the closer structure of the grain, and will therefore last longer. Teak contains oils that help repel rainwater and so protect the material.

💡 *Applied barriers*

Paints and varnishes

Paints can be used on woods, just as they can on metals, but first the material must be cleaned and any knots should be treated to prevent resin leaking. The surface of the wood must be sealed with a primer paint, which helps to key in the next layer of paint and prevent subsequent layers being absorbed by the wood. As with metals, an undercoat can be used followed by a topcoat. To obtain a high-quality finish, it is necessary to rub the surface down with fine sandpaper in between layers of paint.

Oil-based paints are generally used with woods. These are hardwearing, non-porous materials and are available in a range of colours. These paints can be used inside or out and are used for coating windows and door frames.

Polyurethane paints, on the other hand, are used for coating, for example, children's toys. They are extremely hardwearing, being tough and scratch-resistant. If the natural grain of the wood is required, then sealing can be achieved by the use of transparent polyurethane varnishes. For products that are used outside, such as patio tables and chairs, a yacht varnish would be more appropriate. Yacht varnish is not affected by sunlight and the expansion or contraction of the timber in the same way that polyurethane varnish is.

Two-stage stain and varnishes both colour the wood and provide a protective layer. There are varieties that can be used internally or externally and those that can be used on already painted surfaces without the need to strip the old paint.

These products rely on a base coat being applied to the timber product as the first stage. This applies a base colour to the material that represents the original colour of the timber, i.e. a stain. The top coat is a layer of varnish which is coloured to bring out a more defined wood colour. Examples of where this type of finish is used includes window or door frames, interior fittings such as stair balustrades and skirting boards.

Wood preservatives

The four main groups are:

- ▪ tar-oil derivatives (creosote)
- ▪ water-soluble preservatives
- ▪ organic solvent preservatives
- ▪ **tanalising**.

All of these can be applied by brushing, dipping or spraying, or by pressure treating.

Creosote has been traditionally used for the preservation of a range of timber products. The main disadvantage with this method is that creosote will destroy any plants it makes contact with and is generally damaging to the environment. This has led to it being banned from use. An alternative would be the water-based organic solvent preservatives. These can be obtained in a variety of colours. Water-based preservatives will need to be maintained more regularly.

Increasingly, timbers can be obtained that have been tanalised. This is a process where timbers, usually softwoods, are treated by the preservative prior to assembly into a product. The process of tanalising involves the impregnation of the timber with a solution of copper sulphate and other salts in large pressure vessels. The pressure forces the minerals into the structure of the timber which helps prevent water from being absorbed.

Water is first removed from the timber by drying. The pressure vessel is filled with preservative. Lengths of sawn and planed timber are loaded into the vessel which is then sealed. Pressure is slowly increased until the desired amount of preservative has been injected into the timber. The wood is then steam dried before removing it from the pressure vessel.

The main advantage of pressure treating timber is that it can be applied to uncut timber before manufacture of the finished product. Timber products treated in this way could well last up to 50 years.

Papers and cards

Varnishes can be applied in the same way as ink; this is usually the final stage of the printing process and is carried out on the same printing machine. The aim of including this final stage is to extend the life of the printed product.

Laminating is the application of a protective layer of a clear plastic material to the surface of the printed material. It is a separate finishing process, resulting in the protection of the printed material and, in addition, an increase in the strength and durability of the product.

Polymer coatings

Most spectacle lenses are made from a polymer these days. Everyday spectacles have lenses made from PMMA (acrylic). This material makes much lighter lenses than those made from glass, though they can be scratched more easily. In order to reduce the risk of scratching, a coating of another polymer, CR39, is applied to the lens. The process used for this is physical vapour deposition (PVD).

Physical vapour deposition utilises a vacuum chamber where the product to be coated is placed. The coating material (which can be a solid, liquid or gas) is evaporated

▪ **Key terms**

Wood preservative: applied to timbers that are exposed to general weather conditions and which do not have any other means of protection. Preservatives prevent moisture entering the structure of the material, thereby reducing the risk of wet rot.

Tanalising: a process whereby wood is pressure-treated with preservative.

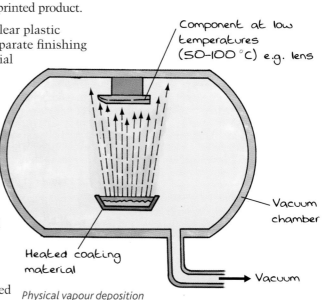

Physical vapour deposition

by intense heat. The heat energy could, for example, be provided by a tungsten filament. Atoms of the coating material are then deposited onto the exposed surface of the product being coated, i.e. the lens. All of this can occur at relatively low temperatures ensuring no distortion to the product.

Additional anti-reflective coatings can also be applied to the lenses using this technique. In this case compounds of silicon dioxide, aluminium oxide and zirconium dioxide are deposited as a number of very fine layers onto the surface of the lens.

Dual layer plastics

Overmoulding The process where a second polymer is injected over specific areas of the component. For example, a toothbrush, originally injection moulded from PMMA (acrylic) is overmoulded with a thermoplastic elastomer to act as a grip. This process uses two injection moulding moulds, one for the acrylic toothbrush shape and the second for the grip. The second stage requires the acrylic toothbrush shape to be inserted into the second mould prior to the overmoulding.

Twinshot injection moulding This achieves similar results but uses a single mould and a specially adapted injection moulding machine with two barrels (injectors) for the two materials being used. An example of twinshot injection moulding is the outer casing for an Apple iPod, where the two layers of polymer can be clearly seen.

The process works as follows. Within the first part of the cycle the basic shape of the product is formed while in the second part of the cycle the second material is applied to the areas requiring overmoulding. The advantages of twinshot injection moulding lie in the much reduced cycle time compared to the previously described overmoulding process.

Activity

Steel gate

Wooden gate

Look at the photos above. Explain how the two gates shown might be protected from the environment.

Further reading

See: www.hardwarezone.com/img/data/nnews/2007/8544/image/full.jpg

✓ Product analysis exercise 4: Finishes and finishing processes

Applied barriers

Study the photographs of:

■ an anodised aluminium Mag-Lite torch　■ silver-plated cutlery　■ plastic-coated pliers

1 For each of the products, use notes and diagrams to show how the finish is applied.

2 For each product, explain the function finish has.

3 For one of the products, name an alternative finish. Explain why this finish is suitable.

■ Properties and materials testing

General properties of materials

All materials have properties to some degree or other. For example, a metal like aluminium will conduct electricity extremely well whereas other metals like lead will conduct electricity, but not as well. A different material, e.g. a polymer such as ABS, will not conduct electricity at all, and is therefore an excellent insulator.

Materials' properties and structures

The properties of a material are determined largely by its structure. Metals are made up of crystals that contain atoms and molecules of the various elements that make up the material. Metals have good strength in both compression and tension, due to the very strong metallic bonds holding the atoms together. These metallic bonds also allow free electrons to be shared amongst molecules, thereby making metals excellent conductors of heat and electricity.

Polymers and woods, on the other hand, have very different structures that do not permit the flow of electricity since there are no free electrons in their atomic structure. This makes them excellent insulators of both heat and electricity.

Although hardwoods and softwoods differ in type and structure, they are all fibrous materials made up of an arrangement of plant cells and resins. This results in the material having greater strength along the grain; woods are generally better in compression than in tension.

Polymers, in the main, are made up of long-chain molecules containing carbon, hydrogen (hence the term 'hydrocarbons') and oxygen atoms, along with other chemicals such as chlorine and fluorine.

The long-chain molecules in thermoplastics are held together by electrostatic bonds (called Van der Waals bonds). When heat is applied to the material, these bonds become weaker and so the material softens. With sufficient heat, the material can be remoulded. This is the basis under which thermoplastic polymers can be recycled.

The long-chain molecules in thermosetting polymers are held together by covalent bonds (very strong carbon-to-carbon bonds) forming rigid cross-links. These are not affected by heat, and so the material cannot be melted and reformed.

Materials' properties and products

One of the main factors affecting the choice of material for a product is the product's functional requirements; two examples are given below.

Example 1: A soft drinks can
The material for a soft drinks can:

■ must not be affected by the acids in the liquid it is holding

■ must not contaminate the drink, i.e. it must be non-toxic

■ must have sufficient strength to withstand any internal pressure if the drink is carbonated

■ must be capable of being formed to the desired shape, e.g. one that is stackable in order to aid transportation. It must be capable of being deep drawn into the required shape. This means the material must have good ductility – the ability to be drawn out under tension without fracture.

When the can is being manufactured, the main body of the can starts life as a disc of material – in this case it would be mild steel. It is then formed into a cup shape, followed by deep drawing. The final process actually reduces the wall thickness of the can, resulting in the wall thickness being about one-third of the thickness of the base.

Example 2: An electric plug

Most domestic appliances are mains powered and so have a 13-amp plug fitted to them. If we consider the choice of materials for the main parts of the plug, i.e. the casing and the pins, we can see that they require quite different properties to function.

The casing

The casing is made from a polymer, either a thermoplastic or a thermosetting plastic. The functional requirement of this component is that it:

- acts as an electrical insulator
- can withstand any heat generated by the flow of electricity
- is sufficiently rigid and durable to withstand inserting and removing from a socket.

The pins

The pins, however, need to be able to conduct electricity and so are usually made from a metal. Durability is also a high priority for this component, since this is the part that actually moves against the contacts in the socket.

Definitions of materials' properties

Mechanical properties

Mechanical properties are those properties that determine how a material reacts to external forces.

Plasticity is the ability of a material to be permanently changed in shape by external forces, e.g. hammer blows, pressure, without cracking. Metals and (thermoplastic) polymers are generally more plastic when heated. Plasticity applies to both compressive forces and to tensile forces and the ability to be deformed in these ways is determined by the material's malleability and ductility, respectively.

- *Malleability* is the ability of a material to withstand deformation by compression. A malleable material, e.g. copper, can be deformed by compression before it shows signs of cracking. Malleability increases with temperature and therefore metals, which need to be bent, rolled or extruded, are heated first. A silversmith would be interested in the materials' malleability for example, when planishing an object or forming a shape by hammering.
- *Ductility* is the ability of a material to be drawn out. Copper is also a ductile material, i.e. it can be deformed under tension before it fractures. The ductility of all materials decreases as the temperature increases, making them weaker at higher temperatures. Soft drinks can makers are interested in ductility as the can bodies need to be deep drawn.

Elasticity is the ability of a material to flex and bend when forces are applied and to regain normal shape and size when those forces are removed. Spring makers need to understand a material's elastic properties in order to produce a spring of the correct rating.

Toughness is the ability of a material to withstand a sudden impact without fracture. It also refers to a material's ability to withstand bending (see also **bending strength**, below). Copper is a very tough material, e.g. copper wire can be bent many times before it fractures; while a high carbon (hard) steel possesses the opposite property – brittleness.

Hardness is the ability of a material to resist abrasive wear, indentation or deformation. It is an important property of cutting tools, e.g. drills. Abrasive papers depend on the hardness of the abrasive medium to be effective. Brittleness is usually associated with hardness, unless the material structure has been altered to provide some measure of toughness, e.g. tempering of metals.

Durability is the ability of a material to withstand wear and tear, weathering and the deterioration or corrosion this may cause. Weathering processes can change the appearance of a material and result in mechanical weakening.

Stability is the ability of a material to resist changes in size and shape due to its environment. Timber tends to warp and twist due to changes in humidity. Metals and some plastics gradually deform when subjected to steady or continual stress. This gradual extension under load is known as 'creep'. Turbine blades are subjected to high temperatures and rotational speeds, therefore the blades need to be produced from a creep-resistant material.

Strength is the ability of a material to withstand force without breaking or permanently bending. Different forces require different types of strength to resist them.

- *Tensile strength* is the ability of a material to resist stretching or pulling forces.
- *Compressive strength* is the ability of a material to withstand pushing forces which attempt to crush or shorten the material.
- *Bending strength* is the ability of a material to withstand forces which attempt to bend the material.
- *Shear strength* is the ability of a material to resist sliding forces acting against each other.
- *Torsional strength* is the ability of a material to withstand twisting forces under torsion or torque.

Physical properties

Physical properties are those properties that refer to the actual matter that forms the material.

Fusibility: the ability of a material to change into a molten or liquid state when heated to a certain temperature, i.e. a melting point. This varies between materials, but is essential to processes such as casting, welding and soldering.

Density: defined as mass per unit volume. Relative density is the ratio of the density of the substance to that of pure water at a temperature of 4 °C.

Electrical conductivity: all materials resist the flow of electricity to some extent. Electrical conductors offer a very low resistance to the flow of an electric current. Metals – especially silver, copper and gold – are good conductors. Liquids (electrolytes) and some gases also allow current to pass through them easily.

Electrical insulators: these offer a high resistance to the flow of electricity. Non-metals are generally good insulators, but vary in their ability to resist the flow of electricity. Wood is a comparatively poor insulator, while ceramic materials, glass and plastics, such as nylon and PVC, are very good.

AQA Examiner's tip

It is vital that you explain why such properties are relevant to a product, making reference to function and so on.

For example, ABS has good strength to weight ratio. This is useful in mobile phones which need to resist impact from being dropped, but also be lightweight.

Semi-conductors: these range between the two previous extremes, allowing electric current to flow only under certain conditions. For example, silicon and germanium in their pure state are poor conductors, but their electrical resistance can be altered by the addition of impurities.

Thermal properties: these relate to a material's reaction to heat.

Thermal conductivity: how heat travels through the material. It is measured in watts per metre per degree Celsius. Metals, especially copper and aluminium, possess high thermal conductivity.

Thermal insulators: materials with low value thermal conductivity, and are generally non-metals. They are used to prevent heat gains and losses, e.g. pan handles, loft insulation.

Thermal expansion: materials generally expand when they get hot and shrink upon cooling. A material's coefficient of linear expansion is the fractional change in length due to changes in temperature. In large civil engineering projects, such as bridges, allowance has been made for movement caused by seasonal variations of temperature. Control mechanisms also use this effect, e.g. car thermostats or automatic kettles.

Optical properties: how materials react to light and heat by reflection, radiation and absorption. This will vary according to whether the material is translucent, transparent or opaque:

Opaque does not allow light to pass through, e.g. house brick, mild steel sheet.

Translucent allows some light to pass through, e.g. one sheet of photocopy paper, a thin acrylic sheet, fine bone china.

Transparent allows light to pass through, e.g. clear glass.

Magnetism is a property possessed by many elements, and is the product of the orientation of electrons about their atoms. Only a few elements, however, are strongly magnetic. Steels are generally magnetic. However, mild steel is not, due to insufficient carbon in its structure, neither is stainless steel.

Materials testing

You need to have an understanding of basic tests that can be applied to materials to identify what they are, and their suitability for the intended application. All of the tests suggested here can be applied easily within the workshop using the equipment usually found there.

Workshop testing

Metals

Metals are readily identified by their density, colour and shine (or the way the light reacts with them). By simply looking at the material and judging these aspects, a metal can be identified. For example, aluminium is silvery in colour but is much lighter than silver. Polished steel can be similarly silver in colour, but is also heavier than aluminium.

Aluminium is a soft metal, so if you were to scratch it with a file or scriber it would make a deeper mark than mild steel. If all else fails, you can test the material with a magnet. Mild, medium and high carbon steels are all magnetic. Stainless steels and most other metals are not.

Woods

Woods can be identified by their grain, colour and density. Beech (a hardwood) has a very close straight grain with very few knots and is a light buff colour, while Scots pine (a softwood) also has a straight grain but is very knotty. Some woods have a distinctive grain such as walnut or yew (both hardwoods), while woods like oak, as well as having a distinctive grain, are heavy.

Plastics

Plastics can be more difficult to identify simply by looking at them and nowadays manufacturers employ an identification code to the materials.

This enables the material to be collected and recycled. However, there are aspects of plastics' properties that can help identify the material.

- Determining whether a plastic is a thermoplastic or thermosetting material can be carried out by the application of heat; if it begins to go soft, then it is a thermoplastic.
- Polyethylene, for example, will float.
- Acrylics and polystyrenes can shatter on impact.

Is the material appropriate?

Workshop testing of metals can be carried out for:

- hardness
- ductility and malleability
- tensile strength
- toughness.

Hardness

Hardness can be tested in a number of ways – two are given here. (Both of the following methods can also be used to compare two materials.)

1 A file can be run over the material. If the file cuts, then the material is soft, i.e. softer than the file; if it does not cut, then it is harder than the file.

2 A dot punch is used to create an indent in the material. It is most important that when comparing materials, the amount of effort used in striking the dot punch with the hammer is the same for all sample pieces.

Ductility and malleability

Ductility can be tested by placing a piece of the material in the vice, then attempting to create a 90° bend. If the material shows cracking on the outside of the bend, then it may not be sufficiently ductile for its intended purpose. If cracking appears on the underside of the bend, then the material may not be sufficiently malleable.

Tensile strength

An indication of tensile strength is the amount of energy required to bend a material. A comparison of tensile strength can be made by clamping sample materials of similar length in the jaws of a vice, and applying the same load to them. In this case, it is the resistance of the material to the load being applied that is being tested.

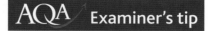

AQA Examiner's tip

For AS level it is a good idea to carry out some workshop experiments to explore properties of materials.

At A2 you will need to know how this is done in industry.

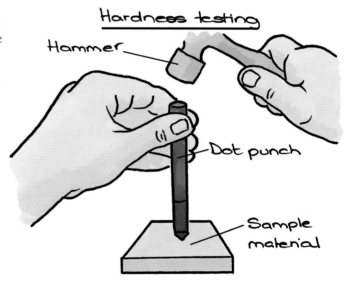

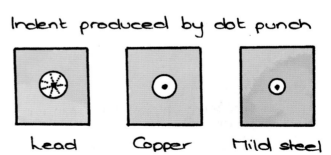

Testing for hardness

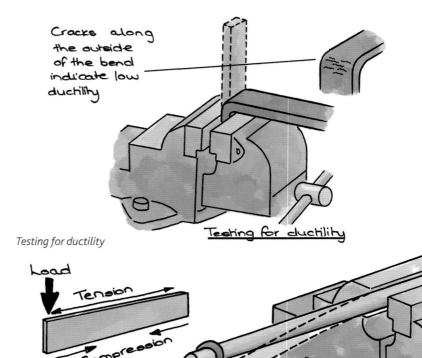

Cracks along the outside of the bend indicate low ductility

Testing for ductility

Load

Tension

Compression

Deflection indicates strength as well as compressive strength

Load provided by weights

Tensile strength test

Tensile strength test

Toughness

Toughness is a material's ability to absorb mechanical shock from, for example, a hammer blow. A comparison of materials' toughness can be made by clamping samples of materials in a vice, then striking them with a hammer.

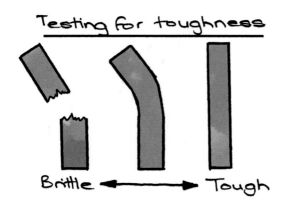

Testing for toughness

Brittle ⟵⟶ Tough

Testing for toughness

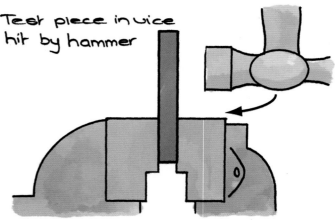

Test piece in vice hit by hammer

**WARNING: Safety spectacles must be worn.
Some materials may shatter.**

✔️ Examination-style questions

1 a Name a Knock Down (KD) fitting you are familiar with. *(1 mark)*

b For the Knock Down (KD) fitting you have named in (a), name a product that it is used in and state an advantage of using this KD fitting in the product. *(2 marks)*

c Name a component used to make temporary joints in sheet metals. *(1 mark)*

d Name an adhesive used to join acrylic and state one drawback that it may have. *(2 marks)*

2 a Name a ferrous metal and explain why it can be susceptible to corrosion. *(4 marks)*

b Name a specific finish that can be applied to metals to prevent corrosion. *(2 marks)*

c Explain in detail how this finish is applied. *(6 marks)*

d Briefly state the main causes of decay in timber. *(2 marks)*

e Name a finish that can be applied to timber to prevent decay and explain in detail how this finish is applied. *(6 marks)*

3 Study the concept design for a kettle shown on p174. The design has to be made into a three dimensional (3D), non-functioning block model.

a Name a material that could be used to make a 3D non-functioning block model of the kettle *(2 marks)*

b Explain two properties of this material that make it suitable to make a 3D non-functioning block model. *(4 marks)*

c Explain in detail how a 3D non-functioning block model of the kettle could be made using the material you have named in **a**. You may use diagrams to support your answer. *(9 marks)*

AQA Examiner's tip

Unit 1 Section 1 questions can be answered in brief bullet point form.

AQA Examiner's tip

Look for key words like 'explain in detail' and look at the number of marks allocated to questions as a guide to how much you should write.

A six mark question will usually need two to three sentences or short paragraph answers to properly explain points.

AQA Examiner's tip

Drawings used in exams only need to be simple line diagrams. Don't waste time rendering drawings with lots of colour or tonal shading as you won't gain any more marks for them.

✔️ *After studying this chapter it is hoped that you will:*

- be aware of the vast array of joining techniques appropriate for use with a variety of materials or combination of materials

- understand the differences between permanent and temporary joining techniques and where they are used

- understand the term 'integral fixings' and give examples of where these are used

- have gained an understanding of the terms 'corrosion', 'decay' and 'degradation' and the applied barriers that help prevent these

- be aware that materials have particularly useful properties that enable them to be used appropriately

- have gained a knowledge of simple workshop tests for a range of materials' properties.

3 Design, environment and ergonomics

Through the study of this chapter it is hoped that you will:

- understand the environmental and sustainability issues that influence Product Design

- practise analytical skills and develop an understanding of how products can be designed to meet human needs

- appreciate how products are designed to meet safety criteria

- understand some of the human and social values in Product Design, such as designing for disabled people and other groups.

AQA Examiner's tip

Where you are asked to discuss a number of things about a product, for example; raw materials, manufacture, use and disposal, you might find it helpful to structure your answer under subheadings for each one.

Environmental and sustainability issues

It is important that you know what the general issues are concerning the environment and how designers and manufacturers can minimise the environmental impact of products.

Why sustainable design?

Currently, we are consuming the earth's resources such as oil, timber, metal ores, etc. at an alarming rate. Only timber can be replaced but not quickly enough at current rates of consumption. The process of converting raw materials, manufacturing products and then using them, consumes a huge amount of energy. This, in turn, creates pollution and CO_2 emissions which are linked to **global warming**. This warming of the earth's atmosphere is creating changes in weather patterns which, if unchecked, will have devastating effects. In addition to this, when products are disposed of, they often go to landfill which wastes resources and creates further environmental hazards.

The role of designers and manufacturers

Many consumers are already recycling packaging waste and products when they reach the end of their useful life. Designers and manufacturers now have an obligation to develop products that use fewer materials and components in their manufacture; consume less energy in manufacture and in use by consumers; and to recover and reuse materials and components after their disposal.

The three Rs

Reduce

Designers and manufactures aim to reduce the amount of materials and energy used in manufacturing a product and the amount of energy the product will consume in its life.

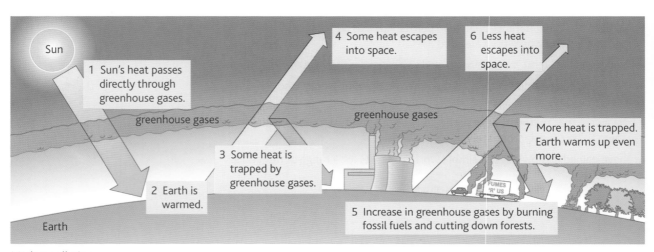

Modern pollution

Recycle

Designers and manufacturers aim to ensure products can be recycled. This means that materials are able to be separated, cleaned and used again in a new product.

Reuse

Designers and manufacturers will aim to ensure that materials and components that have already been used, can be used again in a new product. For example, reusable cartridges in printers and copiers, filters in coffee machines and vacuum cleaners, etc.

Eco-design improvements to a mobile phone

Electronic gadgets such as mobile phones are made from non-biodegradable plastics and electronic components. These components may also contain some metals such as lead, cadmium and mercury which are toxic. This makes recycling of such devices a hazardous and difficult task. Recently, such materials and substances have been banned in the EU by the introduction of the Restriction of Hazardous Substances Directive (RoHS) in 2006–7.

The table below and the diagram on p126 explain how the impact of a mobile phone on the environment could be reduced.

Table 18 *Eco-design improvements to a mobile phone*

Design strategy	Ideas for improvement
Use low-impact materials	Use recycled polymers for the casing.
	Use recycled copper for the electronic components.
	Do not use aluminium in the casing or internal parts (aluminium uses energy in its production).
	Do not use materials banned under RoHS.
Reduction of materials used	Make the phone smaller to reduce the materials needed.
	Reduce the functions on the phone to reduce the number of components needed.
Reduce impact of distribution	Provide human powered or solar powered charger to charge batteries.
	Use recycled materials in packaging.
Reduce energy consumption in use	Provide human powered or solar powered charger to charge batteries.
	Provide a device that switches off chargers when the battery is charged or when the phone is unplugged from the charger.
Optimisation of product life time	Design the phone with classic styling that will not 'date' the phone too quickly.
	Provide downloadable software upgrades to update the functions of the phone.
	Provide interchangeable casings to refresh the appearance.
	Make the phone repairable.
Optimisation of end of life	Make the phone using smart shape memory alloy fastenings and actuators that will loosen and pop the casing and parts open when heated and aid the separation of parts for recycling and reuse.

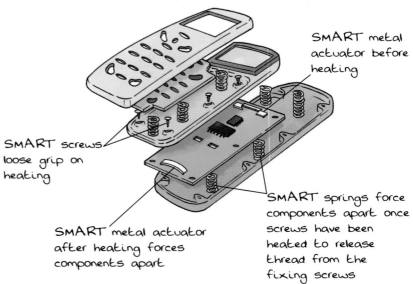

SMART metal actuator before heating

SMART screws loose grip on heating

SMART metal actuator after heating forces components apart

SMART springs force components apart once screws have been heated to release thread from the fixing screws

Fastenings and actuators that could be used in mobile phones

Hand operated mobile phone charger

The impact of a mobile phone on the environment could be reduced by users being provided with a human-powered charger to charge the battery

Key terms

Ergonomics: the study of the interaction between the human body, products and environments.

Ergonomics and anthropometrics

Ergonomics

Ergonomics concerns the interaction between the human body and products, systems or environments. Product designers are particularly concerned with making products that are easy to use.

Ergonomists are designers specialising in ergonomics. They may design:

■ *products:* for example, ergonomists may conduct trials with users to check the usability of a product such as the operation of a games controller, a steam iron, computer mouse, and so on

■ *systems:* for example, the layout of a restaurant kitchen or a manufacturing production cell, in order to make them more efficient and reduce strain injury risk

■ *environments:* for example, the interior of a car or aircraft, to ensure comfort of the user and an efficient interface between the control systems and the driver or pilot.

How does ergonomics influence design?

Ergonomics is a critical factor in the success of a product. If products cannot be used easily; are difficult to set up and need complex instructions; or are difficult to maintain or simply uncomfortable to use, they will be unpopular with consumers. There are many ingredients or factors that can influence ergonomics. Some of these are as follows:

■ *Colour:* This is used in many products such as power switches on a kettle, warning lights on a car dashboard, function keys on a mobile phone and so on. The type of colour used and how it performs in different levels of light are important factors for ergonomists to consider.

■ *Lighting:* The correct level of illumination can be a very important ergonomic factor. Visual displays need to be bright enough to be seen in full sunlight but perhaps adjustable for night time use, so as not to strain the eyes. Many portable cell phones, satellite navigation systems and car dashboards have daylight and night time settings. Light levels are also important in office and workstation situations. For example, special computer grade lighting is needed to minimise reflection from PC monitors.

- *Sound*: Audible instructions and warnings are common in products such as satellite navigation, in-car safety systems, aircraft controls, lifts, self-service tills and many other areas. The sound level and clarity of sound under different conditions such as engine noise are, again, very important factors to consider. Noise such as background sounds from machinery can affect ergonomics. High levels of noise can be uncomfortable and serious health and safety issues.

- *Comfort*: There are many factors that affect how comfortable something is. These factors might include shaping a product to fit part of the body, such as a chair seat. Alternatively, they might include covering products with a soft material to make them easier to hold. Sometimes products can be uncomfortable to use if the user has to stretch or move awkwardly to reach something. This could happen in a poorly designed workstation or kitchen, for example. Comfort can also be affected by temperature. If the temperature is too high or too low – such as in a car interior or computer room – air conditioning is often needed. Other factors such as noise levels and vibration such as that experienced by machine operators can also affect comfort.

Anthropometrics

Anthropometrics involves using body sizes to improve the ergonomics in products, systems or environments. For example, designers of items such as personal stereos would look at data for hand sizes in order to ensure that the product can be comfortably held, and that the controls are positioned to allow easy operation with finger tips.

Anthropometrical data taken from the measurements of hundreds of volunteers is normally recorded as percentiles. The average size is known as the **50th percentile**. Most design activity is for the body sizes between the 5th and **95th percentile**, which would take in the majority of the population.

The photograph opposite shows a pair of scissors made from stainless steel. The scissors could be made more ergonomic in the following ways:

- The metal handles could be made from a polymer to reduce the weight of the scissors, making them easier to hold, and to prevent any allergy reactions. This could be overmoulded with soft TPE to make it cushioned or soft to touch and easier to grip.

- The handles need to be large enough for adults to use. They would need to accommodate at least the 50th percentile male and female user comfortably.

- The handles could be shaped so that they fit the contours of the fingers.

Metal handled pair of scissors

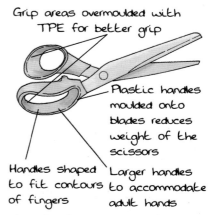

Grip areas overmoulded with TPE for better grip

Plastic handles moulded onto blades reduces weight of the scissors

Handles shaped to fit contours of fingers

Larger handles to accommodate adult hands

Plastic-handled scissors

Product analysis exercise 1: Ergonomics

Mobile phone

Study a mobile phone and note the following ergonomic features:

1   How comfortable is it to hold? Does it fit into the hand neatly? Has it been shaped to fit into the hand?

2   Are the number/letter keys spaced sufficiently to allow easy dialling?

3   Are the keys laid out in a logical sequence? (This can help the user to make calls/texts and prevent errors.)

4   Are the keys backlit to enable the user to dial in dark conditions?

5   Is the screen backlit?

6   How is colour used on the keys (usually green to answer a call, red to end a call – familiar colours for 'go' and 'stop')?

7   Are simple ideograms or pictures used on the buttons or menu to help the user recognise features, for example power button, end call, volume, battery level?

8   How clear are characters/digits on both the keys and the screen?

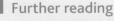
Further reading

■ Henry Dreyfuss Associates, *Measure of Man – Human Factors in Design*, Whitney Library of Design

■ Steve Garner, *Human Factors (Design Topics),* Oxford University Press

 Product analysis exercise 2: Ergonomics and anthropometrics

Personal stereo

Sketch a personal stereo and headphones like the one illustrated. Label and make notes on the following features:

■ overall dimensions relate to average hand size
■ rounded corners for comfort
■ lightweight materials
■ ideograms used on fast forward, and so forth
■ textured wheel for volume adjustment
■ raised buttons for radio/stereo selection
■ enlarged play button
■ easy battery access
■ volume restricted to prevent ear damage
■ fingernail recess for tape removal
■ pocket size.

Headphones:

■ flexible steel band adjusts the headphones to fit different head sizes
■ wire long enough to allow freedom of movement
■ foam padding used on earpiece
■ earpieces swivel to 'best fit'
■ earpieces can be adjusted vertically
■ sculpted to fit average
■ stem fits in natural slot of ear lobe
■ may have foam covering for comfort
■ flex has one piece longer to go around back.

■ Inclusive design

Inclusive design concerns developing products that can be used by disabled people as well as other consumers. Very often, changes in products to accommodate disabled users can have benefits to able bodied people, e.g. more user-friendly kitchen appliances, gardening tools, etc.

Designers working on inclusive design projects will often use techniques to give them the experience of what it is like to be a disabled person. For example, to simulate having arthritic hands, the designer might wear special gloves that restrict hand and finger movement therefore addressing problems with manual dexterity. Designers would also work closely with disabled people and observe them doing different tasks to identify what the specific problems are.

Adapted products

Many products have been changed to meet the needs of disabled people and designers are now taking more care to improve the appearance of such products so that they are more appealing as well as being functional.

One area where many elderly disabled people have problems is in the bathroom, particularly when taking a shower, reaching for the soap or adjusting the shower settings; balancing without slipping when getting in and out of the shower; and drying after bathing.

Possible solutions for this problem might include the provision of :

- ■ a cubicle with built-in warm air drier
- ■ a combined soap dispenser with the showerhead
- ■ a folding seat with hand rails for support
- ■ 'touch tile' controls to adjust the water temperature, dispense soap, etc.
- ■ body jets to allow improved coverage without the need to turn around
- ■ 'wet room' drainage so that there is no step to negotiate.

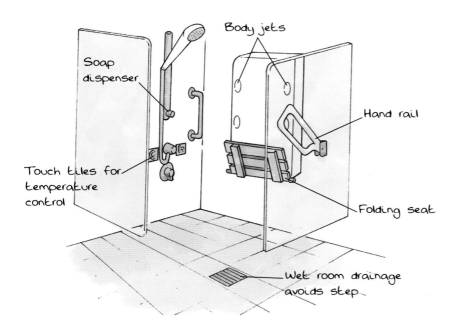

Adapted products: an adapted shower

Products designed specifically for the elderly would focus on making life easier and more comfortable. Generally very elderly people might have reduced mobility or motor skills. They might also have reduced physical strength. As the very elderly are more immobile than the average consumer, it is very important that furniture such as seating and beds are designed and made to be as comfortable as possible.

Examples of products specifically designed for the very elderly include things like:

- lever tap tops (to make turning taps on and off easier)
- kettle cradles (to aid the pouring of kettles)
- universal jar openers (to facilitate jar lid opening)
- elasticated and Velcro-fastening clothing
- seating with memory foam cushions.

As the population is generally living to an older age, design activity for this age group is becoming more and more significant. Indeed, in some parts of the United States and Japan, whole supermarkets and shopping malls are devoted to products that appeal to the elderly.

Designing for other groups in society

In addition to designing for disabled people and the elderly, 'inclusive design' can also include designing for children and those in the lower percentile group, (5th percentile or lower) and the upper percentile group (95th percentile and above).

Designing for children (or the 5th percentile), means designers must take into account smaller body sizes and different physical abilities. Many products are already specifically designed for children such as furniture, car seats, baby products, tableware, e.g. cutlery and plates, and clothing.

Products designed for people in the 95th percentile group need to accommodate their large body sizes. This has already resulted in the design and manufacture of XXL-sized clothing, fully adjustable car seats, steering wheels and seat belts.

💡 Consumer safety

There are many European and international safety standards that influence the safety measures that designers and manufacturers have to adhere to when developing new products. Many products sold in the UK and Europe must comply with standards set by the British Standards Institute and the European Community. For example, toys must meet the European Community Directive 88/378 and (Community law) for Toy Safety and British/European standard BS EN 71. Toys meeting these standards would be labelled with the 'CE' mark and Kitemark.

The British Standards Institution (BSI)

The **British Standards Institution** is an organisation that documents UK national standards for quality and safety in products and services. BSI also represents the UK in European (CEN) and International (ISO) standards production. Companies can pay to have their products tested against national or international standards, and if they meet the standard requirements, and their production processes have been assessed and comply with regulations, they can be awarded the BSI Kitemark. The company is issued a licence to use the Kitemark on its products. This symbol of quality and safety helps to assure consumers they are buying

The 'CE' mark

■ **Key terms**

British Standards Institution (BSI): an organisation dedicated to producing British (BS) and European (EN) quality and safety standards, and testing products against those standards for companies wishing to register their products.

a safe and consistent product. Companies registered with BSI have their product and their production process regularly tested.

A British Standard example

An example of a British Standard is BS EN 71. This means that the standard is both British (BS) and European (EN) and this particular standard is for toys.

BS EN 71 has eight parts as follows:

Part 1 Mechanical and physical properties covers toys to ensure that they have no parts that can stab, trap, mangle or choke.

Part 2 Flammability concerns toys such as Wendy houses, fancy dress costumes and soft toys. It limits the materials used to prohibit some of the more flammable ones, and ensures that if the toy does catch fire the child can drop it, or get out of it and get away.

Part 3 Migration of certain elements concerns limiting the 'release' of harmful substances such as lead, cadmium or mercury from toys, if they are swallowed or chewed by a child.

Part 4 Experimental sets for chemistry and related activities gives safe limits for the amount of chemicals that can be sold in such sets.

Part 5 Chemical toys (sets) other than those used for experiments controls the substances and materials used in toy sets such as water-based paints, modelling clay, etc.

Part 6 Graphical symbol for age warning labelling sets the standard for labelling toys unsuitable for children under three years old.

Part 7 Finger paints controls the chemicals used in finger paints and minimises the risks associated with ingesting paint or prolonged skin exposure to paint.

Part 8 Swings, slides and similar activity toys for indoor, family and domestic use limits the height of such play equipment, reduces protruding parts, requires that a child or a child's clothing cannot be trapped, and ensures stability.

The BSI Kitemark

AQA Examiner's tip

You may be asked to explain how the safety of a particular product could be improved or explain how a designer/manufacturer might ensure the safety of a product. (See the example of the hedge trimmer below and the 3-pin plug featured in the web materials.)

When you use products, think about how they have been made safe.

Safety features in a garden hedge trimmer

A 240 volt electric hedge trimmer can be a very dangerous power tool. Designers and manufacturers have devised a number of features to ensure consumer safety:

- *Electrical wire*: this is coated in thick, heavy duty PVC insulation which is orange coloured. This makes it stand up to wear and tear and stand out against a green/brown hedge.

- *Cable grommet*: this is a thick rubber sleeve that reinforces the cable where it enters the body of the tool. This area is weak and the cable could break leaving exposed wires.

- *Cable hook*: this is a small recess in the handle or casing of the trimmer which feeds the cable down, away from the blades.

- *Double switches*: with one positioned on the top handle and one on the trigger grip, this means that the consumer has to have both hands on the handles where they will be safe.

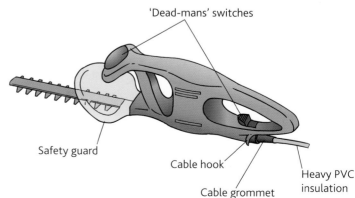

240-volt electric hedge trimmer

■ *'Dead-man's' switches*: when the user lets go of either switch, the blades stop immediately.

■ *Double insulated motor and electric controls*: this means that there are no exposed electrical parts that could conduct electricity into the user. The outer casing and handles are also made from polymers that will not conduct electricity.

■ *Guard*: this is a large plastic guard that protects the user's hands from sharp hedge cuttings.

■ *Safety instructions*: all power tools are sold with safety instructions to advise consumers about their safe use.

✓ Examination-style questions

1 Study the figure of the human powered torch.

a Identify and elaborate ways in which the ergonomic features of the torch could be enhanced. You should use diagrams to support your answer. *(9 marks)*

b Explain how the use of wind up technology and LED bulbs can minimise the impact that a torch might have on the environment. *(6 marks)*

c Describe how the designers and manufacturers of the torch would minimise the impact that it has on the environment. Your answer should make reference to:

■ Method of manufacture
■ Design for disposal *(2 × 6 marks)*

LED torch

Human-powered torch with squeeze lever

✓ *After studying this chapter it is hoped you will:*

■ understand how designers and manufacturers are trying to improve environmental performance of products in the light of environmental and sustainability issues and the government and EU legislation aimed at combating global warming. Approaches include examining whole life cycles and eco-design strategies of reduction, reuse and recycling

■ understand ergonomics – the study of the interaction between the human body and products, systems and environments – and the range of factors involved including sound, light, temperature, colour, textures, comfort and so on

■ understand anthropometrics, defined as the use of body measurements and data needed to design products, systems and environments

■ have become aware that most design activity is based around users between the 5th and 95th percentile. Products need to fit at least the 50th percentile (the average). It may be necessary to make some products adjustable to fit a range of users

■ have gained an understanding of inclusive design – designing products for all users including the disabled – and the need to work closely with disabled consumers when developing products, the appearance for which, is as stylish as any other

■ have become aware that consumer safety is a top priority for designers and manufacturers governed by legislation and consumer demand. An important skill is being able to critically analyse and spot potential safety hazards in products and suggest how these can be rectified.

4 Design and manufacture

You should be aware of the way modern materials are developing. Why are these particular materials being used in products – is it about being 'trendy' or are there serious benefits from using those materials? You should also be aware of the need to conserve energy and raw materials. How does this affect the choice of material for a product?

In this chapter case studies will be used to show these points and an indication given as to how exam questions based on this topic should be answered.

Materials and components

We should first consider the choice of materials. The purpose of design is to provide a solution to a need. Whether it is for people, for the environment in which the product will be used, or for the conservation of energy and raw materials, the designer must always choose materials which are fit for purpose.

Take for example, the need to drink. The main function of any drinking vessel, e.g. cup, glass, drinks can, etc. is to hold the liquid. There will, of course, be other functions such as the material not contaminating the liquid, or even the material being affected by the liquid contents. The designer may wish to put a patterned surface on the outside, the user might want to see the contents or prevent scalding, especially in the case of a child's cup.

The choice of material could also be based on the life-expectancy of the product, i.e. to make the product disposable, as in the case of a polystyrene cup, or to give the owner a sense of quality with a highly decorative surface, for example in a fine bone china dinner set.

The choice of material will depend on a broad range of factors, but the most important factor in this case is that the material will need to hold liquid. Consumer preference, manufacturing and cost will all play a part in the designer's final choice of material.

Drinking vessels made from a variety of materials

Consumer preference refers to the shape or form of the product along with other aesthetic qualities such as colour and finish. Manufacturing refers to how the product is to be made, i.e. whether the materials' properties lend themselves to more efficient, automated processes and so on.

This leads us neatly to cost. There will, of course, be the initial cost of the materials in a form ideal for processing. Then there will be the costs involved in manufacture which give value to the material by turning it into a usable product, e.g. polystyrene powder into a lightweight, heat-resistant cup, or a slice of clay being processed to the shape of a cup or mug.

In summary, materials' properties and characteristics have been covered in some detail in Chapter 2. In this chapter, however, we will use them to help explain the choice of material used in the manufacture of products. When analysing a product yourself you could refer back to Chapter 2 to remind yourself of the terms and definitions used when discussing materials' properties.

Now let's look at some case studies that will help reinforce what has already been said. The products I will be using for these studies are everyday consumer products and include a toothbrush and a 13-amp domestic plug.

Case study 1: Materials and components

Toothbrush

Function To provide an oral cleaning facility, i.e. for cleaning your teeth.

Environment The environment in which a toothbrush operates is usually water-filled. There are also chemicals involved for the purposes of cleaning teeth. The user will also provide a small amount of force to ensure the bristles – the part that carries out the cleaning – reach all the places that need cleaning.

Life expectancy The usable life of a toothbrush according to the advice of dentists is around 6–8 weeks.

Consumer preferences A product such as this toothbrush is brightly coloured for aesthetic appeal giving it a modern look. It is also formed to a shape that is more ergonomic for the user.

Cost A toothbrush is normally a low cost item being priced in the region of £2 per item.

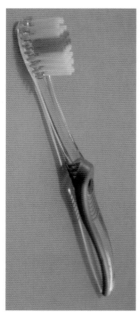

Toothbrush with TPE overmouldings on handle

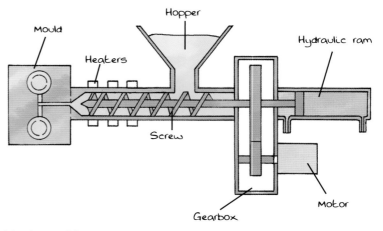

Injection moulding process

The main part of the toothbrush is made from PMMA (acrylic). Acrylic is a thermoplastic polymer that can be moulded to its required form once heated to its softening point. In this case injection moulding is the ideal process since it can be used to produce complex 3-D shapes such as the toothbrush handle.

Acrylics can also be coloured by adding pigments to the material in the hopper of the injection moulding machine.

Injection moulding becomes cost effective for these types of low cost products due to the use of multi-cavity moulds. This means that more than one product can be produced per machine cycle.

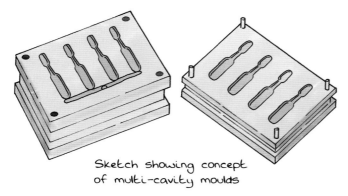

Sketch showing concept of multi-cavity moulds

Multi-cavity mould

For this toothbrush, TPE (thermoplastic elastomer) has been used to provide a 'grippy' surface to help the user maintain a hold on the handle in the wet environment. The process of applying the grip to the handle is called 'overmoulding' (see p116) and is carried out in an injection moulding machine. Thermoplastics are well suited to the injection moulding process.

In order for the TPE material to stay in place (in a wet environment such as a bathroom), the main handle will have grooves and cavities moulded into it in the first machine cycle.

AQA Examiner's tip

Your answers to exam questions should be supported with clear, fully labelled line diagrams where appropriate. Use of colour in your diagrams should be limited.

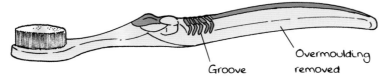

Groove   Overmoulding removed

Toothbrush handle without TPE material

The application of the TPE material will be carried out either as a separate moulding process to that of the handle, or as part of a dual shot moulding process where the two materials are injected into the mould – one following the other – during a machine cycle.

During the injection moulding cycle the nylon bristles are moulded around to secure them. Nylon is a polyamide material with integral toughness, stiffness and strength; this gives the material the properties necessary to brush teeth.

In summary then, the materials chosen for this product meet the demands required of them. Acrylic provides the base colour (or transparency in this case) as well as sufficient strength and

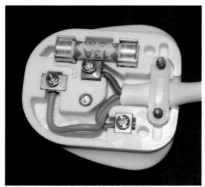

Domestic 13-amp plug

resistance to the water and chemicals in the environment. TPE provides a colourful grip for easy use, while the nylon bristles have sufficient rigidity and resistance.

Case study 2: Materials and components

Domestic 13-amp power plug

The main function of this product is to provide a safe connection between mains-driven portable appliances and the 240-volt a.c. electrical supply in the home.

13-amp plugs are designed to last for a long time with appropriate use. This particular product is coloured white and represents a large part of the domestic electrical plug market.

A number of features have been designed into the product to make it easier and safe to use. These include upper and lower 'wings' which enable the plug to be inserted and withdrawn from the socket without the user's fingers coming into contact with the – potentially live – brass pins.

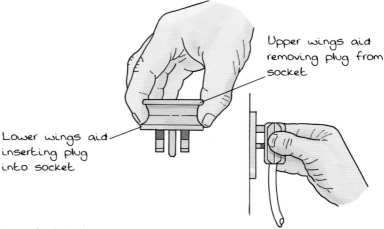

Upper wings aid removing plug from socket

Lower wings aid inserting plug into socket

Power plug 'wings'

Internally, a very complex arrangement guides the cables and secures the brass pins, clamp screws and fuse. This is all achieved through the use of a brass insert – moulded into the top of the product, and a screw – inserted through the bottom part of the product.

The materials used in this product need to carry out different functions. On the one hand, the brass pins must allow electricity to flow to the cables and therefore to the appliance to which they are connected. On the other hand, the two-part urea formaldehyde casing must prevent any contact between user and electricity and between the internal cables.

Urea formaldehyde is a thermosetting polymer. As you will know from Chapter 2, polymers in general are excellent insulators of electricity. The choice of urea formaldehyde provides the necessary insulation and its high rigidity and strength (for a polymer) makes it ideal to withstand the forces applied to it when inserting and withdrawing the plug from the socket.

Portable appliance connected to a socket

Compression moulding would be the most appropriate for forming this material to the shape required. Thermosetting polymers require internal cross-links to form between long-chain molecules. Compression moulding provides the necessary time and pressure for this.

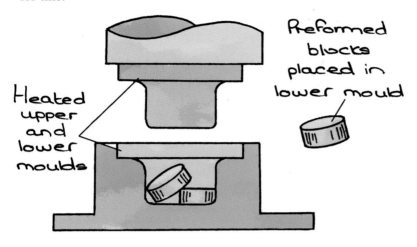

Compression moulding

Why is brass rather than aluminium or copper used for the pins?

Aluminium, although a slightly better conductor of electricity than copper, is a very soft and lightweight material. The use of this material would mean that the pins would wear very quickly. There could also be problems with over-tightening the cable clamp screws, stripping the threads and rendering them useless. Further problems could occur if the current being drawn heated the pins to a point where the material softens. This would clearly make them impractical for their intended application.

Copper has a much higher melting temperature making it more capable of handling the higher currents. Copper has higher strength than aluminium but it still does not have the wear resistance required for longevity.

Brass is an alloy of copper and zinc. The addition of zinc to the copper strengthens and hardens the material giving it greater wear resistance and durability – at the expense of marginally lower electrical conductivity. Its greater strength ensures the cable clamp screws remain secure which, in turn, prevents the cables coming loose and presenting a safety problem.

AQA **Examiner's tip**

Refer back to the terms and definitions of materials' properties in Chapter 2 to help you here.

■ Industrial materials testing

Industrial testing

Why is it necessary to test materials? The most obvious answer is that the designer must know that a material is suitable for its intended purpose, i.e. whether or not it has sufficient strength, toughness, durability, etc.

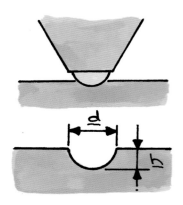

Brinell hardness test

A hardened steel ball indentor is used. Diameter **d** and depth **h** are measured and used to calculate a hardness value.

Brinell hardness test

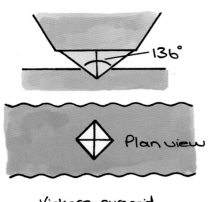

Vickers pyramid hardness test

A diamond pyramid indentor is used. The surface area of the indent and the load are used to calculate a hardness value.

Vickers pyramid hardness test

We will now look at standard methods of testing materials and products that are used throughout a range of industries. Materials tested using these methods are provided with certificates stating their specific materials' properties as numeric values.

Destructive testing

Destructive testing refers to a range of tests that ultimately results in the destruction of a (standard size) test piece. Test pieces are of a standard size and shape for the particular test being carried out.

Hardness test pieces will have small indentations after testing, while impact testing equipment will cause the test piece to bend or break completely. Destructive testing also refers to tests that are applied to products, for example, to test for durability. Tyre companies such as Michelin will run tyres on vehicles to establish wear-rates in use.

Hardness tests

Hardness is the ability of a material to resist abrasive wear, indentation or deformation. Hardness is actually a by-product of strength – generally, the stronger the material, the harder it is. In order to establish hardness of a material, it must be indented or deformed.

There are three basic methods of hardness testing:

Brinell test: a hardened steel ball is forced into the material's surface by means of a suitable load. The resulting surface area of the indent is measured, and used to calculate the hardness number.

Vickers test: this uses a diamond pyramid to indent the material. This is measured using a microscope to give the hardness value.

Rockwell test: this is more appropriate for the quality control testing of finished products. It is a relatively rapid test, with the hardness value being indicated on an attached dial, thus avoiding the need to measure a very small indentation.

All tests produce an indentation of the material or product. The Brinell and Vickers tests produce an indent in the material being tested that has to be measured with the aid of a microscope. Different scales can be used, depending on the material being tested.

Tensile testing

Tensile testing involves putting material under tension by stretching to provide information regarding tensile strength, elasticity and plastic properties, such as ductility and malleability.

A standard test piece is held between two grips. One of the grips is fixed, while the other is attached to a vertical slide operated by an electric motor. The test piece is then put under tension at a constant rate until (i) it breaks, or (ii) it stretches beyond the limits of the machine.

As the test piece is being stretched, the distance travelled by the vertical slide is recorded and plotted against the load being applied, which is sensed by a load transducer fixed to the moving grip. This will result in a graph that can be used to indicate a variety of useful information.

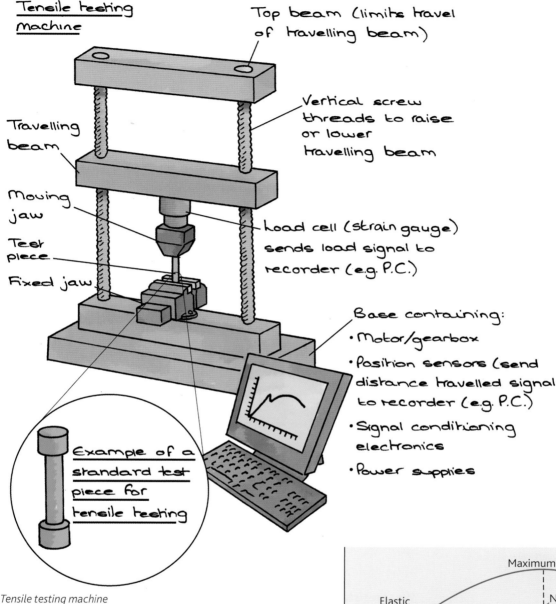

Tensile testing machine

Tensile testing is standard in a range of industries including the rubber industry, where the rubber, steel and fabric used in the manufacture of tyres are tested. This method of testing is also used in the rope-making industry to test the strength of the fibres being used, and in the clothing industry to test the strength of fabrics.

Impact tests

Impact tests indicate the toughness of a material and, in particular, its resistance to mechanical shock. Toughness, (or rather its opposite property of brittleness), is often not revealed by a tensile test.

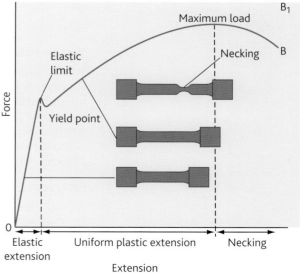

Tensile test diagram for mild steel

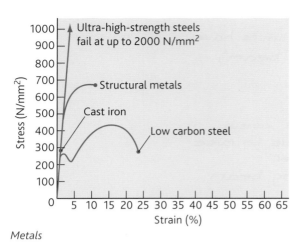

Metals

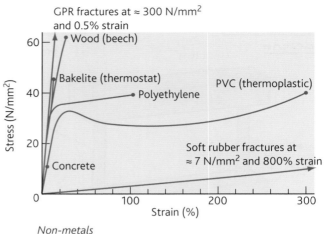

Non-metals

Activity

Suggest reasons why standard shaped/sized test pieces are essential when carrying out these types of tests.

There are three main methods of impact testing:

- the Izod test
- the Charpy test
- the Houndsfield test.

Test pieces have been standardised for each test and are shown below. The more the sample piece absorbs the impact, the tougher the material is.

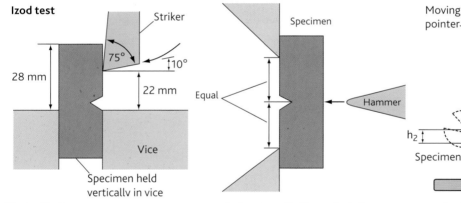

The Izod test

A plan view of a Charpy test piece

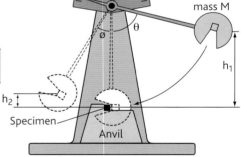

Izod/Charpy impact test equipment

Wear resistance

Wear resistance of a material can be determined by rubbing with an abrasive. A standard test involves weighing a disc of material, e.g. for use in brake discs, rubbing an abrasive disc against the material a given number of times, at a given pressure, followed by re-weighing to give a quantitative value of abrasive wear. In the pottery industry a similar test is applied but in this case the abrasive resistance of the glaze applied to crockery is tested using an object similar to a dinner knife.

Fatigue testing

As with most tests, both materials and products can be tested for fatigue. For example, the wire used in tyres is tested by gripping a sample between two chucks. One chuck is stationary while the other can rotate – being driven by a motor/gearbox. The sample is twisted by rotating one of the chucks for a given number of revolutions. The direction of rotation is changed, and so on, until the sample breaks.

Products such as chairs can be tested for fatigue. In this case a weight (or force) is applied repeatedly to the product. The diagram shows a chair being tested by the application of a force on the seating area. The force being applied is representative of a person sitting on the chair and is used to test the resistance of the material.

Non-destructive testing

Non-destructive tests, as the name implies, are methods of testing that do not damage or destroy the material or product. These methods of testing are usually carried out on the final product, where the aim is to test for surface or near-surface faults or flaws. There are a number of standard methods of testing that can be found in a range of industries, and some methods require the use of sophisticated equipment. Typically, welded joints and castings are tested in this manner.

Surface crack detection

Sound and touch These are methods of testing that can be applied to a variety of products and use basic quality-control techniques.

'Ringing' Just as the term suggests, a bell cannot ring if it is cracked. This method of testing a product is used in both the casting and pottery industries, where ringing is the first line in detecting a faulty product.

As well as a visual check, touch can also be used to sense faults directly on the surface of the product.

Liquid penetrant The penetrant liquid is sprayed onto the surface of the product. Any excess is removed leaving only the penetrant in the cracks. To help make the cracks clearer, a light dusting of chalk is applied. The coloured dye marks the position of the crack in the white chalk.

Magnetic testing

The component is magnetised by making it part of an electromagnetic circuit. Iron particles are dusted over the area, which then highlight where the magnetic lines of force are broken by a defect. This method is particularly useful for finding defects such as cracks and hollows just below the surface, in castings, for example.

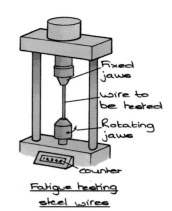

Fatigue testing

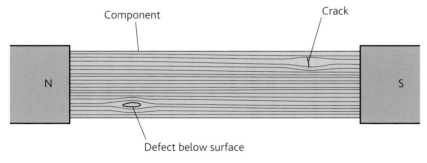

A component within a magnetic circuit

Acid pickling

In order for cracks to be visible it is necessary to clean the surface of the product. Steel castings, for example, can be 'pickled' in a weak solution of sulphuric acid, heated to 50 °C, for a number of hours. This will remove any oxides from the surface of the material, and when washed will make surface cracks clearer.

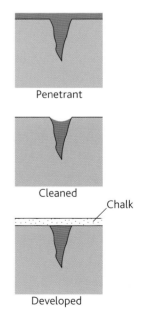

Crack detection

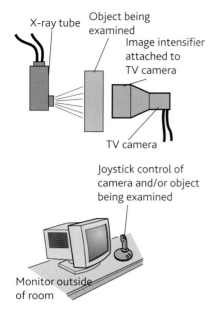

An X-ray arrangement

Internal defect detection

Light Light is utilised in the pottery industry to 'see' through some of the finer ceramics, such as bone china, to indicate faults within the body of the material.

X-ray methods X-rays are used to detect defects under the surface. For example, in the tyre industry X-rays are used to check for air bubbles between layers of rubbers, fabric and supporting wires. An X-ray tube emits radiation through the product and forms an image on a photographic plate, or through an image intensifier and camera, to a monitor. X-rays travel faster through cavities and so produce a darker image where the structural materials have not vulcanised properly, which can result in a potentially dangerous product.

γ-ray methods (gamma rays) Used in the same way as X-rays but since γ-rays are 'harder', thicker and denser, materials such as cast iron and steel can be tested to detect 'air' pockets in the casting.

Both X-rays and γ-rays are lethal to human tissue. γ-rays are produced from strontium-90, present in the 'fall-out' products of nuclear explosions. For this reason, such methods are shielded behind puddle (dense) concrete or lead-lined walls. Also equipment operators wear a photographic film badge, which is monitored to indicate levels of exposure to the X- or γ-rays.

Ultrasonic testing Very high frequency sound vibrations can be used to locate internal defects precisely. Ultrasonic frequencies between 500 kHz and 100 MHz are used. A probe is passed over the component transmitting the high frequencies. Under normal conditions, the vibrations will pass through the material and will be reflected back from the bottom surface of the material. The probe receives this and an amplifier converts the vibrations into a series of blips on a monitor.

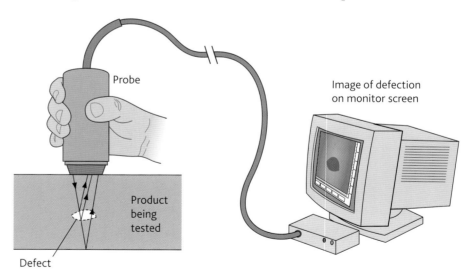

Ultrasonic testing

Ultrasound is used to test sheet, plate and strip materials up to 6 mm thick. It is therefore ideal for pinpointing defects during tyre, aircraft and pipeline inspection.

Case study 3: Steel and alloys used in industry

When products are manufactured, the materials used have to be tested to ensure consistent quality. In the manufacture of cars, the quality of the steel is vital. Specific steel is selected for its mechanical properties, such as malleability and ductility. These properties are crucial in order to press body panels. The steel needs to be malleable so that it can be formed by pressing methods without the steel tearing or cracking. Ductility is needed so that the steel will stretch over the pressing dies.

At Swindon Pressings (part of the BMW group), the body panels for the Mini, Land Rover Freelander and other MG Rover vehicles are manufactured. Test engineers perform random materials testing on the steel that they use, because this is imported from outside suppliers. It is very important that the steel used matches the original design specification. Tests might include tensile tests to check the point at which the material fails under pulling forces. This will give an indication of how ductile the material is. The metal may also undergo impact testing, where samples of the material are snapped under impact and the structure of the steel examined. Samples are examined under a microscope, where a fibrous structure will indicate a ductile material. Such materials testing is known as destructive testing as the sample is damaged as a result of the test.

Following such materials testing, test pressings will be done to assess how the steel performs. These will be checked against 'standard' pressings located in each pressing area.

In the manufacture of products such as alloy wheels, or the undercarriages of aircraft, also made from lightweight alloys, non-destructive tests might be used to ensure quality. Products such as these are made by casting methods. Castings can be prone to internal cavities invisible to the naked eye. X-rays are used to test for such defects. Internal cavities will normally show up as a dark part on X-rays. Hairline surface cracks may also be very difficult to see. These are tested by painting 'engineer's blue' onto the component while the component is hot. The heat evaporates the spirit base of the engineer's blue, and the blue dye will concentrate where there are surface defects.

AQA Examiner's tip

Materials testing is a further area that contains a number of specialist terms and techniques. You should develop an understanding of these terms and techniques and use them appropriately in your answers to exam questions.

✓ Examination-style questions

1 Manufacturer of children's toys need to test materials and components for their safety.

   a Explain what role standards such as those set by the British Standards institute (BSI) and European Community (CE) have in ensuring products like toys are safe to use. *(18 marks)*

   b With reference to specific materials and components used in toys, explain in detail safety tests that may be carried out. *(10 marks)*

2 **a** Name a suitable material for four of the following products:

- fold-up garden chair
- container for a fast-food/takeaway meal
- handmade dining table
- temporary exhibition indoor sign
- high-quality sports trophy award. *(4 marks)*

   b For each material, explain why they are suitable for the products you have chosen. Your answer should make reference to the following:

The function and use of the product	*(8 marks)*
The manufacturing process	*(8 marks)*
The quantity being produced	*(8 marks)*

✓ *After studying this chapter it is hoped you will*:

- be able to identify a material (or materials) from which a product is manufactured and use your knowledge and understanding of materials and their properties to explain their suitability for the intended function and the method of manufacture

- be able to discuss the method of manufacture (including materials used) of a single (bespoke) product

- be able to explain why a different material and process would be used if the product were to be made in a much larger volume, i.e. batch or large-scale production. Chapter 6 talks more about processing

- be familiar with the techniques used to test materials on an industrial basis in order that consistency and quality of product are maintained.

5 Design and market influences

Through the study of this chapter it is hoped that you will:

- understand how the design and innovation process starts, the key stages involved in design and manufacture and the individual roles in the design process

- understand market research, social and economical factors and their influence on the success of Product Design

- appreciate human factors such as ergonomics, anthropometrics and human consumer needs

- understand the constraints influencing design and manufacture such as legislation, safety and environmental factors

- understand how design and manufacture have been influenced by advancements in technology

- understand the influence of contemporary styles and historical practices.

Roles in the design process

The client

The client might be an individual or a group who identify a need or niche that could be met by developing a new product. Clients may often be entrepreneurs seeking to make money by launching a new product into a market. Entrepreneurs are often needed either to directly finance a project themselves or to persuade others to back an invention and fund its development into a commercial product. The client will be the person or group who commissions a designer or designers to develop a product.

The designer

The designer is an individual or group who will work to develop a product for a client. The designer, together with the client, will develop a design brief and formulate a design specification. In a large organisation, this process will also usually involve the marketing department; they work with the designer to ensure that he or she knows exactly what the 'user' wants from a new product. Large companies have developed the role of 'product managers' – people who monitor the progress of a product's development and work between the design, manufacturing and marketing departments to ensure the products made match customer needs.

Inventors

An inventor is an individual or group who produce ideas for a new or improved product. These ideas have to be communicated in a visual form such as sketches and models. In the commercial world, product designers might often take an idea originally created by an inventor and develop it into a product that will sell.

The designer-maker

This role usually describes individuals who design a product and then make it. Typical examples might include craft workers such as potters, jewellery makers, costume makers, and so on. They are associated with small-scale production.

Makers

Makers are the people who will manufacture the product that has been designed. The manufacturer might be a company owned by the client or entrepreneur, or simply be an independent company that is commissioned by the entrepreneur to make the product.

With the expansion of email and internet/intranet systems the concept of **global manufacturing** is made a reality. Designs can be produced in one part of the world and made entirely in another. Lower labour costs, availability of raw materials or expertise in a specific manufacturing process might make it more economical to design and manufacture products in this way.

Key terms

Global manufacturing: modern-day industrial practice of designing in one part of the world and manufacturing the product in another where materials and labour costs may be cheaper.

Users

The user is the individual or group that will make use of the product developed by the designer. In a large company, marketing departments will conduct market research to identify the target market for a particular product (the sector of users likely to purchase the product). Having done this, researchers and the designer may work with user groups within this target market to identify specific features required in the product.

■ The marketing function

The relationship between the user, designers and makers

In the past, the user was only thought about once the product had been developed. There might be some retrospective adjustment to the design or marketing to convince consumers to choose a particular product. Today, designers generally consider the needs of the user at the earliest opportunity in the design process. This makes economic sense because if the product meets user needs, they will typically want to buy it.

Very few manufacturers sell direct to the public. Most items go to distributors who, in turn, sell them to retail outlets. However, for a product to sell well, it is important that the manufacturer understands their customer and builds up as strong a relationship as possible. This would include ensuring that the products they make meet the needs, aspirations and budget of their consumer. It might also include aggressive advertising of a product to ensure customers can see its advantages over products from rival companies.

Designers are also concerned with the same issues and relationships as manufacturers and so the design process is becoming increasingly user-focused. Finding out about the people you are designing for, what they desire, and involving them in the development process, can lead to products that both please users and sell well.

Market research is vital in building up an understanding of user needs and aspirations for both designers and manufacturers.

Consumer profiles

Sometimes organisations will create a user profile which is representative of people in their target market. This helps them to determine the needs and aspirations of users they are designing for. Consumer profiles give designers an understanding of people's lifestyles and buying habits which is then used to shape the appearance and quality of the product. It is also used to help designers decide on how to advertise products, including graphics and packaging; this then appeals to the lifestyle of the intended market.

The marketing mix

In order to produce a design brief and specification, those involved in the decision making within a company will need to consider what will affect the design and what will influence the success of the final product. The factors are known as the marketing mix.

The factors in the marketing mix are as follows:

Product

For a product to be successful, it must attract buyers. Consumers will consider the following issues when choosing whether to purchase a product:

Activity

With your friends list the features that users in your age group might want in a mobile phone.

Now make a list of features for a phone you think might be suitable for a target market of people aged 70+.

What are the main differences and why?

- *Function* What does the product do? Are there any interesting features in the product?
- *Performance* How well does the product do what it is designed to do?
- *Ease of use* How easy is it to use? Is it easy to set up? Are instructions needed?
- *Reliability* How long will the product last? Is it likely to fail?
- *Aesthetics* What does it look like? Is it appealing to look at? Does it fit in with the required image or style of the consumer?
- *Compatibility* Will the product work with other products already owned by the consumer, e.g. a DVD player with a TV set?

Price

One of the main constraints that a designer has to work with is price. The designer must make a compromise between designing a product that can be made as cheaply as possible and providing the user with value for money.

Setting the right price for a product is a difficult task. If it is too high, not enough people will buy it. If it is too low, people may not buy it as they may think it is too cheap to be worthwhile owning. Price is not usually chosen by a designer but it does influence what the designer will develop in the product.

Place

In order to ensure products reach the consumer on time, designers need to work closely with manufacturers to ensure that the products they develop can be made efficiently, packed and distributed easily. Specialist industrial designers would help in planning production lines, 'just in time' systems and in designing flexible or dedicated manufacturing equipment.

Promotion

In order to make a product successful, it must be promoted to the public. This is done through the design of packaging and promotional materials. In small companies, designers might be involved in not only developing the product, but also the creation of its packaging and promotional materials.

Process

How easily can the consumer purchase the product? The easier it is to purchase, the faster the product will diffuse into the market.

Physical evidence

When you buy a product, you have the physical evidence of making a purchase. However, many products have 'bolt-on' services, for example mobile phones and PDAs may have optional broadband internet access. As this is not a physical product, designers would create some form of icon to reassure the consumer that they have purchased such a service and tell them when it becomes active. See **http://my247.com.au/images/demo-sydney.gif**.

Properties

Two very important properties in products are aesthetics and environmental performance. Consumers often make the decision to purchase a product based upon its aesthetic qualities. This is clearly the case in products such as fashion textiles and furnishings. In consumer electronics, the look of the product is often as important as the features that it may have.

Currently, consumers are becoming more environmentally conscious about the products they purchase. For example, white goods such as refrigerators are energy rated, and consumers may look at these ratings

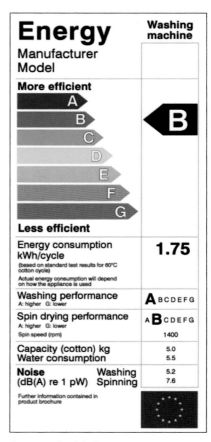

Energy rating label

before making up their mind. As concerns for the environment increase, it is likely that this factor will become significant. Many purchases are already based upon manufacturers' claims of products being 'organic', non-toxic, recyclable or environmentally friendly.

Pleasure

If a product gives the consumer pleasure, it is said to have 'added value'. If a product does everything it is supposed to do and gives pleasure to the consumer using it, it will succeed. Products such as the Sony Walkman and, more recently, the Apple iPod, have attained iconic status because they not only function well but please the consumers using them.

People

If a new product is to sell well (diffuse), the people selling it need to understand the benefits of the product they are selling. This is important to influence purchasers and provide a good after-sales service.

Design methods

How designing starts

Commercial and economic reasons drive most invention. However, most inventions are the product of individual inventors. These individuals invent because:

- they are dissatisfied with an existing product or situation (constructive discontent)
- they want to make money
- they want to do something to help others
- they are interested in technological or scientific progress.

The starting points for innovation can be illustrated with the following examples:

Constructive discontent

When an existing design proves to be unsatisfactory, creative inventors often set about designing a solution with improved properties. James Dyson was dissatisfied with a conventional wheelbarrow. He found them difficult to use on soft ground as the thin wheel digs in making them hard to turn. In 1974, he developed the Ballbarrow. This uses a ball instead of the wheel which turns easily on soft ground and absorbs shock when using the barrow over rough surfaces.

To make money

In 1895 K.C. Gillette realised while shaving, that it was the edge of the razor that was the vital part to shaving. He wanted to make a disposable product that would ensure customers kept buying replacements, thus ensuring a constant demand. So with the help of William Nickerson (inventor of the push button elevator control), he set about designing a razor consisting of a handle, holder and disposable blade. In 1903, the first Gillette 'safety razor' went on sale. With most of the blade covered, it was considerably safer than traditional cut-throat razors. In its second year, sales boomed with 90,000 razors and 12.5 million blades being sold. Today, Gillette is one of the largest razor and grooming product manufacturers in the world (mostly focusing on disposable products) with several billion dollars worth of sales each year.

Did you know?

There were originally four factors considered in the marketing mix, all beginning with the letter P. These were known as the Four Ps. As more factors have been added, the same letter was used to help people remember them.

Further reading

http://newsimg.bbc.co.uk/media/images/39073000/jpg/_39073046_ballbarrow.jpg

AQA Examiner's tip

The freeplay radio is a good product to learn as an example of something tht has changed in response to developments in technology (super capacitors, solar cells, etc.) and market pull (demand for green products).

Wanting to help others

In 1991 while watching a BBC documentary about the spread of HIV/ Aids in Africa, inventor Trevor Bayliss heard that poor people in Africa weren't getting the message about safe sex because they couldn't afford batteries for their radios. Bayliss produced a prototype clockwork radio that would produce 14 minutes of radio play after a 30-second wind. After several years of market research, further development and fundraising, the Freeplay Radio went into production in South Africa. It was initially made by disabled workers who traditionally found it difficult to obtain employment. Now, several years on, the radio comes in various forms, including one with a solar cell that charges an internal battery. Freeplay Radios are now made in China but the Freeplay Foundation distributes the self-powered radios free of charge as part of aid programmes worldwide.

Exploration of science and technology

After the Second World War, Charles H. Townes and Arthur L. Shadlow worked at Bell Labs in the USA. They were experimenting with modified radar techniques using microwaves to study molecular structures. While experimenting with short wavelengths of infrared and optical light, they created the first laser. The laser, (short for light amplification by stimulated emission of radiation), was patented in 1960. The two scientists never considered commercial applications for lasers, thinking that they might be just used in scientific research. Today, lasers are used in a wide range of applications such as eye surgery, CD and DVD players and barcode scanners.

Freeplay Radio – the original model (top) *and a current model*

Design activity within organisations

The majority of design innovation takes place within companies. This is because they tend to have access to facilities such as rapid prototyping, CAD systems and databases, and the financial resources to pursue patents. For companies to remain competitive, they need either to make continual incremental improvements to their existing products or develop new ones. There are several factors that lead to design innovation within a company, including:

- the business strategy of the company
- deficiencies in existing product or method of making
- advancements in materials or technology (**technology push**)
- government legislation or regulations requiring a change in product or making process, e.g. environmental regulations.

The design process

The design of products in an industrial context normally follows a process. This is how the process works:

Identification of the problem

Design activity usually arises because someone identifies a need or a problem that has to be solved. Designers often call this the 'situation' or 'design problem'. Designers can identify the problem themselves, but normally it will be presented to a designer by a client, or perhaps (in the case of a large company) by marketing departments. Whoever identifies the problem, it is the designer who will attempt to find a solution to solve it.

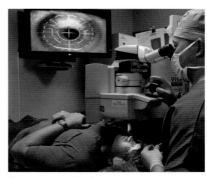

Eye surgery using lasers

Key terms

Technology push: new products can be developed and old products made obsolete by advancements in technology, e.g. smaller, more powerful microprocessors led to the development of computers with improved performance.

The brief

A brief is a detailed document that sets out what is to be designed. It may contain some details of functional requirements, aesthetics, materials, safety and quality considerations, and other design constraints. The brief will guide the designers and help them formulate a performance and marketing specification.

The client is usually the person who has identified a need and provides the brief. This might be, for example, an individual who wants a custom-made kitchen, caravan or boat, or it may be an entrepreneur who has identified a niche for a particular product. It is the responsibility of a designer to work closely with the client to ensure that they get the product they want.

The client who wants a custom-made kitchen, for example, is also likely to be the user. However, often the user is simply someone who will buy the product. It is crucial that designers make full use of market research and fully understand the needs and wants of the 'user' or 'customer base' they are designing for.

In industry, designers may be part of a team, as they are unlikely to have expertise in all areas. In the design of a personal musical player such as the iPod, designers would be split into teams working on styling, electronics, software and control systems, ergonomics and interface systems. These teams will have particular expertise in those areas but may also use external consultants.

Another example is in the car industry: the design of a vehicle would be shared among many designers who would be specialists in specific areas, including mechanical engineering (for engine and mechanical systems), software engineering (for engine management and instrumentation), textiles (for seating, carpets, etc.), and so on. Designers of cars would work with production engineers to plan the manufacture but specialist industrial designers would design the machines that would make the cars.

The specification

The specification is a document that expands upon the brief and sets out very detailed design constraints. It may include:

- details of materials that the product can be made from
- specific functional details, i.e. what the product must do, cost limitations and references to legal and quality standards that the product must meet.

The specification is referred to when designing, and in evaluating designs, to ensure that the product designed meets the original identified need.

When considering what should make up a specification, those involved could refer to a model developed by Professor Stuart Pugh. This is a model of 'total design' where all the factors that might influence the design of a product are given attention.

Pugh makes an analogy between a designer having to balance all the factors that will influence a design and a circus performer balancing plates. The plates represent the factors that the designer must keep in mind throughout the design process. Like the spinning plates, some will require more attention than others at different times of the design process.

The 'total design approach' ensures that factors such as cost, ergonomics, environment or other issues are not given dominance over others.

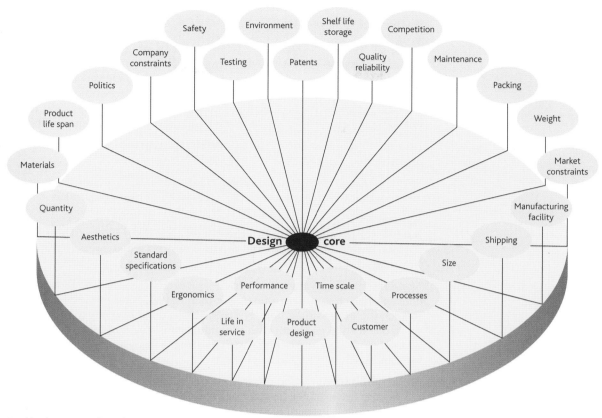

Pugh's plates: a guide to design

Analysis

When designers receive a design problem and brief, they will analyse the problem and look at what they need to research in order to design successfully. Before designing can proceed, designers may have to research into unfamiliar materials or technologies, and may have to consult experts to find out whether a particular material or technology is suitable for their design project. During the analysis stage, research plans would be drawn up to detail what needs to be researched and where the information can be obtained.

Research

There are two broad types of research carried out to inform the design of products. These are market research and user research.

Market research

Market research is a vital component in ensuring products are designed, developed and manufactured successfully, but critically they are designed for a market so that the product will sell. There are a number of ways in which market research is done:

Surveys

One method of collecting data to find out about a market is to conduct surveys. There are different types of surveys, some of which include:

- personal interviews
- group interviews

■ telephone interviews

■ internet surveys

■ postal questionnaires.

As you will realise, surveys have different levels of contact with people. Generally surveys produce quantitative data. This can identify trends, consumer spending habits, and existing products that consumers purchase. This data can be stored on computer database systems and used later to help designers focus on a target market and draw up product specifications.

Personal interviews These can be structured, semi-structured and non-directive.

Structured interviews These will have a list of questions with set possible answers that the interviewer marks off as the interview progresses.

Semi-structured interviews These have a series of prompts for the interviewer to raise topics with the interviewee. This allows them to respond with more freedom and can give unexpected answers that might be useful in the design process.

Non-directive interviews These invite the interviewee to talk about chosen topics freely. The interviewer then makes notes or simply helps to keep the discussion going. Typically this is done in product handling sessions. Testing products with individual consumers or focus groups, can be used to assess the problems with existing designs and identify scope for improvement with a new product.

Structured interviews and questionnaires are not very helpful in identifying the need for new products or the desirable features of a new product. This is better done with 'user-centred' techniques.

User-centred research techniques

User research can help to identify the need for a new product and specific features that consumers want in a product. It is especially helpful when users can be observed interacting with products.

There are several common user-centred research techniques including:

■ observation of people in their own environment

■ observation of people in a useability laboratory

■ bodystorming.

Observation of people in their own environment

Designers can learn a lot by observing people in their own homes. They will watch how people use products, noting any difficulties they may have, workarounds (using a product slightly differently than the designer intended to make it easier for them), or even how products might be adapted. For example, some people may use steps to reach items in a kitchen wall unit, others might balance a phone on their shoulder while working in the kitchen, tie string or fasten tape to handles to hang products up or make them easier to grip. This type of observation is known as ethnographic research. If videoed, it is called video-ethnography.

Observing people in a useability laboratory

Manufacturers will often use groups of people that represent a cross-section of users to test and evaluate products. This may be done in a controlled environment called a useability lab, where the comments of the focus group can be recorded using video and audio to be analysed in detail later. In a useability lab, the focus group might be given a range of

Keeping the cord out of harm's way can be difficult – a design weakness?

products to test along with a worksheet that prompts them to test the product as required. This type of research is particularly useful to identify potential weaknesses in designs, or to identify what features of design work well and are popular with consumers. Some companies will use a prototype of their own product to test alongside products from rival manufacturers.

Bodystorming

This is a form of role-play in which designers act out the process of using a particular product. This might involve using full size mock-ups or prototype products to experience what it is like and observe any problems. Sometimes designers might use wheelchairs or special suits that restrict body movement to assess, what it is like to use products for disabled users.

Other forms of research include:

- ■ *Analysing similar designs* to find out about useful materials, mechanisms or other features that could be incorporated into a design. This may involve testing and disassembling products.
- ■ *Database searches* of materials and components, to review their properties, costs, etc.
- ■ *Testing materials or components*, e.g. testing electronic circuits to assess their suitability for a project.
- ■ *Field testing*.

Some manufacturers will test their own products against the products of rival companies to analyse their comparative strengths and weaknesses. This type of testing helps companies develop their products in order to stay ahead of the competition.

Research may be carried out by designers themselves, or by specialist researchers who have particular expertise in gathering the required data.

Generation of ideas

This is the actual designing stage where sketches of ideas are drawn and evaluated. Once initial concept designs are completed, the designer will select an idea and develop it further. Some concept ideas may be drawn in a CAD system and rendered to show clients for evaluation.

■ Development

This is where a design idea is selected and then developed into a finished solution. This stage may include consideration of alternative ways the product could be manufactured. Component parts would be considered, such as switches, buttons, screens, and so on. The design would be refined, with attention given to the styling features as well as functional aspects. Designers may make use of **scale models** and mock-ups in refining the design. Prototypes may be made in order to take measurements for the manufacture of moulds or dies. Final working drawings, with details such as materials, surface finish and dimensions, will be created.

Manufacture

The maker, or to use the correct term 'manufacturer', is someone who does not design the product but who usually communicates with the designer to ensure that the design is interpreted correctly; they would then make the product to the correct specifications.

> ■ **Key terms**
>
> **Scale models:** used to test designs without the expense of making full-size prototypes; can be used to test ergonomics, construction methods, colour schemes, and so on.

Activity

Use the internet to search for examples of how CAD is used and investigate how this can aid communication between the manfacturer and designer.

Key terms

Video conferencing: a PC desktop system that enables designers to talk to and see manufacturers, clients, etc., while simultaneously working on CAD drawings or other tasks on the computer. Video conferencing reduces the need for key personnel to travel to meetings.

At the other end of the scale, the designer-makers design the product and then make it themselves. Artisans, such as sculptors, jewellery makers, and so on, would fall into this category, because they often design and make one-off pieces for specific clients.

Manufacturing is often done by companies who are specialists in particular manufacturing technologies. For example, one company may design a package for a detergent, but the actual package may be made by a different company that specialises in plastic moulding techniques. This company may be located in a different part of the world, where labour is cheaper or raw material sources are closer.

With the use of ICT today, the manufacturer can be geographically quite distant from the designer. The term 'global manufacturing' refers to the practice of designing a product in one part of the world and making it in another part of the world. This is often done because there may be particular expertise in an area, such as engineering and electronics in Germany and Japan, or for economic reasons because some countries have much lower labour costs than others.

Computer technology enables designs to be emailed to manufacturers. **Video conferencing** enables designers to talk to manufacturers and discuss drawings on-screen simultaneously.

Before large-scale manufacture takes place, companies usually make small production runs:

- to iron out problems during the manufacturing stage
- to carry out product testing and evaluation.

■ Testing and evaluation

Prototype products need to be fully tested before the product goes into final production. Once full-scale production starts, most modern companies would want to be manufacturing to zero-defect standards.

During testing and evaluation, products are compared against the original specification to ensure that the final product meets the requirements of the specification and solves the design problem.

The design process should not be seen as a linear process with designing taking place, then manufacturing and, finally, evaluation. In reality, designing often takes place alongside research work; evaluation takes place while analysing the research, considering design ideas and developing a final design; there is also evaluation of the finished solution.

How are ideas formed?

There are several ways in which ideas can be formed including:

- chance
- act of insight
- associative thinking
- adaptation
- transfer
- analogy
- combination.

Chance

Sometimes, inventions can be the product of chance. While working on one thing, scientists and technologies can stumble upon something new. For example, in 1933 road mender Percy Shaw saw the headlights of his car reflected in the eyes of a cat while driving at night near his home in the north of England. Shaw was inspired to design a 'cat's eye' reflector that is embedded into the centre of the road at regular intervals. These reflect the light of car headlamps and thus make it easier to see the course of an unlit road.

Another example of a chance invention is when, in 1948, Swiss engineer George de Mestrel found that seed pods stuck to his clothing when he was out walking his dog in the countryside. He examined the seed pods under a microscope and found they had hundreds of tiny hooks. He then examined his woollen trousers and found these had hundreds of tiny loops and so the hooks of the seeds caught in the loops of the fabric. From this, he eventually developed the hook and loop fastening system, known by the commercial name Velcro.

Act of insight

One of the most famous acts of insight was that of Archimedes who leapt from his bath and ran down the street shouting 'Eureka!' ('I've found it!'). Legend has it that he had been tasked by the king of Syracuse to determine if the gold in the royal crown had been substituted for silver while being repaired. When Archimedes got into his bath and saw it overflow, he suddenly realised he could use water displacement to work out the volume and density of the king's crown. Archimedes had realised that silver was less dense than gold and would need to be bulkier to make the same weight. It would therefore displace more water. He had found a way to test if the crown was pure gold or silver.

Another act of insight was made by Barnes Wallis, inventor of the bouncing bomb made for the dam busting raids of the Second World War Two. While skimming stones along the surface of a pond, he realised that it might be possible to skim a bomb along the surface of a stretch of water and make it land or sink precisely where it was needed (in this case, at the foot of the dam where it would cause maximum damage).

Associative thinking

Drawing a conclusion by bringing together apparently two unconnected ideas such as in the examples above, is known as bisociation or associative thinking.

Adaptation

Adaptation is where a design solution is found by adapting a solution for another design problem. When developing the DC01 bagless vacuum cleaner, James Dyson looked at adapting the cyclone technology used in industrial dust and fume extractors to make a miniature cyclone in his product. See the case study on p104.

Transfer

This is when a technology, material or process is transferred from one application to another in order to provide a design solution. For example, lasers originally used in molecular science research were transferred into products such as CD players.

Did you know?

In 1945 Percy Spencer melted a chocolate and peanut bar in his pocket while standing in front of a radar magnetron. He realised that the high frequency radio emissions had melted the bar. He did the same with a bag of corn which exploded to make popcorn. This led to the development and patent of the first microwave cooker.

Analogy

This is where designers use similar situations, either in the natural or man-made world to inspire ideas. The Wright brothers observed how birds twist their wings to balance in flight. They adapted their aircraft wings to do likewise. George Carwardine used the principles of the human arm to design the 'Anglepoise' lamp. Alexander Graeme Bell made the analogy of the human ear when designing sound receiver apparatus for his experimental telephones. These analogies went on to become major innovations and inspired many more.

Combination

This is where two or more devices or products are combined into one to produce a new product. For example, power tool manufacturers are currently making a range of multi-functional tools combining a drill, circular saw, light or other tool with an interchangeable handle and battery.

Patents

Protecting designs (patents and intellectual property)

From the point of invention to the release of products into the market and their continued diffusion, ideas are at risk of being copied. To prevent this happening, inventors need to use a form of legal protection.

If an inventor or designer can prove that an invention is theirs, they can be granted a patent. This gives the designer the intellectual property rights of ownership of the design and legal action can be taken against anyone trying to use their invention without their permission.

Patents are granted by the state exclusive rights to make, use or sell a new invention for a set period (normally up to 20 years) in most countries. In exchange, patent holders must allow the details of their invention to be made public. This allows the state to build up a knowledge base that can encourage further invention and advance technological development for the benefit of everyone.

Patent applications contain the details of a product sufficient for it to be made by a third party. This will be a detailed description including drawings and technical detail that may be used by manufacturers actually making the product or seeking to improve upon it in the future.

Once a patent is granted, the invention becomes the legal property of the inventor. The owner can sell it, or they may authorise others to make, use or sell the invention in exchange for royalties.

The UK Patent Office has four criteria for a patent to be granted. These are as follows:

1 It must be new. It must not have been shown or discussed publicly anywhere prior to the patent application being filed.

2 It must involve an inventive step. The idea must not be obvious to someone with reasonable prior knowledge of the subject.

3 It must be capable of being industrially made. It must take the physical form of a substance, product or an industrial process.

4 It must not be excluded. An invention is not patentable if it is on the excluded list issued by the Patent Office.

These lists vary but generally, in the UK, exclusions include things such as discoveries, mathematical methods or scientific theories, art, literary

AQA Examiner's tip

Methods of protecting designs feature in A2 exam questions. You should learn some examples of products that have been patented.

and dramatic work, computer programs or other areas that don't include a physical product.

There are other methods of protecting intellectual property. Where designers or manufacturers have similar products but they each have different design features, the different features can be protected as registered designs.

When designers produce drawings of new ideas, these drawings can be protected under design right. This is similar to copyright which protects the work of artists or authors.

Product brand names, slogans, logos and other branding material can be protected by trade marks.

Patenting a design can be expensive, especially if worldwide patents are required. This can be very difficult for lone inventors who often need initial investment in a product in order to afford the patent process. This puts them in a vulnerable position as their designs are at risk of being copied after presenting their ideas to potential backers. The only way to challenge an infringement of a patent is through the courts. This can be hugely expensive. In 2000, James Dyson, famously took Hoover to court over infringements of his 1980 patent for his bagless vacuum cleaner using cyclones. At the time, Hoover was manufacturing a Triple Vortex bagless cleaner, using the same cyclone invention. Dyson had to put everything he had into paying for legal action. He eventually won the case and with the proceeds was able to set up his own UK factory to build the DC01.

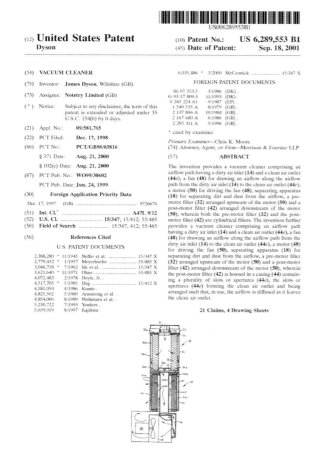

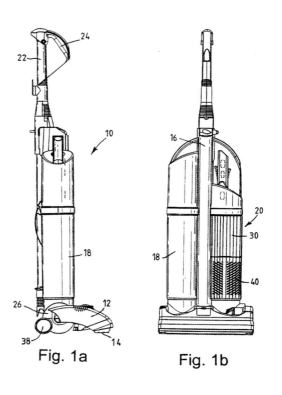

Extract from Dyson's 1980 bagless vacuum cleaner patent

> **i Activity**
>
> Think about projects that you have done and answer the following questions:
>
> **1** What research methods did you use and how useful were they in gathering the information you needed?
>
> **2** Write an example specification and explain its purpose.
>
> **3** For a specific product you are familiar with, explain how you would test and evaluate the product.

Ron Hickman, inventor of the Workmate portable work bench has spent over £1 million fighting infringements of his patents for the Workmate. Made under licence by Black and Decker since 1972, over 10 million have been sold but, over the years, there have been many rival companies who have tried to copy the design. See **www.blackanddecker.com**.

Products are often most at risk of being copied when they are first launched. Rival companies can easily reverse engineer products (take them apart and look at how they can be improved) in order to modify them and launch a similar product with added features. Some argue that because patents are made public, getting a new product to market first can be very difficult. For this reason, some companies take the risk not to patent a product. They hope that being first to market they can capture a large market share before rivals can develop a competing product.

■ Communication and representation of design ideas

During your course, you should try to develop illustration techniques and experiment with a range of graphical communication methods.

Here are some common communication methods used in the design process.

Mood boards

Mood boards are usually a collection of images/photos, e.g. of similar products to those being designed, colour **swatches**, fabric/material samples, finishes, etc. Mood boards are normally used by a designer as a style reference, when designing. They may also be used with a client, to agree on a particular style with the designer.

2-D/3-D sketching

These are sometimes known as '**thumbnail sketches**'. They are quick, rough sketches to explore concept ideas. Designers may add critical, evaluative comments or just notes of their own thoughts as they design.

Rendering

This is the use of line, tone and often colour to make 2- or 3-D drawings look realistic. This could be done by hand, using pencil or marker, or on 3-D CAD systems such as ProDesktop, 3-D Studio Max or Pro Engineer. Both CAD and traditional techniques enable the designer to experiment with textures and colour to represent alternative materials and surface finishes.

Orthographic projection

Orthographic drawings are technical line drawings, usually showing the product in a front, plan and end view. They are used to convey design details necessary for manufacture, and may:

■ be drawn to a scale, e.g. 1:10
■ be dimensioned
■ include details of materials/finishes
■ be known as 'working drawings'
■ include a tolerance, e.g. ± 0.01mm (meaning that it is acceptable for the product or component to be made bigger or smaller by 0.01 mm to the dimensions on the drawings).

AQA Examiner's tip

Graphical communication and modelling techniques used in the design process are common topics in exam papers. You should try some of them out in your coursework.

■ Key terms

Swatch: sample showing colour, texture, etc. (e.g. of fabric, paper), used as a portable source to select from.

Thumbnail sketches: rough sketches of a design idea.

Orthographic drawings: drawings showing the front, plan and end views of a design. These may include dimensions and details of materials.

■ Activity

Look up examples of CAD software on the internet

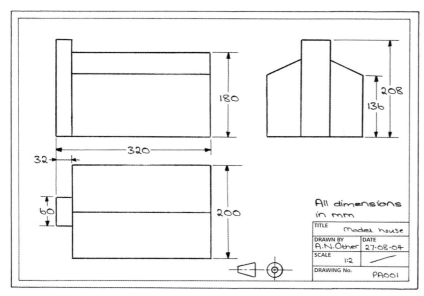

Orthographic drawing

Clay model of an Audi TT

■ **Key terms**

CAD models: the production of computer-generated drawings using vector or raster graphics. CAD models can be simple dimensioned drawings or, at the other extreme, animated 3-D simulations.

Mock-ups: rough models, often full-size, made from low-cost materials, such as card, MDF, etc.

Modelling

Models may be in the form of 3-D photo-realistic **CAD models** that can be used to select and develop ideas, or they may be physical models made with resistant or compliant materials.

To ensure a design is correct, designers may use scale models before the product is developed any further. For example, architects would often make a scale model of a building to check proportions, aesthetic considerations, etc. They may also use the model to present designs to clients and the public.

Mock-ups

Mock-ups are a type of rough prototype, possibly made in low-cost materials such as card, MDF, plywood, etc. For example, in developing the Euro-fighter airplane, designers used a full-size plywood mock-up to test the ergonomics of the cockpit area with test pilots. On a smaller scale, product designers often make modelling clay mock-ups for things such as handles, again to test ergonomics.

Prototypes

A prototype is usually a high-quality model or functioning product that is produced to realise a design solution. This prototype would be tested and evaluated before the product is considered for production. The products you make for coursework may fall into this category, for example a concept travel iron that you may model in MDF and acrylic.

High-quality prototype model of a travel iron

Presentation boards

Presentation boards usually display high-quality renderings, and possibly technical line drawings, showing the details of a design. A designer may use these when presenting ideas to a client, colleague or to the public. For example, architects would present their designs in the form of an artist's impression, elevation drawings at exhibitions, (such as public consultation events), or to local authorities to receive planning permission for projects.

Further reading

- Dick Powel, *Presentation Techniques – A guide to drawing and presenting design ideas*, Optima

- David Fair and Marilyn Kenny, *Design Graphics – Drawing and presenting your design ideas*, Hodder and Stoughton

- Jennifer Cottis, *Design Topics – Product Modelling*, Oxford University Press

Sustainability and environmental concerns

Introduction

Manufacturers and retailers are becoming increasingly concerned with the impact that the products they make may have on the environment. The main reasons for this are, first, government and international law, and, second, that consumers are much more environmentally aware and will choose greener brands.

Environmental legislation and regulation

The following is intended as a brief summary of recent legislation and regulations concerning products and the environment.

Ecolabel

The EU Ecolabel is a voluntary scheme which was established in 1993. Manufacturers are encouraged to label products that have a reduced impact on the environment over their life cycle. European consumers can identify such products with a flower symbol.

Packaging Directive

The EU Packaging Directive, introduced in 1994 and amended in 2004, sets targets for the reduction of packaging waste by means of designing out waste in the initial package design, recycling, and re-use. It also sets limits for the amount of toxic metals used in packaging. EU member states have to meet the following targets: by 2008, 60 per cent of all packaging waste is to be recovered and a minimum of 55 per cent of this waste is to be recycled.

Energy Labelling Directive

This EU directive was introduced in 1996. All electrical appliances such as refrigerators and washing machines are labelled with a rating from A to G to indicate their energy use for consumers to refer to when making a purchase. The directive also aims to phase out inefficient appliances.

End-of-Life Vehicle Directive (ELVD)

This directive was introduced in 2003 to encourage the reuse and recycling of waste from vehicles when they reach their end of life. It restricts the use of toxic metal in new cars and requires manufacturers to label plastic parts to aid recycling. Manufacturers also have to publish information on how to dismantle the vehicles.

Waste Electrical and Electronic Equipment Directive

This EU directive known as the WEEE Directive was implemented in 2006. It encourages manufacturers to develop electrical and electronic products that can be dismantled and the parts reused or recycled. Manufacturers have to include instructions to consumers not to discard the old product but take them to WEEE collection points. The directive also requires manufacturers to arrange collection of WEEE.

Restriction of Hazardous Substances Directive (RoSH)

Introduced in 2006, this EU directive bans the use of some hazardous materials and chemicals such as lead, mercury and cadmium in electrical and electronic equipment. This is to safeguard human health when electrical equipment is disposed of and recycled.

EU Ecolabel

Green design, ecodesign, sustainable design and sustainable innovation: what's the difference?

Green design

This is an approach in design to reduce impact on the environment.

It focuses on one or two areas such as conserving materials through using recycled materials in the manufacture of a product or by conserving energy in the use of the product. For example, the Dyson contra-rotating washing machine uses a water jet system to reduce the amount of water used and the agitation caused by the two tubs turning in opposite directions reduces the time taken to wash clothes, thus saving energy.

Ecodesign

This is an approach to design that goes further than green design. In this approach, designers and manufacturers will try to reduce the impact of a product through its entire lifecycle from raw materials extraction to final disposal. For example, a company developing a new washing machine might take the following areas into consideration:

- selection of low impact materials
- reduction in materials useage (both in manufacture and packaging)
- reduction of impact during use and optimisation of initial lifetime
- optimisation of end-of-life systems (for recycling and recovery of materials and components).

Sustainable design

In this approach, the main function of a product is analysed and a more environmentally sound method of performing the same function is sought. In addition to lessening the effect on the environment, sustainable design often has wider socio-economic benefits such as improved welfare and safety for workers producing the product, fair trade schemes and so on. For example, instead of using tumble dryers to dry clothes, it may be possible in some homes to use an alternative such as a cabinet that is heated by solar energy.

Sustainable innovation

This is a radical approach that goes beyond sustainable design to look for new ways of doing things using a mix of products and services. For example, instead of each home having a washing machine to clean clothes, a community based laundry services could collect your washing at the same time as your recycling waste (using biodiesel powered vehicles), then clean your clothes using efficient washing machines powered by alternative energy systems such as solar, wind or micro CHP (Combined Heat and Power). Your clean clothes could then be returned with your weekly grocery shopping.

Green design products

Examples of green design include clothing made from organically grown, naturally coloured cotton (reducing the need for pesticides and chemical dyes), sandals made from recycled denim (most waste denim would go to landfill), folding bicycles (encouraging commuters to conserve fuel and reduce carbon emissions), condensing gas central heating boilers (with over 90 per cent efficiency, saving much more energy than traditional boilers at around 50–60 per cent efficiency), coffee machines that utilise reuseable plastic filters instead of paper, biodegradable carrier bags, pencils made from recycled polystyrene cups and so on.

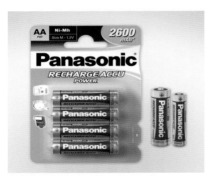

Plastic cell packaging

■ Key terms

Cathode ray tube (CRT): still used in most television sets for displaying a transmitted image and in computer monitors for displaying data or graphics. The large face of the tube is the screen of the television or monitor.

🔋 *Green design packaging*

Due to the EU Packaging and Packaging Waste Directive, much design and development work has gone into reducing packaging materials and packaging waste.

Some examples include companies such as Motorola who have replaced polystyrene inner packaging with moulded cardboard, and Duracell who have replaced high impact polystyrene blister packs with a simple card wrapper.

A recent development in packaging is the use of inflatable LDPE 'cushions'. These significantly reduce the quantity of polymer used in packaging and can be easily deflated and returned to the manufacturer for recycling or even reuse.

Eco design: redesigning the jug kettle

Eco design or life cycle design (LCD) as it is sometimes known aims to tackle two or more of the following environmental problem areas:

■ material consumption

■ fossil fuel energy consumption

■ pollution and toxic waste.

Designers involved in LCD think about the product's impact on the environment at every stage of its life, from raw materials extraction to final disposal, and will then try to quantify this. This is done through a process of life cycle assessment or LCA.

🔋 *Environmental impact of consumer electrical goods*

If a lifecycle assessment were to be carried out on the average TV set, it would identify the phase of the lifecycle that causes most damage is the 'use' phase. Approximately 80 per cent of the CO_2 emissions created in the lifecycle of a TV are accounted for in this phase. Typically when TVs are in use they use around 100 watts and between 3–6 watts when in standby mode. The remaining CO_2 emissions are created in the manufacture of the materials that make the TV and in the manufacture of the TV itself. There are other hazardous materials in the electronics of TVs and significant quantities of toxic lead oxide in the **cathode ray tubes** (CRT picture tubes).

Possible ecodesign ideas to make a 'green' TV:

■ Combine the TV with a DVD recorder to reduce the materials and components used.

■ Remove standby features so that the TV has to be switched off.

■ Use low-energy circuits and components to reduce operating power.

■ Replace the picture tube with an LCD display that uses less power.

■ Replace polymers and metals used in casing with wood to facilitate recycling and reduce energy consumption in manufacture.

Technological development in eco light bulbs

Compact fluorescent light bulbs

Fluorescent light bulbs work by heating an electrode which emits electrons into a tube of mercury vapour. This makes the vapour emit ultraviolet light. On the inside of the bulb a coating of phosphor reacts to the UV light and emits a visible white light. Compact fluorescent light bulbs (CFLs) introduced in the 1980s to domestic consumers, last about 10 times longer

Table 19 *Life cycle assessment and eco design approaches for a polymer jug kettle*

Life cycle phase	Environmental impact	Design approach
Raw materials extraction and processing	• Polymers processed from crude oil (exhaustible material). • Copper and zinc used in wire and metal parts (exhaustible materials). • All polymers and metals used in the kettle consume large amounts of energy in extraction and processing (greenhouse gas emissions). • Mining or metal ores and oil exploration can have an impact on the site of extraction (toxic waste).	• Minimise the quantity of material required in each kettle, e.g. a reduction in weight by 15 per cent. • Use a significant percentage by weight of recycled polymer. • Use a cordless design to minimise the use of copper cable. • Reduce the number of different materials and components used.
Manufacture	• Material wastage. • Injection moulding and final assembly. • Consumption of energy (greenhouse gas emissions).	• Efficient mould design to mould as many parts in one cycle as possible. • Snap fittings and ultrasonic welding to replace adhesives and screws (speeding up manufacture and reducing toxic materials found in adhesives). • Elimination of wasteful steps in manufacture to speed up 'tac time' (saving energy).
Distribution	• Transport from point of manufacture to distribution centre and onto retail outlets (greenhouse gas emissions and consumption of fossil fuels). • Packaging material waste, e.g. expanded polystyrene (EPS), LDPE film and printed card.	• Efficient box design to maximise number of units to a pallet. • Moulded card insert to replace EPS. • Bio-additive included in LDPE film to biodegrade.
Use	• High amount of energy consumed in the life time of a kettle (significant greenhouse gas emissions) and solid waste/ash from coal fired power stations.	• Easy to read filler gauge positioned on the top to aid precise filling. • Thermochromic patch to show if it is necessary to reboil the kettle or not. • Use an insulating double wall with an air gap to keep the water hot. • Use a water reservoir that dispenses the correct amount of water onto the heating element for one or more cups as desired.
Disposal	• Polymers could take several hundred years to degrade in landfill. • Electronics are difficult to separate from a circuit board.	• Design the kettle in a form that is 'classic' or timeless to extend its useable life. • Use the international identification code on polymer parts to aid recycling. • Use one type of thermoplastic polymer to facilitate recycling. • Use surface mount components that can be separated from a circuit board when passed through an infra-red oven.

than incandescent bulbs and they use about 20 per cent of the electricity. While they have significant environmental benefits in the 'use' phase of their lifecycle, CFLs use a number of toxic materials in their manufacture.

Light-emitting diodes

Light-emitting diodes (LEDs) produce light when electrons pass between two pieces of semi-conducting material held within them. LEDs are used in a wide variety of applications from digital displays to car brake lights. LEDs are very robust and energy efficient (converting about 90 per cent of the energy they use into light).

 Key terms

Light-emitting diode (LED): a semi-conductor made up of a single junction of n- and p-type materials. As with all semi-conductors current will flow when the junction voltage has been reached but in this case light is emitted. Various colours of LEDs can be used.

Bang and Olufsen Beovision Avant TV-DVD with a fibreboard casing

Electrodeless induction lamp

White LEDs can be made by coating the inside of the bulb with a phosphorescent coating which emits white light in response to the LEDs' light emission or by mixing the light from several primary colour bulbs. With an estimated lifetime of over 100,000 hours, falling costs of production and increased technical development, white LEDs could begin to replace CFLs, halogen and incandescent bulbs in most domestic situations.

Electrodeless induction lamps

These are an innovative type of lamp developed in the 1990s by Intersource Technologies of California. They work by using a magnetic coil to generate radio waves which excite gas contained in the lamp. The inside surface of the lamp is coated with a phosphorescent material which glows. The estimated lifetime of the bulb is around 20,000 hours. This compares extremely well against incandescent bulbs with a life around 700 to 1,000 hours. These bulbs do not have a filament or electrode that wears down. However, the gas eventually degrades requiring the glass cover to be changed. Only the cover is replaced with the electronic base unit being retained. This makes for low running costs.

The environmental impact of cars

The main materials used in cars are aluminium, mild steel, copper, glass and polymers. The extraction and processing of these materials consumes large amounts of energy and water, and emissions to the atmosphere or water system, in addition to solid waste. During production, the manufacturing processes and painting also consume large amounts of energy and produce more emissions and solid waste.

It is during the useful life of the car that the highest impact on the environment occurs. The use of petrol or diesel produces emissions of CO_2, carbon monoxide, nitrogen oxides and unburned hydrocarbons. These are hazardous to human health and to the environment. On average the private motor vehicle contributes 30 per cent of the total carbon emissions for the UK. Consumable parts such as the tyres, battery and exhaust are regularly replaced and therefore consume more energy and resources. At the end of the vehicle's useful life, the metals and polymers are recycled (involving further energy consumption) but textiles, glass and rubber are more difficult to recycle and so are often disposed of in landfill. Approximately 80 per cent of the impact of cars on the environment occurs during the 'use' stage of their lifecycle.

Green or eco design in cars

Generally, car manufacturers have tended to adopt green design strategies focusing upon single issues such as optimisation of end life recycling or improvements in manufacturing to save energy. In the early 1990s EU regulation meant the adoption of catalytic converters to reduce exhaust pollutants. EU regulations now focus upon fuel economy requiring manufacturers to label cars in sale rooms and publicity material to indicate their CO_2 emissions per km.

To achieve better fuel economy, car manufacturers have tended to focus on reducing the weight of cars and making them more aerodynamic.

Generally most cars feature the following fuel-saving measures:

■ aerodynamic body (reducing drag)
■ lightweight aluminium engines

- use of polymers to reduce vehicle weight
- thin section mild steel or alumininium body and sub-assemblies (reducing weight)
- electronic engine management systems to optimise burning of fuel
- stop/start systems. These are electronic starter motor systems that turn off the engine when the driver brings the vehicle to a halt, but re-start the engine when the clutch is depressed to move off. This feature makes a significant fuel saving and reduces CO_2 emissions. The Bosch system fitted to new BMW-1 series cars reduces fuel consumption and CO_2 emissions in heavy traffic by about 8 per cent. If the stops are longer, the savings are much higher.

In addition, most cars also feature other green features such as:

- asbestos-free brakes and clutches
- a percentage by weight of recycled textiles in upholstery fillings and soundproofing
- natural fibres/textiles and dyes utilised in upholstery
- a finishing of water-based paints
- international coded polymer parts to aid recycling
- digital recycling manuals to assist in efficient recovery of materials and components.

Hybrid cars

Some manufacturers such as Toyota and Honda have developed hybrid cars which run on a petrol engine and an electric motor. At slow speeds such as in an urban area, the vehicle runs only on the electric motor and therefore has no emissions. At higher speeds the petrol engine takes over and at the same time charges the batteries that run the motor. This means that the vehicle doesn't have to be plugged in and charged which is a weakness of purely electric vehicles. A petrol engine also allows for features such as air conditioning, stereos and other items that would normally cause a drop in speed or range in electric vehicles.

Critics of hybrid vehicles argue that they are only beneficial at slow speeds and once they need to run on their petrol engine, the increased weight from the motor and batteries reduces the overall fuel efficiency gains.

Hydrogen fuel cell

Most of the major car manufacturers are researching and developing hydrogen fuel cells as a means of fuelling cars. Some have produced limited production runs of road going vehicles as part of this process, e.g. the Daimler-Chrysler F-Cell car. Hydrogen fuel cells are electrochemical energy conversion devices that convert hydrogen and oxygen into water. In the process, they produce electricity which can be used to drive an electric motor. The most likely fuel cell to be used in cars is the 'polymer exchange membrane fuel cell' (PEMFC). This has a high power output and operates at relatively low temperatures so it will produce electricity at temperatures of 60 to 80 degrees Celsius. Their only emission in use is water vapour. Unfortunately, at present, the components that make up a fuel cell are extremely expensive (in particular the catalysts that are made from platinum). Research is centred on reducing the size of fuel cells, finding safe ways to store the hydrogen and alternative catalyst materials.

Hydrogen fuel cell-powered car

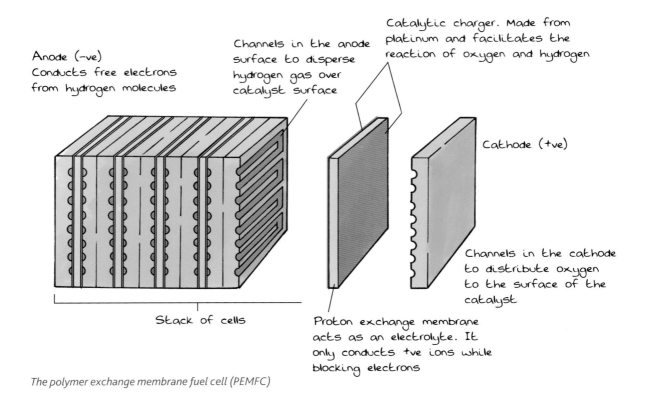

Anode (-ve)
Conducts free electrons from hydrogen molecules

Channels in the anode surface to disperse hydrogen gas over catalyst surface

Catalytic charger. Made from platinum and facilitates the reaction of oxygen and hydrogen

Cathode (+ve)

Channels in the cathode to distribute oxygen to the surface of the catalyst

Stack of cells

Proton exchange membrane acts as an electrolyte. It only conducts +ve ions while blocking electrons

The polymer exchange membrane fuel cell (PEMFC)

Electric cars

There are several electric cars commercially available with both an impressive range and acceleration, e.g. the now iconic G-Wiz designed and manufactured by the Californian based Indo-US Reva Electric Car Company. This commuter car, now commonplace in the City of London, is capable of speeds of up to 45 mph and a range of 48 miles on a single charge. This has been made possible with developments in efficient a.c. electric drive motors, lithium-ion batteries and advanced lightweight alloys and composites used in the chassis and body. The G-Wiz, like many electric and hybrid cars, also employs regenerative braking. This is where under-braking (the kinetic energy from the moving vehicle) is transferred from the wheels to the motor that acts as a generator. This helps to charge the batteries and extend the range of the vehicle on a single charge. See **www.goingreen.co.uk**.

Unfortunately all battery powered electric cars have to be charged. This has serious drawbacks as the vehicle obviously has to be parked overnight in a place with suitable charging facilities (usually the user's home). It would require a massive change in infrastructure to provide charging points in public places. An even greater disadvantage is that if everyone changed to electric cars, there would have to be a huge increase in the number of power stations to provide the necessary increase in electricity. If that electricity is generated by burning fossil fuels, the resulting CO_2 emissions would be far greater than those currently produced by petrol and diesel cars.

Bio diesel

Bio diesel is diesel made from vegetable oil extracted from crops such a rape seed and palm. Diesel made from plant materials is 'carbon neutral' because the diesel produces the same amount of CO_2 when burned as would be absorbed by the plant when growing. It can be used in all diesel engine vehicles and produces roughly the same miles per gallon as standard diesel. Enthusiasts sometimes make their own bio diesel by recycling used cooking oil. This is itself an ecologically sound practice as waste cooking oil would normally go to landfill. There are drawbacks with bio diesel, the most serious being loss of natural habitat where rainforest is being cleared to grow palm trees, and utilising valuable farming land that could be used for food production.

Bio power

This is a fuel made from grain crops that is converted to make ethanol which, in turn, is blended with diesel. This reduces the amount of fossil fuel diesel needed and has lower CO_2 emissions. Some manufacturers are producing dual fuel cars capable of running on bio power or diesel. This is necessary as it will be some time before bio power fuel is available in large numbers of filling stations. Currently bio power produces fewer miles per gallon than standard diesel which is a significant drawback. Scientists are trying to improve this and aim to develop fuel that can be made from the whole plant rather than just the grain, making more efficient use of the crop.

The rebound effect

This is a phenomenon that describes how society reacts to improvements in the environmental performance of products. As manufacturers make products such as cars more fuel efficient and therefore cheaper to run, the more people will use them. So in the case of cars, there is a pattern of consumers trading up for larger cars and travelling further and faster in them. This wipes out any gains in environmental performance that manufacturers achieve through technological advancements. The same type of effect can be observed in other goods such as clothing and domestic electrical items. As manufacturers find cheaper ways to make products, the savings are often passed onto consumers and so products become more accessible to more people. Therefore, even though products are becoming greener, their increased use cancels out any environmental benefits.

Plastics and the environment

Manufacturers often prefer to use plastics rather than other materials. One major reason for this is that the use of plastics sometimes has less impact on the environment than the use of some metals or timbers.

Plastics in the car industry

Most car manufacturers use a wide range of polymers in building cars. Plastics can be used for a large number of components including front and rear bumpers, front grill and headlight surround, door mirrors, headlamps, dashboard fascias, steering wheels, door trims, and so on.

Vehicle dashboards tend to be made from ABS (acrylonitrile butadiene styrene). This thermoplastic material is very hard wearing and more than able to cope with daily use, handling, cleaning, and so on.

Advantages of using plastics in car manufacture

- They are available in a range of colours to suit consumer taste for vehicle interiors.
- The moulding can be given a surface texture, such as a leather-grain effect, by engraving the surface of the mould.
- The dashboards can be made in a variety of ways, the most common method being injection moulding. This enables all of the apertures for instrumentation, heater vents, controls and switches to be made at the same time in one moulding.

Activity

Use the internet to research some of the following innovations that reduce the environmental impact of cars:

- Aerodynamics (low drag).
- Catalytic converters.
- Liquid petroleum gas (LPG) and other advanced fuels.
- Small commuter vehicles, e.g. Smart car.
- Hybrid vehicles, e.g. Toyota Prius.
- Diagnostic engine management systems.

AQA Examiner's tip

When explaining how products change with advancements in materials/technology you might use plastics and composites.

Traditionally, dashboards would have been made from pressed metals, such as steel, and either paint sprayed or covered with leather-effect vinyl or timber veneers. This is time consuming and expensive, as more machines and labour are required than for modern, injection-moulded designs.

In volume production models, manufacturing processes need to be as fast and streamlined as possible, therefore injection moulding is used.

In addition, final assembly is much faster because plastics such as ABS can be joined using self-tapping screws or 'click fastenings'. This enables fast fitting of the smaller components, e.g. instrumentation into the dashboard housing.

The use of plastics not only speeds up manufacturing but, also, the properties of plastics can be more desirable than traditional materials. For example, headlamp assemblies are usually covered in transparent polycarbonate. This has superseded glass headlamp assemblies, which had a tendency to chip or smash in small impacts.

The use of plastics for smaller components also helps to reduce the net weight of the cars they are used in, and this will ultimately improve performance and fuel consumption.

Further reading

Dorothy Mackenzie, *Green Design: Design for the Environment*, Thames and Hudson

Intermediate Technology Development Group, *Make The Future Work: Appropriate technology*, Longman

www.plasticresource.com

 Product analysis exercise 1: Design and the environment

Plastics in packaging

Study the photograph of the package shown and answer the questions:

1. Under the following headings, explain what impact the package may have on the environment:

   a raw materials extraction

   b materials processing

   c manufacture

   d distribution

   e use

   f disposal.

2. Explain why fast food restaurants might use paper and card as packaging materials.

3. Making reference to environmental issues, list the advantages and disadvantages of using PET (polyethylene terephthalate) as a material for drinks bottles.

 Product analysis exercise 2: Design and the environment

Pepsi can

1. a Name a specific material or materials suitable for the manufacture of this product.

   b Explain why this material is suitable, or why these materials are suitable.

2. Using notes and diagrams, describe how this product is manufactured.

3. Explain how the following influence the design and manufacture of this product:

   a function

   b aesthetics

   c environmental matters.

■ Safety

Before reading this section, you should refer back to Chapter 3 which introduces safety standards and legislation in Product Design. You will need to have an understanding of British, European and International standards that affect safety in products and their safe manufacture.

Risk assessments

You need to understand the concept of **risk assessment**. Risk assessments can be applied to both the design and manufacture of products, and the outcome of these risk assessments can determine things such as the physical appearance, the materials, components and finishes used, the method of manufacture and consumer advice issued with products.

The example in Table 20 is a risk assessment applied to a child's sit and ride plastic car

■ Key terms

Risk assessment: a document assessing the type of hazard, the level of risk, who might be affected by the hazard, and a description of control measures taken to minimise the risk associated with using specific materials and manufacturing processes.

Table 20 *Child's sit and ride plastic car*

Hazard	Level of risk	Control measure (design)	Control measure
Hazards in use			
Entrapment in mechanisms or moving parts	Low	• Design out potential areas for entrapment such as door hinges by removing doors altogether. • If pedals are used these would be direct drive to the front wheel(s) so there is no chain or gears to guard. • Sufficient space between the pedal crank and the wheel to prevent entrapment.	
Tipping over	Medium	• Design car with wide wheel base and thick wheels. • Add seat belt/straps to keep rider in. • Add a parental handle.	
Toxic materials and finishes	Low	• Specify non-toxic materials, pigments and additives from suppliers. • Applied finishes are designed out; colour pigment to be added in moulding process.	• Random testing of materials to ensure hazardous materials are not present or fall below safe limits.
Accident through use, e.g. road traffic incident	Medium to high	• Give clear instructions about adequate parental supervision and safe use of the product.	
Manufacturing hazards			
Toxic fumes			• Protect employees by using fume extraction and fully automated moulding processes.
Molten polymer			Fully guarded machines (guards are safety interlocked and machine will not operate without guards in place).
Hot products (post moulding)			• Fully guarded machines (guards are safety interlocked and machine will not operate without guards in place).

Control Of Substances Hazardous to Health (COSHH): regulations dealing with the safe handling, use and storage of hazardous materials.

Health and Safety Executive (HSE): a government advisory service that helps companies meet health and safety obligations under the Health and Safety at Work Act. The HSE publishes safety posters, books and copies of specific Health and Safety regulations. Local HSE officers visit employees to check they are complying with regulations and to investigate accidents.

Safety legislation & manufacturing

There is specific legislation to protect employees involved in manufacturing. The main ones are the Health and Safety at Work Act 1974; the Personal Protective Clothing Regulations 2002; and the **Control Of Substances Hazardous to Health Regulations (COSHH)** 2002. Generally this legislation is designed to protect employees in the workplace. Under this legislation, employers are generally obliged to do the following:

■ Make the workplace safe and free from risks to health.
■ Ensure machinery is safe and safe working practices are followed.
■ Ensure dangerous items and substances are removed and stored safely.
■ Provide sufficient welfare facilities.
■ Provide information, training and supervision as necessary for health and safety.

In this section, we will look at how manufacturers actually conform to health and safety law.

Manufacturers ensure the safety of employees in a variety of ways. The main methods are as follows.

Training

Employees would normally be trained in the safe operation of the equipment they use. This may include taking health and safety courses and being tested against **Health and Safety Executive (HSE)** standards to prove competence.

Guarding of machines

HSE regulations require most machines to be guarded to prevent employees hurting themselves. Guards range from devices to cover saw blades, such as those on band saws and circular saws, to sophisticated infra-red light beams that switch off the power to a machine if the beam is broken. These can be seen on larger machines, such as press formers or CNC (computer numerically controlled) punches.

Personal protective clothing

Depending on what tasks employees have to do, they may be issued with protective clothing, such as overalls, dust masks, safety boots, goggles and so on.

Extraction

If dust or fumes are produced in the manufacturing process, extractors are used to protect employees. Dust extraction is particularly important when machining composites such as MDF (medium density fibre), carbon fibre reinforced plastic and glass-reinforced plastic, because the dust produced is very hazardous.

COSHH

COSHH or the Control Of Substances Hazardous to Health is a set of HSE regulations and guidance for the storage and handling of potentially dangerous materials. The regulations include details of how the materials should be labelled, safely used and stored to protect employees.

Risk assessments

A risk assessment is a calculation of the hazards associated with a manufacturing process or job, an assessment of whether the risk is a low, medium or high one, and a description of how the hazard can be controlled. All employers are legally obliged to carry out risk assessments for their operations.

Case study 1: Safety in JCB manufacture

Here is a brief summary of how safety is ensured in the manufacture of JCB earth-moving equipment at JC Bamford Ltd, in Rocester, Staffordshire.

Safe zones

In a busy factory such as JCB, vehicles are delivering parts 'just in time' and the parts are distributed throughout the factory using a variety of means, including fork-lift trucks. Pedestrian walkways are clearly marked throughout the factory to help minimise the risk of collision.

Safety screens

At JCB, the manufacturing process makes extensive use of laser cutting, plasma cutting and electric arc welding. Exposure to laser light can cause instant and permanent eye damage, and exposure to ultraviolet light from arc welding can cause severe eye irritation. Prolonged exposure to such UV light can also cause permanent eye damage. Heavy, black, opaque screening is used around production cells that use such processes, to protect passers-by and those working in the vicinity.

Guarding

JCB uses huge presses to fold heavy-gauge steel plate into the components used to make vehicle chassis and so on. These machines do not have any physical barriers, such as screens or cages, as they would make it difficult to load and unload the components. Instead, light beams protect them. The operator has to stand at their control pedestal, or the beams are broken and the machine won't work.

Personal protective clothing

At JCB, employees involved in arc welding have to be issued with protective welding visors. These visors darken instantly as the welding begins, and have a forced air system that blows air over the welder's face, blowing away the fumes from the welding process. This would be complemented with flame-retardant overalls, welding gloves and so on.

Use of robotics

Robots are not used to replace labour at JCB, but to take out the heavy lifting during the manufacturing process. This helps to prevent strain injury. Robots can also be used in some of the more unpleasant jobs, such as spray powder coating for the finishing of components. This removes the need to have employees working in such environments.

Job rotation

If an employee is at risk of repetitive strain injury (injury caused by doing tasks repeatedly), they can be rotated to another production cell to work on an alternative job.

Health and safety management

JCB trains all employees to be responsible for their own safety, but also has cell managers and production managers with specific roles

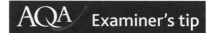

in the management of health and safety. They conduct detailed risk assessments for each stage of the manufacturing process, and ensure that each employee is appropriately trained. Health and safety managers also keep detailed records of any accidents and any 'near misses' that occur. (Near misses are incidents where something went wrong, e.g. a part fell off a trolley or conveyor, and could have potentially caused an accident.) These are analysed to assess how they can be avoided in the future.

Safety legislation and the user

There is a range of consumer protection laws determined and enforced by the Department of Trade and Industry (DTI) and the European Union.

The Trading Standards Agency is responsible for the day to day enforcement of consumer safety law. Trading Standards officers have the power to remove unsafe products from the market and prosecute offenders. Supplying an unsafe product can result in a £5000 fine and/or imprisonment for up to six months.

One piece of important legislation concerns the safety of electrical consumer goods. This is influenced by the Electrical Equipment (Safety) Regulations 1994. This requires mains voltage items to be well insulated and contain measures to protect consumers from electric shock or fire. If used with 240 volts mains power, electrical plugs have to be fitted. These, in turn, must conform to the Plugs and Sockets etc. (Safety) Regulations 1994.

The European Union (EU) have put in place a number of Product Directives, covering a wide range of product areas such as:

- General product safety.
- Machines.
- Toy safety.
- Noise emission from domestic products.
- Low voltage electrical equipment.

Products that meet the relevant EU directives can display the CE mark. This mark is a statement by the manufacturer that it conforms to the directive that is applicable to it. It means that the product can be sold in the EU. Manufacturers wishing to display the CE mark on their products usually have them tested by the British Standards Institute. The BSI tests the products against agreed standards. On passing the tests, the product can also display the BSI Kitemark. Both the CE and Kitemark reassure consumers that they are buying a safe product.

Case study 2: Safety features in a domestic, 3-pin electrical plug

A standard 240-volt, 3-pin plug is packed with safety features. They are as follows:

- The wires are colour-coded: earth (yellow with green stripe), live (brown), and neutral (blue) to help ensure plugs are wired to

Further reading

- More information about UK and EU consumer safety legislation can be found on **www.dti.org.uk**.

appliances correctly. The earth wire is striped to aid users with colour blindness.

- Three-pin plugs are supplied with a card label fitted to the underside of the plug. This gives a clear wiring diagram to help ensure that the user correctly wires the plug up. The underside of the plug also has the letters E (earth), L (live) and N (neutral) embossed on the surface to help the user, should the card label be lost.

- Three-pin plugs are supplied with a fitted fuse (usually 3- or 13-amp). The fuse is designed to fail if there is a sudden power surge, or if a fault develops in the product. The conducting wire within a fuse breaks and cuts the power from the appliance. This gives the user some protection from electric shock, and protects the appliance from further damage.

- The earth pin on a 3-pin plug is the longest pin. This ensures that when an appliance is plugged in, the earth pin connects first. Should there be a fault in the appliance, the electric current will flow safely to earth and not make the outer casing or power switches of the appliance live.

- The live and neutral pins have a small section at their base coated with a polymer sleeve. This ensures that the user cannot accidentally touch a live pin when it is being inserted or retracted from a mains socket.

- 3-pin plugs are fitted with a cable clamp. This fixes the appliance cable firmly and helps to prevent the wire at the terminals or pins becoming loose or breaking.

- The casing of a 3-pin plug is usually made from urea formaldehyde. This is a hard, durable, thermosetting plastic. These properties are desirable to prevent the plug becoming damaged through general use. As a thermosetting polymer is used, the plug retains its shape and integrity in the event of it becoming hot through a power surge or even a minor fire.

- 240-volt, 3-pin plugs are usually marked to indicate that they meet the requirements of the British Standards Institution standard for electrical plugs and fittings BS 1363. This standard sets out a detailed specification for electrical plugs.

13-amp, 3-pin domestic plug

Human needs and human factors

Ergonomics and anthropometrics

Before you read this section, you may want to refer back to Chapter 3 which covers the basic definitions of ergonomics and anthropometrics and explains some of the factors influencing these two critical areas in Product Design.

You need to be able to critically analyse a range of products in terms of their ergonomics and anthropometrics. We have included some exercises for you try out in this section of the book.

Study the two kettles pictured on the next page. They each have different ergonomic and anthropometric features. Tables 21a and b illustrate these features.

AQA Examiner's tip

It is common to be asked to compare and contrast the ergonomic and anthropometric features of several different products. You could answer this type of question using written notes and diagrams or a table can sometimes be useful.

It is a good idea to practise analysing products in this way. The next time you use a torch, a power tool, an MP3 player and so on, think about how easy they are to use and why.

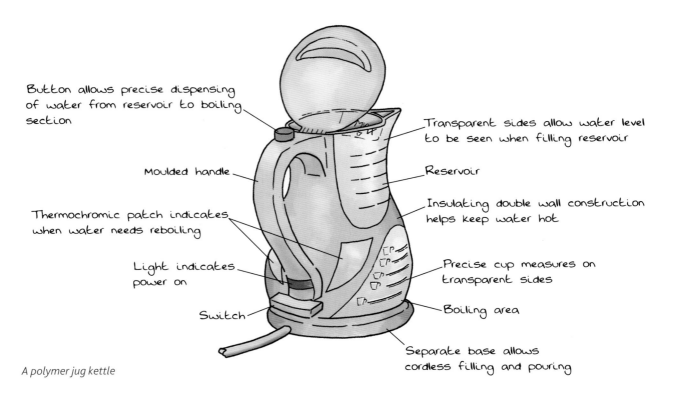

Button allows precise dispensing of water from reservoir to boiling section

Moulded handle

Thermochromic patch indicates when water needs reboiling

Light indicates power on

Switch

Transparent sides allow water level to be seen when filling reservoir

Reservoir

Insulating double wall construction helps keep water hot

Precise cup measures on transparent sides

Boiling area

Separate base allows cordless filling and pouring

A polymer jug kettle

A traditional stainless steel kettle

Table 21a *Ergonomic and anthropometric features of a stainless steel kettle*

Stainless steel kettle parts	Ergonomic or anthropometric feature
1 Main handle	Made from a thermoset polymer, the handle doesn't conduct heat from the body of the kettle so it is more comfortable to hold.
	Mounted on the top of the kettle, the pouring action can be uncomfortable on the wrist. This can be difficult for the elderly.
	When pouring, the steam rises up over the hand; again this can be uncomfortable.
2 Lid	Mounted under the man handle, it is awkward to lift off for filling.
	The small handle on the lid is possibly difficult to grip.
3 Pouring spout	Angled to allow pouring without causing splashes. Fairly easy to direct water into a cup.
	Narrow spout is difficult to use to fill the kettle; often water is accidentally spilled.
4 Flex	Has to be removed from the kettle before filling. This is dangerous as many consumers might not do so and there is a risk of electric shock.
5 Filler gauge	There is no filler gauge so it is difficult to estimate how much water is in the kettle.
6 Body	Made from stainless steel, the body gets very hot when the kettle is boiled. This can burn the user.
7 Power switch	Convenient location for thumb operation. Red illuminated switch to make it easy to distinguish from body/handle.

Table 21b *Ergonomic and anthropometric features of a polymer jug kettle*

Polymer jug kettle parts	Ergonomic or anthropometric feature
1 Side mounted handle	Large chunky handle with plenty of finger space making it easy to grip.
	Side mounting make pouring easier with comfortable wrist position and no risk of steam going over the hand or body.
2 Lid	Positioned on top of the kettle with textured finger grips to aid removal of the lid for cleaning, etc.
3 Spout	Large enough to allow filling and therefore the lid does not need to be frequently removed.
4 Detachable base	Isolates kettle from mains power when the kettle is lifted. Much safer to use when filling over a sink.
5 Filler gauge	Allows easy measuring of water for one cup boiling, etc.
6 Body	Polymer body acts as an insulator and therefore in the event of touching the hot side of the kettle, although warm, it will not burn the user.
	Slim design allows one cup boiling and therefore the weight of the kettle when lifting and pouring is reduced.

 ## Product analysis exercise 3: Computer workstation

Make brief notes to explain the ergonomic and anthropometrical features identified by each label.

Desk and computer

  a Foot rest

  b Leg room under table

  c Computer grade lighting

  d Ambient temperature, + 15 °C

  e Adjustable monitor

  f Wrist rest

  g Screen filter

  h Document holder

  i Window blinds

Chair

  j Cushioned seat and backrest

  k Adjustable height/gas strut

  l Adjustable backrest

  m Seat avoids pinching knee joint

  n Backrest allows free movement of shoulders

  o Fabric made of breathable materials

  p Five spoke wheels

  q Backrest hugs curvature of spine

Further reading

■ Henry Dreyfuss Associates, *The Measure of Man – Human Factors in Design,* Whitney Library of Design

■ Steve Garner, *Design Topics – Human Factors,* Oxford University Press

AQA Examiner's tip

In preparing for exams, critically analyse how products could be designed for use by disabled customers.

✓ Product analysis exercise 4: Car interior

Study a car interior and note the following ergonomic features:

a Adjustable seats – to take account of different body sizes and driving positions. How easy are they to adjust? What parts are adjustable and what is the range of adjustment?

b Shaped and padded seats to provide comfortable seating.

c Adjustable mirrors.

d Layout of the dashboard. Note that the instruments such as speedometer, temperature gauge, and so forth, are usually visible either over or through the steering wheel. Controls such as heater controls, light switch, hazard warning light switch, and so on, are within easy reach.

e Use of colour on instruments. Note the use of red and blue on temperature controls. Red is used on engine warning lights, for example for the low oil indicator and brake fluid level indicator. Red is used on the speedometer to indicate the 30 mph mark and on rev counters to indicate high level engine revs.

f Light level of instruments. The brightness of instrument lighting can usually be adjusted to allow for different consumer preferences.

g Heating/air conditioning. Interior temperature control is an important aspect of maintaining passenger comfort.

Design for disabled people

Introduction

In an inclusive society, it is extremely important that designers take into account the different needs of different groups of people. Disabled people make up one such group of consumers – though it's important to note that, of course, different disabled people have different needs.

Adapted products

Many domestic products have been adapted to meet the requirements of disabled people and with an ageing population the demand for such products will continue to grow. Often, as a result of changing products to meet the needs of disabled people, all users benefit from the improvements.

Some examples of adapted products include:

■ kettles with tipping devices for one-handed operation (to assist amputees or stroke victims)

■ tap lever attachments to aid opening and closing taps (especially helpful for arthritis sufferers or stroke victims who may find it difficult to grip)

■ hand controls: retrofitted to cars to enable acceleration and braking instead of using foot pedal controls.

Some products specifically designed for disabled people might include:

■ stair and bath lifts

■ lightweight and manoeuvrable sports wheelchairs

■ clothing using Velcro fastenings (much easier for arthritis sufferers to use than buttons.

Public buildings

Legislation now requires architects involved in planning new public buildings, such as schools, libraries and hospitals, to ensure access and facilities for disabled people.

Activity

Use the following checklist to assess how well your school has been designed to meet the needs of disabled people.

Car parking

- Are there clearly marked disabled parking spaces near the entrances?
- Are the car parking spaces wide enough apart to allow for wheelchair users to get in and out of cars?

Entrance

- Is the car park on the same level as the entrance? If not, has a ramp been installed to help wheelchair users?
- If there is a ramp, how steep is the slope?
- Are there steps to negotiate entering the building? If so, has a handrail been installed to help people who are unsteady on their feet?
- Is the door easy to open? Is it automatic?
- Is there a threshold or step in the doorway? Could this be difficult for wheelchair users to get over?

Corridors

- Are corridors wide enough to allow for wheelchair users and able-bodied users to pass comfortably?
- Are there internal doors? If so, are they easy to open and are they held back on catches or magnets?
- Are there refuge points for wheelchair users in the event of a fire?

Toilets

- Are disabled toilets provided? If so, are they clearly signposted and positioned in an accessible place?
- If a disabled toilet is available, note how it may have been adapted.
- If a door is fitted, is it a lightweight sliding door and wide enough to allow wheelchair access?
- Look at the level of sinks (they should be at wheelchair height).
- Taps should have a lever attachment on the top to make it easier to turn them on and off.
- Toilet cubicles should be wide enough to take wheelchairs and allow the user to slide from the wheelchair onto the toilet. There should be grab rails near the toilet to help with this.

Lifts

- If lifts are provided, note how they may be designed to help the disabled user.
- Is the call button at a sensible height for wheelchair users?
- Is the lift door wide enough for wheelchair users? Does it close slowly and re-open if the door is obstructed?
- Is there a threshold or step between the floor level and the interior floor of the lift?
- Are the interior call buttons easily accessed? Are they illuminated to indicate to the deaf that the floor has been selected? Are they engraved in Braille for the visually impaired?
- Are there audible indicators for the door closing/opening and for the different floor levels?
- Are there handrails fitted to the interior of the lift to provide a steady movement?

Product analysis exercise 5: Design for disabled people

Study the photograph of the kettle tipper. This is a device used to help disabled people tip a kettle in order to pour drinks safely.

1 Who would find this kettle pourer a useful item (what kind of disabilities)?

2 Use notes and sketches to show how the kettle tipper functions.

3 Use the internet to research living aids for disabled people that would help with the following routine activities:

a turning water taps (with arthritic hands)

b dressing (with the use of one hand only)

c making a cup of tea (with poor eyesight)

d driving a car (without the use of legs).

Make notes and diagrams to show how each living aid functions.

Further reading

■ The Disabled Living Foundation is a UK charity with comprehensive information about disabilities, products for disabled people and ways in which homes, gardens, cars, and so on can be adapted for them. Its web address is: **www.dif.org.uk**

■ Henry Dreyfuss Associates, *The Measure of Man – Human Factors in Design*, Whitney Library of Design

■ Steve Garner, *Design Topics – Human Factors*, Oxford University Press

⚲ Major developments in technology

Introduction

Continuous technological development has had a significant impact upon the way we live and the way society and commerce operate.

The supply of electricity cabled overland resulted in increased urbanisation and allowed for the development of an industrialised society. That same electricity also allowed the development of long distance communication systems – initially the telegraph then the telephone and radio. Advancements in science have allowed the development of synthetic materials such as polymers, fibres, pigments, dyes and composites. This has led to an increase in the variety of products available to the consumer.

In more recent times, there have been scientific breakthroughs with the development of new 'smart materials' and in the creation of materials using nanotechnology. These materials offer significant advantages over traditional materials. At the same time, there have been many advancements with electronics which have had a major impact on information and communications technology (ICT). This section of the book will consider the effect of these new technologies on Product Design and the impact on society.

Over the last 70 years there has also been significant development in electrical and electronic products, which has worked hand-in-hand with the materials and processing developments to produce the commercial products we have today.

Four examples of products to illustrate these major developments in technology are shown below: radios, batteries, TVs and the telephone.

Technological developments and the radio

1930s

Radios became commercially available from the late 1920s and early 1930s. At that time, there was still a strong reliance on handcrafted furniture and the radio casing reflected that. The electronics inside consisted of a mains (240 volt a.c.) powered circuit using thermionic valves. These were the forerunner of the transistor, and operated by emitting electrons when the valve components were heated. An internal grid controlled the flow of electrons (and therefore the current), making them an effective amplification stage for the incoming sound signal. A

AQA Examiner's tip

You might find it very useful to practise sketching products like kettles, razors, hairdryers, etc. and label up the ergonomic features and consider how anthropometrics might have been used in their design.

number of amplification stages were used, together with a local oscillator, an aerial, and a big (approx. 200 mm) diameter loudspeaker.

Other components included dozens of resistors and capacitors, and a large amount of copper wire used for connecting all of the components together. There was a large space around the components to allow for the dissipation of the heat (40 watts or so) generated by the valves and other components. The whole product was extremely heavy due to the weight of the wooden case, the metal chassis supporting the electronic components (including the valve holders) and the large transformer used to alter the voltage from 240 volt to 6.5 volt for heating the valves. This radio would have been very expensive to buy, probably costing the equivalent of a couple of months' wages, although by today's standards the quality of reception would be considered poor.

1940s and 1950s

During the 1940s and 1950s, radios tended to be made from the newly developed plastics. In particular Bakelite (a thermosetting polymer) was being used for various external components, such as volume and station-control knobs.

The transistor

At about the same time, in the early 1950s, the transistor was introduced. These are made from two kinds of semi-conducting materials, i.e. materials that will only conduct electrons when a particular voltage is applied. These two materials are known as **n-type** and **p-type** materials, and refer to the special arrangement of particles in either silicon or germanium. Transistors work as an electronic switch: switching on when the current at the p-n-p junction is above a minimum value. They can be used to control the flow of electrons, making them effective at providing an amplification stage for the radio.

The introduction of transistors revolutionised the electronics industry. Since the transistors needed considerably less power than a thermionic valve, their use allowed circuits to be developed that required considerably less power. This also resulted in the reduction in the size of supporting components, such as resistors and capacitors. The radios could now be powered by a 9 volt battery, and so became truly portable.

This miniaturisation of electronic components required a new form of circuit construction. The heavy metal chassis and solid copper wires were now being replaced by a pattern of conductors fixed to one side of a substrate – very similar in structure to fibreglass. Each electronic component needed to be placed and soldered by hand, although some level of mechanisation existed for creating the printed circuit boards.

1960s

Up until, and including, the 1960s, the cases of radios were still being made from a wood material in the form of bent wood veneers. These were a much coarser construction than the cabinets of the 1930s, and were consequently covered in a plastic 'leatherette' (mock-leather) material. The sound quality of these radios was much improved, and was being more suited to listening to music.

1970s

From the 1970s onwards there was increased use of thermoplastics such as acrylics, and acrylic-based polymers such as ABS (acrylonitrile butadiene styrene). With the introduction of these plastics, it was

A 1930s radio (top) *and internal construction showing valves*

A 1960s radio

possible to use injection moulding to manufacture the cases of the radios. These modern plastics have replaced the Bakelite and laminated/plywood cases of the past. They have also made it possible to mould styling and ergonomic features, while the continued reduction in size and power consumption of the electronics has enabled the production of much smaller radios.

The method of manufacturing with plastics has provided huge benefits, as they can include mountings for circuit boards, handles, fixing brackets and strengthening ribs. Also, this can be done in an all-in-one single moulding process.

A further benefit of manufacturing with plastics is the little finishing required, along with the ability for the product to be self-coloured – achieved by mixing pigments with the plastic granules prior to manufacture.

Electronics have become much smaller, even miniaturised, and will fit into a much smaller space. Hundreds, if not thousands, of transistors and other supporting components can be grown onto a single silicon chip, called an **integrated circuit (IC)**. The energy required for these components to function is extremely low, thereby reducing the need for a large battery to power the unit or for extra space to dissipate any excess heat. The product has now become much smaller, fitting into the hand or pocket.

1970s to recent years

The introduction of the microchip in the 1970s revolutionised the design and manufacture of electronic products. The microchip has made it possible to miniaturise products like radios and to increase the range of features available to the consumer. The Sony Walkman exemplifies this. The modern Walkman is truly pocket-sized and:

- ■ has ergonomic features
- ■ is very comfortable to hold
- ■ is lightweight
- ■ is simple to use.

The carbon rod aerial used in the 1960s radio has been replaced by using the wires to the headphones as an aerial, thereby further reducing the size and weight of the final unit.

Many electrical goods now have a **GUI (graphical user interface)**, or a visual display either in LED (light-emitting diode) or LCD (liquid crystal display), made possible by the microchip. We take it for granted that the quality of sound can be adjusted through a graphical equaliser to suit the listener's taste. Also, in CD and MP3 players, there is the opportunity to play tracks in random order or an order determined by the user. All of these programmable features are made possible by the microchip.

In recent years there has been an explosion in the development of digital sound recording and playback equipment, due to advances in microelectronics.

The development of MP3

MP3 is a method of audio file compression originally developed for use with high definition digital TV transmission and digital satellite systems. MP3 is a standard similar to British (BSI) or International (ISO) standards

A 1990s Sony CD Walkman

set by the Motion Picture Experts Group (MPEG). MPEG compressed files remove the frequencies inaudible to humans and produce digital audio files that are much smaller than previous sound files.

MP3 players first started to be retailed in the 1990s but they were slow to take off. At the time, personal audio playing was well catered for by cassette players like the Sony Walkman and portable CD players. It wasn't until personal computers became more widespread and the internet became available to the home user, that MP3 players really started to capture the interest of consumers. The success of MP3 also required advancement in the storage capacity of digital devices and the development of file handling software to enable the downloading of music.

MP3 devices have significant advantages over cassette and CD players. Digital compression of audio files allows the size of recordings to be much smaller without noticeable loss of sound quality. This allows the storage of many files to the extent that today's devices can store many hundreds of tracks. Being compatible with PCs means that music can be downloaded from the internet, or copied from CD. Tracks can be arranged in a desired order of play by the user.

In the 1990s and up until 2003, most music was downloaded from illegal sources (illegal because it infringed the copyright of the artists and music producers and so was a form of intellectual property theft). In 2003, Apple launched its i-Tunes Music Store with some 500,000 songs. This made legitimate downloadable music available and significantly contributed to the iPod player being one of the most popular electronic devices of all time. This innovation has sparked the growth of a number of similar MP3 devices and music website services in addition to the development of music editing software. To keep ahead of competition, several versions of the iPod have been launched each with an ever increasing array of features and storage capacity. See iTunes at: **www.apple.com**.

Technological developments and the battery

The reduction in energy requirements has made a whole range of electronic devices portable. Whether they use standard alkaline batteries or rechargeable nickel-cadmium batteries depends entirely on the application. The reduction in size of portable equipment such as mobile telephones has been helped by developments in battery technology and their subsequent reduction in size.

How do batteries work?

Batteries are made up essentially of two electrodes in an electrolyte. Energy is produced by one of the electrodes decomposing into the electrolyte. Electrolytes can be acids, alkalines or salts. When salts dissolve they release positive and negative ions, which are then free to carry an electrical charge between electrodes. **Ions** are electrically charged atoms. One of the electrodes will then collect atoms, while the other electrode will lose atoms and slowly decompose into the electrolyte. The rate at which it decomposes depends on the materials used for the electrodes and electrolyte.

Types of battery

Modern types of battery use a variety of chemicals to provide energy, as shown in Table 22.

An early Apple iPod

AQA Examiner's tip

Often you will be asked about why products might be thought of as being an example of 'good design'. The iPod is a useful example to learn.

Key terms

Ion: a charged atom formed when, for example, copper comes into contact with oxygen in the air. Two free electrons in a copper atom move over to an oxygen atom. This makes the copper atom a positively charged ion while the oxygen atom becomes a negatively charged ion.

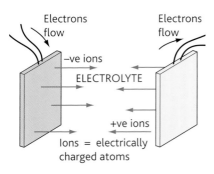

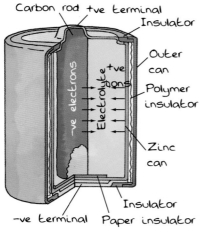

How a zinc–carbon battery works

Table 22 *Types of battery*

Battery type	Made up of	Uses
Zinc–carbon	Zinc and carbon electrodes with acidic paste electrolyte	Inexpensive AA, C, D sized dry cell batteries
Alkaline	Zinc and manganese oxide with alkaline electrolyte	More expensive brands of batteries, e.g. Duracell and Energiser
Lithium photo	Lithium, lithium iodide and lead iodide	Used in cameras, copes well with power surges for the flash
Lead–acid (rechargeable)	Lead and lead oxide electrodes with acidic electrolyte	Used in cars, etc.
Nickel–cadmium (rechargeable)	Nickel hydroxide and cadmium electrodes; potassium hydroxide is the electrolyte	Used in a variety of products as rechargeable standard-sized batteries
Nickel–metal–hydride (NiMH) (rechargeable)	Alloy and nickel-hydroxy-oxide electrodes; potassium hydroxide electrolyte	Generally replacing nickel–cadmium batteries
Lithium ion (rechargeable)	Lithium ion and lithium atom electrodes. The electrolyte also contains lithium	High-end laptops and mobile telephones; good power to weight ratio
Zinc–air (rechargeable)	Zinc and oxygen (from air) are the electrodes. Electrolyte in potassium hydroxide	Lightweight and rechargeable
Zinc–mercury oxide	Zinc and mercury oxide electrodes. Electrolyte in potassium hydroxide	Small sized; used in hearing aids
Silver–zinc	Silver/manganese oxide and zinc electrodes. Potassium hydroxide in the electrolyte	Aeronautical applications; good power to weight ratio
Metal chloride	Typically electrodes are sodium and sulphur with ceramic alumina as the electrolyte	Used in electric vehicles

Technological developments and the TV

Analogue television

Televisions have been around for well over half a century. The most common type of TV remains the analogue type. A composite signal is fed to the television from a transmitting station or from a videocassette recorder. The signal being transmitted comprises a beam of varying intensity as it creates a 'line' providing:

■ the image on the screen

■ a signal to send the beam back to the beginning of the line

■ a signal to send the beam back to the top of the screen to start the cycle again.

The signal also includes sound information.

The signal for colour televisions includes the additional information that is used to switch the phosphor dots on or off to provide the image. The signals received by the colour television can be received through an aerial, VCR or DVD player, cable television or satellite via a set-top decoder (through the aerial socket at the back of the TV).

Digital television

The signal received by a digital television is in the form of 0s and 1s – in the same way that computers receive their signals. Being digital, the image produced is a lot more stable and of very high resolution. The signal conditioning electronics are more sophisticated in a digital TV because of these higher resolutions.

HDTV (high definition television)

HDTV provides a higher resolution, producing greater clarity along with high-quality sound.

Types of HDTV include the use of:

■ **thin-film transistor (TFT)** technology
■ LCD technology
■ plasma technology.

With these types of television the depth of the unit is much reduced, therefore reducing the weight of the unit resulting in flat screens that can be supported on a wall just like a picture.

Projection television

TFT and plasma technology can provide large screen sizes. However, where screens are larger than 40 inches projection television is used. A small CRT (cathode ray tube) or liquid crystal display forms an image that is shone onto a large screen by one of two methods:

■ rear projection
■ front projection.

In rear (or reflective) projection the image is projected onto a reflective surface and then onto a screen. All components are housed in one unit, for use in the home as a home theatre system. Front projection (or transmittive) TVs require the projector to be used in one part of the room with the screen at the other, much in the same way as digital PC projectors are used.

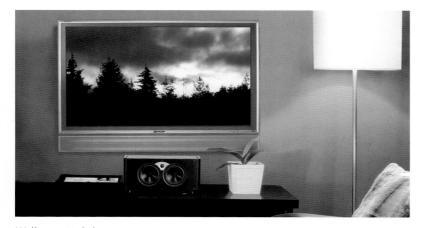

Wall-mounted plasma screen

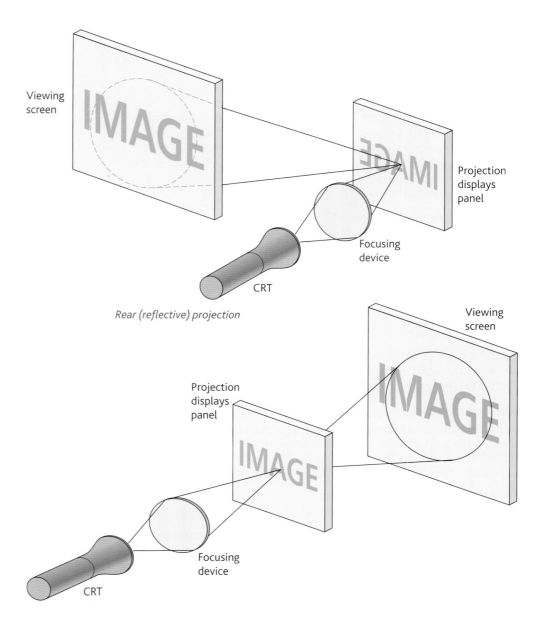

Rear (reflective) projection

Front (transmittive) projection

Technological development in the telephone

The design and manufacture of the telephone has changed considerably over time due to advancements in technology including changes in materials and components and manufacturing processes.

The telephone was invented by Alexander Graeme Bell in 1876.

At the time, long distance communication was carried out using a telegraph system. This consisted of sending electrical pulses through a wire to an electromagnet at the receiving end. The sender completes an electrical circuit by pressing a key. At the receiver's end, a pen makes a series of marks on a paper tape. Samuel Morse invented a code consisting of the alphabet being represented as a series of dots and dashes. As the telegraph operators learned the code, the tape was replaced with a speaker making the sound of the dots and dashes.

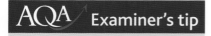

AQA Examiner's tip

When describing the development of materials and technology, you will need to refer to specific products and the benefits these developments have had to manufacturers and consumers.

Bell was a teacher of the deaf who at the time was developing a device to turn sound into visible patterns so that the deaf might be able to 'see' people's speech. While developing this device, Bell realised that the telegraph could be improved by using a long undulating wave current instead of the usual pulses. This allowed more information to be transmitted along the wires, each one using a distinct musical note. In much the same way as today's fibre optic systems, this removed the need to erect more wires to cope with the increase in users.

On 14 February 1876, Bell filed a patent for the 'harmonic telegraph'. This device allowed the transmission of 'sounds or noises' and was intended to be an improvement to the telegraph system. On 6 March of the same year Bell, using his prototype telephone, transmitted the first intelligible words, 'Mr Watson, come here I want you'.

Bell's early telephone systems were simple – consisting of one telephone being wired to another. They were not connected in a network of telephone systems. The maximum distance they could transmit and receive signal was about two miles – the signal strength diminishing with distance. For quite a number of years until there were further advancements, telephones were mainly used by businesses to connect one building to another.

The telephone offered many advantages over the telegraph system, the most obvious being speech. To use a telephone, no specialist training or skills are needed. To use a telegraph, the operator needs to know how to send and translate Morse code.

Early telephone systems had a transmitter telephone at one end of the line, and a receiver telephone at the other. This did not lend itself to two-way communication. By 1877 Bell developed a wall-mounted device with a separate transmitter and receiver requiring an earpiece and a mouthpiece wired to a terminal board. This was cumbersome to use and clearly the user could not move around with the telephone, but it did allow two-way communication.

Bell's telephone and terminal board

Further developments

By 1900 Thomas Edison had developed the classic 'candlestick' tabletop telephone which featured a transmitter (with mouthpiece) mounted on heavy cast iron and brass stem with an earpiece receiver connected by wire to the base. This advancement enabled the telephone to be a little more portable and would fit conveniently on a desk top or hall table.

As technology improved, the transmitter and receiver were made smaller and could be mounted into a single hand set making telephones more ergonomic. As more and more people saw the advantage of the telephone, and they began to be more widely used, it was necessary to develop automatic telephone exchanges. This required telephones to have a dial to make calls to specific numbers via the exchange. These dials were a large rotary electro-mechanical switch and until the development of electronic push button telephones in the 1970s, influenced the minimum dimensions of the phone and became the standard way to dial a number.

The Strowger automatic dial telephone

In the 1920s the introduction of Bakelite enabled telephones to be moulded into new shapes. Handsets became much lighter in weight and could be moulded to make a grip more suited to fit the hand, with the mouthpiece and earpiece contoured to fit the mouth and ear.

Later, from 1959 onwards, acrylic and other polymers started to be used in telephones. This enabled them to be made in different colours (limited to a choice of six colours at the time). This saw the black bakelite

The 1980s 800-series telephone

A contemporary cordless telephone

telephone become obsolete. It also made the handset much lighter than bakelite models. However, the basic dial mechanism had changed very little and the internal bell ringer operated by an electromagnet still made the base heavy and large by today's standards. The overall design was still very similar to that produced more than 40 years before with a dial on the front of a large base unit and a handset that sat in a cradle on top of the base.

In the 1970s with the advent of the microelectronics, the first electronic telephones were developed. One classic design was the 'Trimphone'. The first Trimphones still had the rotary dial but the electromechanical bell was replaced by an electronic buzzer that made a distinctive 'trill'. Advancements in the transmitter and receiver enabled them to be miniaturised and so the handset was styled into a thin, lightweight design.

Later the rotary dials became superseded by push buttons which made dialling numbers much easier and drastically reduced the weight of the telephone.

During the 1980s there were many advancements in microelectronics, in particular the miniaturisation of components. Printed circuit boards replaced the need for hard wiring of components together. Combined with microchips and **surface mount components** (tiny electronic components such as transistors, resistors and capacitors mounted directly onto the copper track of the board) meant that telephones became smaller but had the ability to perform additional functions such as last number redial and other programmable features such as a directory of contacts.

In the late 1980s, the first cordless telephones were developed. These used an analogue radio transmitter and receiver in the handset and were linked to a base unit by an aerial. As the signals were analogue, they tended to be a little unreliable, suffering from radio interference, and had a limited range. However, this development meant that the telephone was now truly portable and the user could move around the home or office while still making a phone call.

In the 1990s digital technology was developed and this was soon adopted in telephones. Now, cordless phones have a much greater range around the home and they do not normally suffer from interference. As microchips have become more powerful and smaller, these phones have an ever increasing number of features packed into a much smaller handset. Such features include a choice of ring tone, directories for over 100 numbers (displayed on LCD screens – another development), caller identification and text or email facilities, to mention just a few.

Continuous scientific discoveries together with developments in materials and technology have led to the development of telephones that are significantly different to Bell's early prototypes. The same technologies have enabled the development of cellular phones and other electronic communication devices.

The impact of information and communication technology (ICT)

There are four areas of development with ICT that have had a major impact. These are: the change from mechanics to electronics, miniaturisation, digitalisation and developments in software.

Change from mechanics to electronics

Technology with moving parts has been replaced with solid-state components. For example, the telephone which had a rotating dial now has push buttons which make tones. The removal of moving parts generally means fewer parts are needed and they are less likely to break down. (Moving mechanical parts are subject to friction and wear and tear.)

Miniaturisation

Developments in electronics such as the invention of the transistor in 1947, the integrated circuit in 1959 and the microprocessor in 1971 have enabled the size of devices that switch electrical signals or control the flow of electricity within a product to become smaller and smaller. At the same time, these devices have enabled the increase of computing power of products. This process of reduction in size and increase in function seems to be almost continuous. In addition, as advanced manufacturing processes develop, such as robotics, the cost of electronic products continues to fall.

In 1965, Gordon Moore (co-founder of the microelectronics firm Intel) predicted that the number of circuits that could be etched onto a piece of silicon could be doubled every year. In fact, this happens approximately every 18 months. This means that potentially every ten years, PCs could become a hundred times more powerful.

The first electronic computer in 1946 ENIAC (Electronic Numerical Integrator and Calculator), contained 18,000 valves, weighed 30-tonnes and covered an area of $120\,\text{m}^2$. By 1971, the first single-chip microprocessor contained 2,300 transistors and was the size of a thumb. Today, a typical microprocessor used in home computers contains over 55 million transistors.

Digitalisation

The switch from using analogue systems to digital has made ICT products much more efficient.

Information can be represented as a series of binary digits (0 and 1). Microprocessors can read this information in less than a millionth of a second. Digital data can be transmitted electronically and reassembled at its destination without loss of data.

Software

ICT enables computer programs to be written to perform tasks for the user. This often means that small changes to products can be made without the need for changes in hardware. For example, Microsoft regularly provides free upgrades for anti-virus and operating system software. Programs can be modified to meet the needs of individual users. For example, control software for artificial limbs can be adjusted to alter speed of movement, degrees of movement, grip pressure, and other variables to suit different users.

Intelligent systems and interlinked products

The use of microchips in products has allowed them to be programmed and controlled. This is now well established in products from DVD recorders to washing machines and microwave cookers and more. The next stage was to use microprocessors to enable products to communicate with each other. Appliances can now exchange information and respond. Such products may use wireless connections systems such as infra-red or Bluetooth for mobile phones and satellite navigation aids. This makes the product easy to use for downloading photos from a camera phone to a photo developing booth without the need to insert a memory card or physically wire the device to the printer.

You will be fully aware that computers can send and receive information via email; music and video can be downloaded, edited and played.

Did you know?

While surface mount components and microchips make telephones smaller and more powerful, their small size makes them virtually impossible to repair and very difficult to recycle.

AQA Examiner's tip

If you learn the major advancements in electronics and materials for the last 50–60 years, you can apply them to questions on most electrical consumer goods.

A digital camera

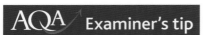
Transactions can be made via the internet. All this was made possible by developments in microelectronics and software.

Many products are now multifunctional. Telephones are not simply used for voice communication. Mobile phones can take photographs, play video and access the internet. Through wireless connection, mobile phones can transmit data to and from computers and laptop computers can be used in public places with wireless networks. Such innovations have allowed users much more freedom to work, exchange information, shop or simply keep in touch with friends while on the move.

ICT and the internet

The internet was developed from US military research in the 1950s and 1960s to devise a computer system that could maintain communication in the event of a nuclear missile attack. This research, together with the advancements in technology already discussed allowed a number of users to access a computer at the same time. This early work enabled the development of email and conferencing systems. A source code that allows information to be shared was developed and this enabled the internet to become a method of mass communication. Linux is one operating system code for the internet used by about a quarter of the market. Microsoft Windows is used by most home users.

The web is the 'public face' of the internet. It was invented by English physicist Tim Berners-Lee in 1989 while he was working at the European particle physics lab in Geneva. In his role, he needed to communicate with a wide number of scientists working on different projects and they all needed access to complex information on a range of subjects. He designed a searchable linked information system using hypertext. This allowed any user to access data using searches that would be able to find documents stored in other servers and across networks. There are now over 600 million internet users worldwide and over 20 million users in the UK.

Radio Frequency Identification Tags (RFID)

RFID tags are an example of a product developed through advancements in microelectronics and software development. They are electronic tags that can be attached to products and can contain information about the product such as ingredients, batch number, date of manufacture, price, use by date and so on. This technology is set to make bar codes obsolete.

RFID tag systems are made up of three main components:

■ A tag that contains an electronic circuit and an antenna. The tag stores the data on the product and will act as a transponder, sending the information when scanned by an electronic reader.

■ A reader that sends a signal to the tag and receives the information.

■ A computer database that receives the information from the reader and processes it.

RFID tags have several advantages over traditional bar codes. They are robust and can withstand rain, and other damage and still function. They can be scanned from several metres away and don't have to be in direct line of sight with the readers, for example, they can be read through obstructions such as the walls of containers, vehicles and so on.

RFID tags are available in two forms; passive and active. Active tags have their own power supply and can have the information modified. They can also transmit information over a greater distance.

Common applications for RFID tags include stock control. They are used in Kanban systems that control the flow of components and products as they move through a factory to a store room and then onto despatch. The progress of products as they are being made can be tracked as the tag passes by readers along a production line.

In some stores, RFID tags are used on individual products and 'smart shelves' read the tags as the product is removed from them. The system then automatically re-orders the product to maintain stock levels. The technology is also used in pet identification chips implanted under the skin, door control identity cards, hospital patient identity bracelets and in new UK passports.

Fluidic self assembly (FSA)

Fluidic Self Assembly (FSA) is a new manufacturing technique developed to manufacture very small integrated circuits like those used in RFID tags on a large scale at a low cost. The technique devised by the American company Alien Technology Corp, uses its 'NanoBlocks' which are tiny circuits floated in a suspension liquid. This is spread over a substrate that has holes in its surface matching the shape of the circuits. These settle and self-align into the holes making the electrical connection. This technique allows the placement of millions of NanoBlocks with a high degree of accuracy on a range of materials within minutes. It makes it possible to manufacture flat screen PC monitors, high definition TV screens and flexible polymer film.

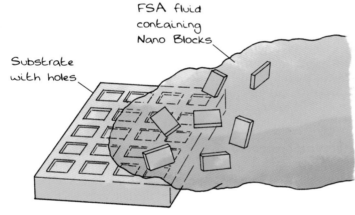

NanoBlocks settling into a substrate in FSA process

Nanotechnology

The previous section discusses the miniaturisation of electronics – putting millions of transistors onto a microprocessor. This involves working in measurements of micrometres (one thousandth of a millimetre). Nanotechnology involves working on materials at the atomic level. Here, scientists and engineers are using measurements in nanometres (one thousandth) of a micrometre which is some 40,000 times smaller than the width of an average human hair.

Nanotechnology can be defined as the manipulation and rearrangement of individual atoms to create useful materials, systems and devices.

Scientists hope that in the future, the scale can be reduced to the molecular level known as molecular nanotechnology. This may allow the manufacture of machines a few nanometres big such as robots, motors, and other devices that would be smaller than a cell.

Electron micrograph showing nanotechnology gears next to a fly's leg.

Currently highly accurate mechanisms can be made so small that they can only be seen clearly through an electron micrograph.

With nanotechnology, materials can have the physical and mechanical properties of their constituent parts modified. This means that the resulting material could be made far superior to the original. Typical properties that could be improved might be: stiffness, strength, flame resistance, electrical conductivity, permeability or impermeability and optical clarity.

Products using nanotechnology

Vehicles

Car manufacturers such as Toyota have used nanocomposites in the manufacture of car bumpers and other vehicle components. Nanotechnology can make these parts 60 per cent lighter and increase resistance to denting by 100 per cent. This again has benefits for the environment because it will allow cars to be made with reduced weight (using less fuel), and more durable so they will not need to be changed as frequently.

Tiny pressure sensors made from nanomaterials can be used in airbags. These are small plates embedded into a circuit board that move under rapid deceleration to make an electrical circuit, triggering the rapid inflation of the air bag.

Carbon nanotubes can be embedded into plastic car body parts to make the surface electrical conducting. This can be used in powder coating where paint particles can also be electrically charged to improve adherence and remove the need for a primer coat.

A pressure sensor used in air bags (pencil point shows scale)

Clothing

Nanotechnology is currently used in clothing to increase stain resistance. Embedded nanoparticles can be bonded to the fabric so that liquids simply run off the surface rather than soaking in. Companies such as Gap and Dockers are using this technology in making stain resistant khakis. The use of this technology means that the clothes won't need washing as much which has benefits for the environment as energy, water and detergent are saved.

Electrical consumer goods

Kodak has developed colour screens made from nanostructured polymer films. These films combine organic light-emitting diodes (OLEDs) which enable them to be made into lightweight, flexible displays for use in mobile phones, PDAs, laptops and other applications. OLEDs also give very good brightness and consume extremely low levels of energy in use.

Companies such as Hewlett-Packard and IBM are experimenting with nanotechnology in computer chips. These chips will allow the manufacture of computers that boot up instantly. Known as NRAM chips (non-volatile random access memory), the chips remember how to run programs and so don't need to go through the usual installations sequences as computers boot up when switched on. Improved conductivity in these chips will make computers run faster and use less energy.

Flexible, organic light emitting diode display

Medical

By manipulating calcium and phosphate at the molecular level, scientists have developed a substitute for natural bone. This can be used to make synthetic bone replacements for bone that has become too damaged to repair or has been removed.

Nanofilters have been produced which are so small that they can stop viruses and other biological agents. This makes it possible to filter even the most contaminated water to make it drinkable. Such products may have applications in emergency survival situations or in developing countries in times of drought.

Scientists have suggested that in the future, nanotechnology will allow the manufacture of tiny machines small enough to be used inside the human body. These might be able to carry out operations, remove tumours or deliver medicines to specific parts of the body.

✓ Product analysis exercise 6: Major developments in technology

Mobile phones

Study the photographs that show a 1980s 'brick' mobile phone and a contemporary mobile phone.

1 Make notes under the following headings, explaining what advancements have been made in technology to enhance the performance and function of mobile phones.

   a Batteries.

   b Visual displays.

   c Microelectronics.

2 Explain how developments in technology have led to improvements in the ergonomics of mobile phones.

3 Explain how developments in smart materials can make electrical products easier to recycle.

Technology push and market pull

So far we have discussed examples of how advancements in technology can drive product development. We have also seen that the design process often starts with the recognition of a need or a market for a product. These two drivers in invention are often referred to as the 'technology push model' and 'market pull model'.

The technology push model is a linear process where a scientific or technological advancement – often conducted in a research and development department (R&D) – is passed to a design and development team to design a useful product using the technology. In turn, these designs are passed to manufacturing to build the product, and marketing and sales to promote and retail the finished item. This approach is often called the 'over the wall model' as departments may work in isolation from each other and the end user. The finished item is metaphorically thrown over the wall to the consumer who the team believes will want the product, and will understand how to use it. This is a high risk strategy that can have its successes and failures.

Basic science drives invention	Design and development	Manufacturing	Marketing	Sales

Linear technology push model

A 'technology push' success

An example of a success is the Sony Walkman first designed in 1979 and manufactured from 1980. Akio Morita, president of the Sony Corporation and other Sony colleagues complained that their existing portable stereo and standard headphones were too big for personal use. Company

The first Sony Walkman

Activity

Study the photo of the Sony Walkman. Using the following headings as starting points, analyse the reasons why it became so successful:

■ Function
■ Performance
■ Aesthetics
■ Ergonomics

The Sinclair C5

engineers removed the recording circuit from their small cassette recorder (the Pressman) and then replaced it with a stereo amplifier. They also developed a lightweight headphone set. The development of the headphone set required a number of technological innovations but the remainder borrowed existing technology. The Walkman did not have a specific market need and many thought it might fail to diffuse into market. However, Morita pushed the project forward and with some aggressive marketing, the Walkman achieved almost instant success. Sony managed to convince consumers to buy a product that they hadn't known they wanted.

A 'technology push' failure

An example of a technically sound and inspirational product that failed to become successful, is the Sinclair C5. This is an electrically assisted vehicle invented by Sir Clive Sinclair and launched in the UK in January 1985. Financed personally by Sir Clive Sinclair (famous for development of the first pocket scientific calculator and early home PCs such as the Sinclair Spectrum and ZX81), the C5 was a battery driven tricycle, steered by two handles either side of the driver's seat. It had a top speed of 15 mph (low enough for the driver not to need a driving licence), and was made in the Hoover factory at Merthyr Tydfil. It cost over £12 million to develop and put into production. Unfortunately, when it was launched it was perceived by the public as being impractical for the British climate (it being an open design and close to the ground), and perhaps a little unsafe in terms of visibility to other vehicles.

In addition to these perceived problems, there were several serious design flaws such as the weight of the vehicle, the lack of gears, the short pedal cranks and lack of adjustability of distance from seat to pedal. In use on long hills, the rider had to pedal to assist the motor which was prone to burning out.

By August 1985, fewer than 17,000 C5s had been sold. Production ended and Sinclair Vehicles Ltd went into receivership in October 1985. The C5, like many other products is an example of a product that was developed without careful consideration of user needs and even with promotional campaigns using ex-Formula One racing champion Sir Stirling Moss, the C5 failed to capture the imagination of the consumer.

Market pull

This model describes how the stimulus for new products comes from the needs of society or a specific section of the market. Detailed analysis of market research would identify what needs exist, how existing products might meet these needs and how a new product might be better.

Having conducted this research, the product that is subsequently developed should be successful because the product has been specifically designed to meet a need.

Market need drives invention	Design and development	Manufacturing	Marketing	Sales

Market pull model

The market pull model can be criticised. Consumers are good at identifying weaknesses in existing products and can voice their demand for new ones. However, they can't demand products that don't exist, where the technology or science isn't available. Just because a need exists, there is no guarantee that a new product can be developed to meet that need.

Coupling model

This is an alternative model to technology push and market pull. It suggests that successful design can emerge by getting the balance right between technology and market considerations. The coupling of market needs and state of the art technology is vital in all of the stages of the design process. In other words, from the first spark of inspiration, the designer would consider both market needs and existing technology, through to design and development, manufacture, marketing and sales.

Product life cycles and historical influences

The term life cycle can have several different meanings. First it can be used to describe how long something will last before it wears out. Second, it can be used to discuss the environmental impact of a product through the stages of its life from raw materials extraction, to manufacture, use and disposal. Finally, it is used to describe the stages that a product goes through from its introduction to its eventual **obsolescence**. It is the latter that will be discussed here.

The life cycle of a product can be divided into several stages. These are:

- introduction
- growth
- maturity
- decline.

How long a product's life cycle lasts depends on several factors:

- changes in materials and technology (often known as the 'technology push')
- changes in consumer demand (often known as the '**demand pull**')
- sales (is the product selling?)
- what the product is
- how technically complex the product is.

Introduction and launch

The introduction stage of a product's life cycle is the period when a product is newly released onto the market. At first sales can be slow, as consumers may not recognise the benefits of a new product. At this stage, there are many costs associated with launching a new product and very little profit if any will be made.

Growth

As advertising takes effect and consumers see the benefits of new technology, sales start to rise, the product begins to diffuse and there is a steady increase in profit. During this stage of a product's life cycle, competitors may start to introduce their own brand of the product. This can be seen in the MP3 player market with many brands being launched, each with slightly different features.

Maturity

At this point in the life cycle, sales begin to level off. The market becomes saturated with competitor designs that may have different or improved features. Major companies, such as Sony, monitor the market very carefully and have new designs ready – in order to

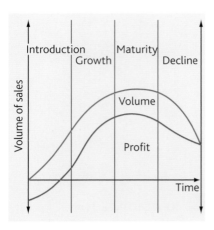

Product life cycles

maintain their market share. Alternatively, companies have to market their product aggressively to stay ahead.

Decline

This stage begins when the market is completely saturated and sales start to drop off. Profits fall. At this stage companies have to decide whether to accept reduced profits or stop making the product and launch a new one. This might be accelerated by changes in technology.

As new technology develops, products can be made obsolete. This is clearly illustrated with the replacement of vinyl records and audiocassette tapes with the compact disc. More recently, Sony developed the minidisc, reducing the size of personal stereos. Then they developed the MP3 player, making a personal stereo truly pocket size. The introduction of internet marketing of music and the MP3 player has the potential to make CDs obsolete. 'Consumer pull' is clearly contributing to this as a whole new generation routinely downloads music from the internet, rather than purchasing CDs.

Planned obsolescence

Some companies deliberately plan to keep the lives of their products short. They produce new or improved products at short intervals choosing not to wait until the current product reaches maturity or decline. Such companies aim their advertising at convincing consumers that they must have the latest version of their product. This system of updating designs is known as 'product churning'. This strategy can be seen clearly in consumer electronics products where new versions of a product are released each year.

There are several reasons why companies 'product churn':

- to maintain a steady volume of sales
- to maintain a market advantage over competitors
- as a result of technological advancement, e.g. developments in microelectronics.

Some products need to have a built-in obsolescence for safety or hygiene reasons, for example, the hypodermic syringe or disposable razor. Others, such as cars, may have a shorter life cycle than is actually possible, in order to keep the overall cost of the vehicle at an affordable level. It is possible, of course, to make cars from very durable materials, such as stainless steel, but it is very expensive.

The influence of fashion

Consumer fashions, trends and the demand to keep up with the latest technology, all help to contribute to obsolescence. Many people change their wardrobe on an annual basis, and their home interiors every three to five years, and this therefore feeds the demand for new products.

The influence of fashion and trends on product design cannot be over-estimated. Manufacturers today employ agencies to predict what the latest fashions will be. Such agencies will advise on colour and fabric trends for interiors and for the fashion industry. This results in seasonal colours and fabrics being manufactured together with a full range of coordinating accessories.

As consumer tastes change, the season's colour can become obsolete. Today, many people like to express a more individual taste and demand products that will enable them to achieve an individual look. This poses a challenge to manufacturers, who have to respond quickly to market pressures.

▪ The work of past and present designers

This section of the book will outline how new designs have evolved over time and introduce you to the most influential stages in the history of product design. The scope of this book can only allow us to give you a brief introduction and you are strongly recommended to read further into the subject. We have printed a list of some suitable titles for you later in this chapter.

The machine age

Making items by machine can be traced back as early as the fifteenth century when, in Germany, Johanns Gutenburg invented a moveable type printing press. This enabled the fast and economic reproduction of printed text. Prior to this, text was mostly printed using hand-carved wooden blocks, which was obviously slow and expensive.

With the development of steam power, machine manufacture became more commonplace. The Industrial Revolution in the late 1700s brought significant innovation in manufacturing equipment and processes, such as the Spinning Jenny invented by James Hargreaves in 1764. This was a machine that could spin 16 yarns at a time and was one of the innovations that brought textiles out of a cottage industry into large-scale industrial production. Potters such as Josiah Wedgwood perfected known ceramics processes and converted them to an industrial scale.

Before the Industrial Revolution, products were mostly made at home or in workshops. People worked in shops and were sometimes members of craft associations or guilds. With the Industrial Revolution, and organisation of workers with power driven machinery, products were able to be made economically. They were, however, not necessarily better than if they had been made by hand.

The Great Exhibition held at Hyde Park in the Crystal Palace (designed by Joseph Paxton), intended to showcase the products of the machine age. It actually highlighted how products had become over decorated and elaborate – to the point where they were sometimes difficult to use and often disguised poor workmanship.

The product age

Partly as a result of the Great Exhibition, manufacturers and industrialists of the time began to realise the need for 'product designers' who would use their knowledge of what people wanted and needed, and of materials and processes, to actually determine the form of the objects being made. The involvement of designers in this way gradually resulted in products that were more functional and attractive to consumers.

Design movements

Since towards the end of the nineteenth century, there has been a series of 'movements' that have shaped the history of product design. These movements are approaches to the style of design that often determined the form, colours and textures of products. The movements were often influenced by political, social and economic circumstances at the time,

AQA **Examiner's tip**

Product life cycles are a common theme in exam questions. You should be able to explain the life cycle of the following:

▪ Seasonal or fad products, e.g. children's toys.

▪ Products that have a sustained volume of sales, e.g. design classics such as the Barcelona chair or everyday items such as a light bulb.

▪ Products with a slow rate of adoption, e.g. micro electricity generation wind turbines.

▪ Products that decline due to technological advancement, e.g. Mini DV Digital tape video cameras.

Practise drawing simple graphs of such product life cycles.

and developments in materials, components and manufacturing processes. While they were often started by individuals in one country, their influence quickly spread across Europe and the United States, which in turn sparked further movements and international styles of art and design.

The Arts and Crafts Movement

The Arts and Crafts Movement was one of the first 'movements' in design which was at its height between 1890 and 1910. It was founded by William Morris who was a talented designer of furniture, wallpaper and textile products such as carpets and soft furnishings. Morris was also a socialist writer opposed to poor working conditions of factory employees, the inferior quality of goods being manufactured at the time, and the damage to the environment that industrialisation had caused.

Morris and other designers in the Arts and Crafts Movement believed that products should be simple and functional. They should be made from natural materials (not the synthetic imitation materials being produced at the time), and they took their style inspiration from shapes and organic forms found in nature. Morris believed in the pride of craftsmanship and wanted to see a return of skilled workers organised in 'guilds' of self-supporting cottage industries. He thought that machines should be used only to assist the craftsman by taking on some of the tedious or arduous tasks and not as a replacement for skilled labour. Unfortunately, as a result, much of the work produced by the Arts and Crafts Movement was very expensive and only the wealthy could afford it.

Art Nouveau

Art Nouveau refers to a style of art and design that became fashionable in Europe and America in the late nineteenth and early twentieth centuries. Literally meaning 'New Art', it took its name from a shop that opened in Paris in 1895. The Art Nouveau style is characterised by free-flowing, organic lines and shapes. In Europe, (especially France) the use of sinuous lines and 'whiplash' tendrils and curves were applied to everything from architecture to printed graphics, wallpapers, jewellery, vases and lamp shades. A famous example of this can be observed in wrought ironwork on the Paris Metro station entrances designed by Hector Guimard. In Barcelona, the work of Antoni Gaudi with a blend of Gothic, Moorish and his own ideas demonstrates a different interpretation of the Art Nouveau style. This is seen in simple objects such as street lamps and furniture to grander architectural projects such as the Palacio Guell (1885–90), the Casa Mila (1906–12) and the Sagrada Familia which is still being built today.

The natural forms and sinuous lines of Art Nouveau are ideal for designing and making in glass. In America Louis Comfort Tiffany was famous for his glassware, especially his multicoloured lamp shades which often depict dragonfly motifs. Tiffany glass became the international symbol of Art Nouveau and is highly sought after today.

In Britain, a more rectilinear version of Art Nouveau was observed in the work of Charles Rennie Mackintosh. Amongst other things, Mackintosh was famous for his designs for the Glasgow School of Art buildings where he designed almost every detail from the form of the building right down to the ash trays. Inspired by Japanese design, Mackintosh's furniture made use of rectilinear patterns finished with stylised motifs loosely derived from Celtic art and natural forms.

In 1900 Mackintosh was invited to exhibit his work in Vienna for the Secession exhibition. His work was well received and he became a key figure

Activity

Look up the work of some of the leading practitioners in the Arts and Crafts movement.

Did you know?

Some of the other leading practitioners in the Arts and Crafts Movement were: Charles Robert Ashbee, Walter Crane and Christopher Dresser, to name a few.

Casa Mila roof line

Paris Metro entrance

in a group of international architects and designers. His work and that of Arts and Crafts designer C.R. Ashbee influenced other European groups of designers such as the Weiner Workstatte of Austria to work in a similar style.

Deutsche Werkbund

The Deutsche Werkbund was an association set up in Germany in 1907. It aimed to bring together arts, crafts, industry, business and education. It was organised in a similar way to the English Arts and Crafts guilds and promoted the role of design in industry.

One of the key principles that the Werkbund believed in was the standardisation and machine manufacture of products. This principle had a major influence on the Modern Movement.

In 1925, the Berlin architect Ludwig Mies van der Rohe led a project to design residential housing for families with small and medium incomes in the city of Stuttgart. He assembled architects from five European countries to submit their designs for what they felt future living should be like. Some of the outcomes included a green terraced building by Berliner Peter Behrens, open-plan free-floored buildings (made from reinforced concrete slabs and supporting pillars) by Le Corbusier and Pierre Jeanneret from Paris, and prefabricated houses by Walter Gropius from Dessau. The project was named the Weissenhof Settlement and it became the archetype or symbol for new building. Mies van der Rohe, Gropius and many of the others involved in this project went on to become leading figures in the Bauhaus and the Modern Movement and were hugely influential in 20th- and 21st-century design.

💡 The Bauhaus and Modernism

The Bauhaus or 'Building House' was a school of art and design founded in Germany in the 1920s by architect Walter Gropius. At the Bauhaus, students followed a foundation course where they experimented with materials, form and colour (especially new materials for a machine age, geometric forms and primary colours). Students then specialised in areas such as architecture, furniture, textiles, graphics, metalwork and so on, working with leading experts in those fields such as Marcel Breuer, Wassily Kandinsky and Ludwig Mies van der Rohe.

The Bauhaus

The work of the Bauhaus was very much influenced by the following set of design principles:

'*Form follows function*' An object's appearance should be influenced mainly by what it is intended to do. In other words, a product's appearance should not be the most important factor. Above all it should function well.

'*Everyday objects for everyday people*' Products should be affordable to a wide range of consumers.

'*Products for a machine age*' Products should be designed to be made with the use of mechanised processes and modern materials.

'*Geometrically pure forms*' Designs should use vertical, horizontal, geometric shapes and clean lines with no fuss or clutter. They should also use basic tones and primary colours.

The Bauhaus tutors and students went on to design what have, in many cases, become design classics such as the 'Wassily Chair' (designed by Marcel Breuer in 1924) and the Barcelona Chair (designed by Mies van der Rohe for the Royal Pavilion at the 1926 Barcelona Exhibition). These chairs, and many other Bauhaus products, are still in production today.

The Bauhaus moved to Chicago in the 1930s to flee Nazi persecution. Many of the Bauhaus designers went on to become very influential in shaping American architecture. Mies van der Rohe was one of the pioneers in using reinforced concrete and glass to make affordable, open-plan buildings. This style of architecture became the principal method of constructing high-rise buildings.

In addition to these lasting designs, the most influential contribution to design that the Bauhaus made was the principle of 'form follows function'.

The idea that products can be made ergonomically correct, using appropriate materials and with the minimum of applied decoration became the doctrine of what is known as the 'Modern Movement' or 'Modernism'. Designers whose work reflected this style were known as Modernists. The principles of good design form the basis of contemporary industrial practice.

Barcelona Chair by Mies van der Rohe

Art Deco

Art Deco was a fashionable design movement from 1920 to 1939. It affected many areas of design such as architecture, interior, graphics, fashion and product. In many ways, Art Deco brought together several styles and movements of the early 20th century including Modernism, Cubism, Constructivism, Bauhaus and Art Nouveau.

Art Deco was a decorative style that was seen as being ultra modern, functional and elegant.

The origins of Art Deco lie with a group of French artists who formed an organisation called *La Société des Artistes Décorateurs*. The founders included Hector Guimard and other leading artists who wanted to promote the French decorative arts and show how modern and stylish it was. In 1925, they organised the *Exposition Internationale des Arts Décoratifs et Industriels Modernes* from which the name for the style movement 'Art Deco' was later taken.

Chrysler building spire

Art Deco took influences from a wide range of sources. Typically, shapes, colours and styling features were taken from Egypt (inspired by the discovery of Tutankhamen's tomb in 1922), the stepped forms of the Aztecs, modern aviation of the time, streamline styling in cars, ocean liners, skyscrapers, radios and electric lighting.

Typical styling features seen in Art Deco were:

- zigzagged, trapezoid and geometric shapes
- jumbled shapes (as seen in Clarice Cliff Bizarre range ceramics)
- stepped block forms
- sunburst motifs
- chevron patterns.

Art Deco styling features were used on many buildings, interiors, products and printed materials. For example, the sunburst motif can be seen on English 1920s and 30s housing in doors and windows, and on a grander scale the spire of the Chrysler building.

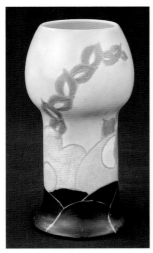

Bizarre ware item

Case study 3: Clarice Cliff (1899–1972)

Clarice Cliff was born in Tunstall, Stoke on Trent, England. At the age of 13 she started working in the potteries and in the evenings, studied at Burslem School of Art. Her first job was a gilder (applying the gold lines to the edge of ceramic ware). In 1916, she took a job at A. J. Wilkinson's to learn how to be a modeller. Clarice spent her early career learning the different skills such as enamelling, tube-lining and modelling.

In this process, Clarice's skills were recognised and she was given the task to decorate some of the company's white ware. She used bright vivid colours and geometric shapes to paint often very traditional ceramic products. These were instantly popular and the designs became known as Bizarre ware. Clarice was eventually given a studio with over 70 painters who worked under her guidance.

In 1930, Clarice became the Art Director at the Newport Pottery and A. J. Wilkinson's two factories made her pottery. By then she had launched several new ranges of designs such as Fantasque which used abstract trees and cottages alongside other Art Deco inspired ranges. In the late 1920s Clarice designed her own shapes for pottery and these often featured cubist forms, angular shapes and bright colours. Typical examples of this can be seen in her conical shaped 'Ravel' pattern ware.

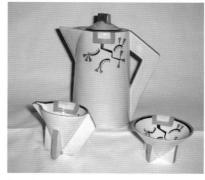

Ravel ware items

During the Second World War it was illegal to make decorated goods as it was seen as a waste of time and resources that could be spent on the war effort. Therefore, only white goods could be produced and so Clarice moved into a more managerial position within the company. In the post war years, most of the company's products were sold in the US market where tastes were more traditional and didn't demand Clarice's creative and bold style. A.J. Wilkinson and their Newport factory continued to sell pottery under the 'Clarice Cliff' name until 1964 when the company was sold. In 1972, Clarice held her first exhibition in Brighton but sadly died that same year.

Today, original Clarice Cliff items are highly sought after by collectors and items can reach high prices at auction. As a result of this, companies like Wedgwood (who were able to acquire the brand name) launched their own limited range of Clarice Cliff pottery in the 1990s which included the most sought after and expensive pieces. Some of these, in turn, have become collector's items.

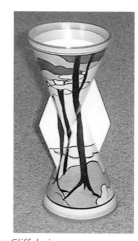

Clarice Cliff design

1930s streamlining

In the 1930s there was much interest in streamlined vehicles, boats and aircraft breaking a number of speed records. With this, streamlining began to appear as an aesthetic feature in a wide range of more static products such as radios, kettles and other domestic items.

This coincided with advancements in materials and manufacturing processes such as the use of Bakelite which enabled more complex aesthetic features to be moulded. As the national electricity grid expanded in the 1930s, demand for new consumer electrical goods increased. The new materials and processes of the time were utilised to meet this demand.

1940s utility

In the 1940s during the Second World War, Britain was not self-sufficient and relied upon imported timber. At the time, many homes were bombed out and families needed replacement furniture. To meet demand, the Utility Furniture Committee was established, headed up by designer Gordon Russell. The committee produced design plans

A 1930s radio

1940s utility furniture

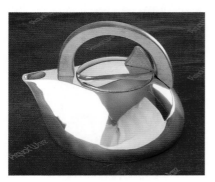

The K3 kettle

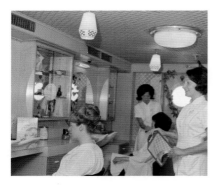

1960s acrylic lighting

for furniture that was strong and well made but made best use of scarce timber supplies. The furniture resembled early Arts and Crafts work, being simple in form and minus surface decoration. It was manufactured by over 600 different companies across Britain. Utility furniture continued to be produced after the war as rationing continued and the scheme didn't end until 1951 when the public, fed up with the austere times of war, demanded more extravagant and colourful designs.

Post war design

After the Second World War, companies previously manufacturing for the war effort, suddenly had to turn their attention to the domestic market. During the war, there had been many advancements in materials and electronics and much research into ergonomic or user requirements. Many of these developments were utilised in early post war products.

This is illustrated in the K3 kettle designed and made by Burrage and Boyd Ltd in 1946. It was made mostly from aluminium (at the time quite possibly sourced from recycled aircraft), and it took some of its styling cues from pre-war streamlining. With its uncluttered smooth lines it has a timeless quality and became a design classic, continuing to be manufactured many years after streamlining had become unfashionable.

In the 1950s there was much interest in science and space. This influenced aesthetics of products, often taking on the shape of rockets, or other 'futuristic' forms. This is illustrated by products from the Festival of Britain exhibition in 1951.

In the late 1950s and throughout the 60s there was an explosion of youth culture and, with that, a demand for new, bright and colourful products that would offer the consumer more choice and the opportunity to be individual. New polymer materials made it possible to make products in volumes at a lower cost. Later in the1960s, interest in science and space gave way to the psychedelic patterns, colours and typefaces reflecting popular music tastes.

💡 British industrial design

One of the most influential industrial designers of the twentieth century is Kenneth Grange. His career has spanned over 50 years and he is responsible for the development of many household products such as food mixers for Kenwood, cameras for Kodak, razors for Wilkinson-Sword, clothes irons for Morphy Richards, washing machines for Bendix, pens for Parker and many more. He was also responsible for the aerodynamic design and interior styling of the Intercity 125 train and Britain's first parking meter!

Grange believed products should be designed with careful consideration to their function and useability. He thought that products should be pleasurable to use as well as utilising modern materials and manufacturing processes. These ideas form some of the principles of 'good design' that many contemporary designers consider in the product development process today.

Post Modernism

Post Modernism is a 'style label' associated with groups of designers, architects and artists whose work reacts against the principles of the Modern Movement.

The basic principles of Post Modernism include:

- focus on aesthetics rather than the function of a product
- the use of ornamental and decorative finishes to enhance aesthetics
- design to appeal to fashion, popular consumerism and youth culture
- a borrowing and mixing of styles from other periods, such as ancient Egyptian
- drawing on influences from the media and fashion, and the use of everyday materials.

The Memphis Group

The Memphis Group was a group of designers based in Milan, Italy during the 1980s. Its founder member, Ettoire Sottsass, produced several designs that typify Post Modernism.

The Carlton Dresser, designed by Sottsass in 1981 and shown here, is typical of the Memphis Group and of the Post Modernist style. Its design is intended to give maximum visual impact rather than to function as a dresser (used to store and display items). This is achieved by the use of a striking mixture of bright colours and an angular structure that is reminiscent of a piece of Ancient Egyptian art.

The angular structure of the shelves makes the dresser barely functional. There is little useable space on the shelves on which to display anything, and there are only two small drawers to store things in. The dresser uses everyday materials such as MDF, finished with melamine laminates to provide colour, and the 'stone effect' base.

The Carlton Dresser is intended as a statement piece. It looks, like many Memphis products, at home in a museum of art and design rather than in a home as a functional piece of furniture.

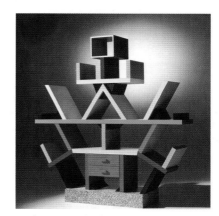

Carlton room divider in plastic laminate by Ettoire Sottsass

The Etruscan chair pictured opposite, was designed by Danny Lane in 1984. Lane is an established designer whose most recent works include a glass balustrade at the Victoria and Albert Museum in London, and a stone, steel and glass sculpture at the GlaxoSmithKline headquarters. Lane specialises in using industrial glass and contradicting materials and forms.

The Etruscan chair is also a typical Post Modernist piece. Although it would have some function as a chair, it is really a work of art. It is an aesthetic piece, designed as a one-off gallery exhibit, or to be made in small numbers for private clients. The Post Modernist aspects of the chair can be shown if it is briefly analysed.

- The use of glass is normally associated with quite a different function – glass is thought to be brittle and sharp.
- The transparent glass allows you to see the sculptural qualities of the legs, but it is a cold, hard surface to sit on.
- The use of glass with a serrated edge gives an interesting aesthetic feature but, again, would be uncomfortable.
- The contrast between the artistic craft form of the legs and glass and the appearance of the accurately engineered fittings also contributes to the chair's aesthetic appeal.

Etruscan chair

In conclusion, the aesthetics of this chair are its most important feature, while its function as a chair is merely secondary, quite different from Modernist designs described earlier.

💡 Twenty-first-century design

The development of 3-D animation software has enabled designers to create organic, free flowing forms by stretching and joining spheres and cylindrical objects, without the need to make complex mathematical calculations or physical models. This has led to many products taking on the appearance of a 'blob' or a bulging amoeba form, typically made from injection moulded polymers, pressed or cast metals. Cars such as the Volkswagen Beetle, Citroen C1 and C3 and products such as the Apple iMac are typical examples of 'blobjects'.

Recently there have been a number of buildings designed in this way – known as 'blobitechture'. A good example of this is the Sage in Gateshead designed by Norman Foster. Another trend in Product Design is the use of 'anthropomorphism'. This means the application of human characteristics to inanimate objects, for example, by making controls on a product such as a portable DVD player or hand held electronic game look like the abstract features of a face. This is done to make products more appealing to use or to 'soften' the interface between the product and the user. An extreme example of this is ASIMO, the anthropomorphic robot developed by Honda. See **www.dld-conference.com/**.

Finally, with advancements in microelectronics and miniaturisation of components, there has been an explosion in the creation of multi-functional electronic communications devices such as mobile phones and personal digital assistants with a wide range of user features. These products are collectively known as gizmos. As companies compete in what is becoming a crowded market, more and more features are added to gizmos. Although this adds value, it often makes them more complex to use.

A blobject – an Apple iMac

The work of past designers inspired by nature

Introduction

Designers often use things found in the natural world to inspire new designs. For centuries craftsmen and craftswomen have observed nature and recreated it in the form of jewellery, textiles and art. Alternatively, designers and inventors have looked towards nature in order to find solutions to design problems.

Craft inspired by nature

The Arts and Crafts Movement designer William Morris (1834–96) used natural things, such as birds and plant life, and re-interpreted them into stylish wallpapers, tapestries, tiles and stained glass. Morris did not simply copy nature; he instead produced stylised designs from it. This idea became popular with later designers such as Charles Rennie Mackintosh (1868–1928) who used motifs based on natural forms, such as flowers, in many of his designs at the Glasgow School of Art.

Charles Rennie Mackintosh chair

Flight inspired by nature

The first powered flight was achieved by the Wright brothers in 1903, but people had been studying flight and how birds fly for centuries before this. It was long realised that the study of birds would one day provide the solution to powered flight.

The shape of a bird's wing creates high pressure over one surface and low pressure over the other, which in turn helps to create lift. Most aircraft wings have a similar shape in cross-section to that of birds.

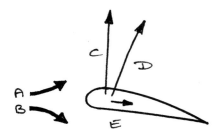

Principles of flight

Aircraft designers also noted that birds are able to adjust their wings and tail feathers in order to make turns. This information helped in the development of the flaps and tail rudder controls in aircraft. It could also be argued that the shape of a bird's body may have helped to influence the aerodynamic shaping of early aircraft, in order to minimise drag.

The principle of flight

■ As air hits the front of the wing, it is split by the leading edge (A, B).

■ As air flows over the top of the wing, a low-pressure area is created (A).

■ Air flowing under the wing travels at the same speed as that over the top (B).

■ There are drag effects due to the air hitting the wing then being divided over the top and under the bottom, but the net result is that lift is created (C, D).

■ The greater the speed of air passing over the wing, the more lift is created (E).

Inventions from plant life

The hook and loop fastening system (known more commonly by its trade name 'Velcro') was invented by George de Mestral in 1948. De Mestral was said to have been inspired by seed burrs that stuck to his trousers when he was walking his dog. He examined the seed burrs under a microscope, together with the fabric of his trousers. He discovered that the seed burr had hundreds of tiny hooks that stuck in the weave of the material, which made lots of loops. He later commissioned weavers to produce the hook and loop fastening system that is today used in a wide range of commercial applications.

The Catseye

The Catseye system, used to mark the centre or edge of a road, was invented by a road repairer from Yorkshire called Percy Shaw in 1933. The story is that he invented it after the reflection of his headlights from a cat's eyes saved him from going off the road on a dark and foggy night. He realised that if the 'eyes' could be manufactured, he could make a product that would help people drive more safely.

A Catseye for road use is typically made from glass with a piece of foil in the back to act as a reflector. The Catseye is housed in a rubber block, so that when a vehicle runs over it the eyes are pushed down in the block and are cleaned by the sides of the block at the same time.

The 'Anglepoise' lamp

George Carwardine was an automotive engineer specialising in suspension systems. He realised that he could use springs to act as 'muscles' to balance an incandescent light bulb in space. He commissioned Herbert Terry & Sons of Redditch to manufacture the springs. He designed two lamps: one for industrial use and one for domestic use. The springs hold the lamp in any desired position within its range of movement.

Table 23 *Construction of an 'Anglepoise' lamp*

	Material	Construction
Lamp housing and base	Mild steel	Spinning and piercing
Arms	Mild steel	Cut to length from stock square, hollow, section tube Pierced (for fastenings to 'elbow' pivot)
Support bracket	Mild steel	Blanked from sheet material Press formed and pierced
'Elbow' pivot	ABS	Injection moulded

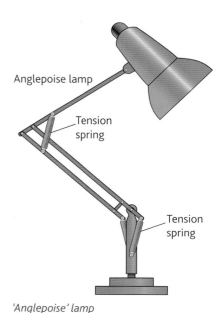

Anglepoise lamp

Tension spring

Tension spring

'Anglepoise' lamp

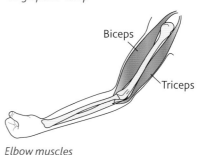

Biceps

Triceps

Elbow muscles

The 'Anglepoise' lamp has an 'elbow' pivot, which allows it to straighten and bend in much the same way as a human arm – giving approximately the same range.

The tension springs on the lamp work in the same way as the biceps and triceps of the upper arm. When the lamp is lowered, or bent, one set of springs is relaxed, while the other is in tension. In the same manner, when the forearm is bent the biceps contract and the triceps relax.

 Product analysis exercise 7: Historical influences

Bauhaus chair

Study the picture of the B32 chair designed by Marcel Breuer. Describe how this product was influenced by Bauhaus principles. Your answer should make reference to materials, construction method, function, aesthetics, and so forth.

 Product analysis exercise 8: Historical influences

Super Lamp

Study the picture of the Super Lamp, designed by Memphis Group designer, Martine Bedin. Explain how its design was influenced by Post Modernist principles. Your answer should make reference to materials, construction method, function, aesthetics, etc.

AQA Examiner's tip

Where you are asked to discuss a number of things about a product, for example; raw materials, manufacture, use and disposal, you might find it helpful to structure your answer under subheadings for each one.

Examination-style questions

1 With the aid of annotated sketches explain in detail how four of the following communication methods would be used by designers:
- colour renderings
- perspective drawings
- block models
- full-size mock-ups
- exploded views
- orthographic/working drawings. *(4 × 7 marks)*

2 Designers and manufacturers often assess the whole life cycle of their products to reduce pollution and environmental damage. For two different specific products that you are familiar with, assess their potential impact on the environment. You should make reference to raw materials, manufacturing methods, consumer use and disposal *(4 × 12 marks)*

☑ *After studying this chapter it is hoped that you will:*

■ understand that the origin of design starts with human need. This can be identified by constructive discontent, acts of insight or through user research

■ be aware that the design process is not ususally a linear process. It is much more complex with many 'stages' taking place in parallel with essential feedback loops between the people involved in the process

■ appreciate that user research techniques produce the most valuable information for designers and the relationship between the designer and the user is very important

■ understand (i) that well-designed products take account of ergonomic and anthropometric issues to ensure that they are easy and comfrotable to use, and (ii) inclusive design takes into account the needs of all users including disabled people, the young and elderly

■ be aware that safety is a major consideration for designers and manufacturers and is regulated by EU and government legislation

■ understand that government and EU legislation is a driving force behind innovation to meet environmental problems, and that designers and manufacturers are approaching envirnmental concerns through stategies of green design, eco design and sustainable innovation

■ be aware that design innovation can also be the result of technological advancements. As a result of advances in technology, products have become smaller and portable. Many products incorporate ICT and this has added value for the consumer

■ appreciate that the style of Product Design has changed over time as a result of changes in fashion and social or poiitical factors.

Further reading

■ Volker Albus, Reyer Kras and Jonathan Woodman (edited by), *Icons of Design – The 20th Century*, Prestel

■ Penny Sparke, *A Century Of Design – Pioneers of the 20th Century,* Mitchell Beazley

■ Magdalena Droste, *Bauhaus-Bauhaus archiv*, Taschen

■ Magdalena Droste and Manfred Ludewig, *Marcel Breuer*, Taschen

■ Judith Carmel-Arthur, *Bauhaus*, Carlton

■ Brigitte Fitoussi, *Memphis*, Thames and Hudson

■ Judith Carmel-Arthur, *Philippe Starke*, Carlton.

6   Processes and manufacture

Through the study of this chapter it is hoped that you will:

- gain a thorough understanding of the factors affecting choice of process, along with the systems available that support those processes. There are a range of example examination questions available on the web

- be aware of the diversity of modern manufacturing systems including the use of ICT and robotics in manufacturing.

This chapter will discuss the factors affecting choice of process. It also provides a view of modern manufacturing systems including the use of ICT and robotics in manufacturing.

Selecting a process

In order to manufacture a successful product there has to be a match between material, shape or form of the product, function, scale of production and cost (selling price). We can take a look at this more closely by looking at a high volume product such as a soft drinks can.

The majority of soft drinks cans are made from an aluminium alloy. Looking closely at the can we can see that it is made from two parts (or three, if you count the ring-pull), i.e. the can body and the top. The body is made from a single piece of material – there are no seams down the side. Production time is saved with no bonding or welding. In order to achieve this, the material has to be stretched or 'drawn' to form the shape.

Pure aluminium can be drawn out but not to the extent that is required from this product. Consequently aluminium has been alloyed with small amounts of manganese and magnesium which has the effect of increasing the material's ductility and so its ability to be drawn out to its final shape.

Consider the process of manufacturing the main body of a drinks can.

The body of the can begins the process as a disc of aluminium alloy that has been blanked from sheet material. At this point the manufacturer must produce as little waste as possible. This has resulted in a more close-packed arrangement of discs being cut from the sheet material.

Close-packed arrangement (aluminium alloy)

Why should we be concerned about the amount of waste from the sheet of the material when (as with all metals) aluminium is recyclable? The sheet material has already been processed to the required thickness with the necessary surface finish. There is a cost attributed to this processing, so to send the material through the process again will increase those costs. In addition, the processing itself will require further use of resources, e.g. energy to melt the material, power to hot roll the material from the ingot and cold roll it to give the final thickness and smooth surface.

The discs are first cupped and then deep drawn by forcing the material through a series of ironing rings.

The process of drawing means that the material will need to have high ductility which is provided by adding manganese and magnesium to aluminium.

Activity

List at least 10 products that are manufactured using materials that have been modified by the addition of other materials. Identify the original material and those that have been added.

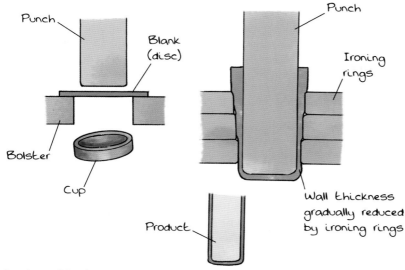

Cupping and drawing

The advantage of the drawing process is that, as the shape forms, the thickness of the can sides is reduced. If you were to measure the thickness after drawing you would find it was about a third the thickness of the base (which doesn't change). This, in turn, saves material – ultimately reducing the size of the blank at the beginning of the process.

The much reduced thickness of the can wall is still capable of supporting the can shape and withstanding the forces from the liquid being held. In fact, the liquid works with the can material to give the side wall strength. It is only when the can is empty that the sides become very weak and collapse under little external force – a 'feature' that helps with collection and recycling.

Modern manufacturing systems

Introduction

In industry today, a number of systems are used to ensure that customers get the products they want, on time and to the correct level of quality.

You should be familiar with manufacturing systems used in some specific industries.

Quick response manufacturing (QRM)

In today's market, consumer demand changes rapidly with changes in fashion. This means that many industries can no longer manufacture items to go into stock or storage before sale. Companies that do manufacture in this way run the risk of not being able to sell their products if there is a sudden change in market demand. Instead, manufacturers today often prefer to 'make to order'. For example, at Jaguar Cars, every vehicle made has a customer before its assembly is started. One immediate advantage of this is that it avoids expensive storage costs while waiting for the car to be sold. The main disadvantage of manufacturing in this way is that the customer may have to wait longer for the product. The use of **QRM** systems reduces this waiting time.

> ### Key terms
>
> **Quick response manufacturing (QRM):** the organisation of production to manufacture to customer demand, rather than manufacturing items to stock.

Electronic point of sale (EPOS)

Electronic point of sale refers to the technology of using bar-coded products that are laser scanned at the point of sale. This system enables the sale of an item to be registered with distributors, warehouses, etc. who in turn can electronically re-order stock from the manufacturer. EPOS, therefore, enables manufacturers to produce items **'just in time'** (**JIT**), rather than storing them. This is an essential part of QRM.

Bar codes or 'data communication tags' are not only used at the point of sale, but also in the identification of a component or a finished product while it is being processed or stored.

Just in time (JIT)

'Just in time' is a system devised to ensure customers get the products they want at the right time, and to ensure that manufacturers do not have to stockpile raw materials or components.

Using JIT, manufacturers organise their suppliers to deliver materials and components just in time for when they will be needed for production. This avoids the need to have large amounts of stock cluttering up assembly lines or the need for costly storage. In practice, companies such as Jaguar may have enough stock to make the cars planned for assembly in one shift.

JIT places the responsibility of ensuring parts and materials arrive on time with the supplier. In order to supply companies such as Jaguar, manufacturers would have to guarantee not only high quality at the right price, but also that supplies arrive exactly on time.

Kanbans

The control of stock levels is managed using computer systems. Many parts or components that are used in the manufacture of cars are delivered in containers, and then placed at the work cell in which they are needed. Each container is labelled with a bar code containing information to identify both (i) the part, and (ii) the quantity contained in the box. Inside the container, a card is kept which holds the same information. This is known as a 'kanban' (Japanese for 'card signal'). As the operator working in a cell starts to use up the items in the container, the kanban is placed in a chute, where it will go into a small box for later collection by the store's workers. When the kanbans are collected, they are scanned and, using **electronic data interchange** (EDI), the parts can be automatically re-ordered from the supplier.

Although the term 'kanban' is, strictly speaking, the card system described above, it is also a term generally used to describe a computer system that controls the flow of products and components through a system.

Sequencing

An essential part of a JIT system is the **sequencing** of work. Once parts or materials have arrived at a factory, they need to go to the individual work cells at the right time. This is controlled, again, by the use of computers.

Master production schedule (MPS)

MPS is a computer-controlled scheduling system that sets the quantity of each product to be made in a given time period. In the car industry, this is done using 'order-based' scheduling, because cars are made to individual order. (Customers choose body colour, individual accessory packs, interior finish, etc.) In this system, cars would be assembled in order priority. In planning this, **materials requirements planning (MRP)** software is used to order the required materials and components for each vehicle.

Telematics

Telematics is a system used to electronically track a product from receipt of customer order through to assembly and dispatch. In the car industry, customer orders are converted into electronic data programmed into a 'black box'. This is placed on the car as it goes through each part of assembly. The progress of the order can then be tracked at monitoring stations, and operators can check that the components they fit, such as engine type, stereo options and so on, match the specific customer order.

Flexible manufacturing systems (FMS)

Manufacturers who mass-produce items such as aerosol cans, toothpaste tubes and so on, will use dedicated, automated equipment that produces only those items. Investment in such production systems is relatively 'safe', because the demand for such mass-produced items is fairly constant. In other markets, items may have to be made in batches. In order to do this, the equipment used needs to be more flexible.

The following equipment can be made to be flexible:

- press formers
- CNC (computer numerically controlled) punches
- CNC laser cutters
- CNC lathes and milling machines
- robot arms.

Press formers

Press-forming equipment can be flexible, because it is possible to change the dies so that different products can be made. Obviously, this is limited to the number of dies available.

Car manufacturers will typically change press dies so that they can make more than one model of car on the same assembly line. For example, at the Jaguar Halewood factory, the X-type Jaguar and the X-type estate are made on the same line.

CNC punches

Computer-controlled punches can be programmed to punch a variety of designs out of sheet metals. Usually, they have a magazine of tools that can be changed automatically as required for the work they are doing.

CNC laser cutters

Computer-controlled lasers and flame cutters can be programmed to cut out a wide variety of profiles, slots, holes, etc.

JCB uses CNC lasers to cut the steel used to build vehicle chassis. As different models are made, it is necessary to be able to download new programs quickly to the same machines.

CNC lathes and milling machines

Lathes and milling machines can be programmed to do highly accurate one-off jobs or batches of items.

Typically, lathes are used to turn the diameter of bars, machine screw threads, and face and drill bar ends. Milling machines can be used to

CNC punching

Key terms

Computer-aided design (CAD): the use of software that can convert CAD drawings into CNC machining data.

Computer-aided manufacture (CAM): the use of computer numerically controlled (CNC) machines to increase efficiency of production.

End effector: robot arms are terminated with an end effector. This is a gripping hand, paint sprayer, welder or other device for moving objects around.

cut slots, pockets, drill holes or cut profiles. The use of **CAD/CAM (computer-aided design/computer-aided manufacture)** software has made re-programming such machines relatively easy.

Robot arms

Robots can be programmed to do:

- the same job all of the time on one product
- the same job, but on different products
- entirely different jobs.

They can be provided with different tools, or **end effectors**, so that they can do tasks such as spot welding, spray painting, applying adhesives, lifting components, and so on. Again, re-programming is relatively easy, and such robots are therefore quite flexible.

Robot arms used to spot weld Jaguar cars can have alternative programs, so that they can weld the different-shaped body or chassis panels according to the model that is being made.

FMS cells

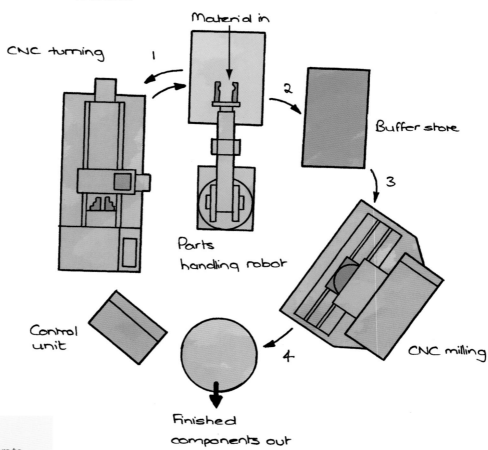

Plan view of a typical FMS cell (flexible manufacturing cells)

Flexible manufacturing machines can be organised into cells. In addition to the machines, they may also include a buffer store. This is a temporary store used to hold partially completed work. As some machines will work faster than others, and some jobs will take longer, work that is partially completed will need to be held while the other jobs take place.

Key terms

Flexible manufacturing: refers to organising production into cells of machines performing different tasks. They are typically laid out in a U-shape, rather than a production line, to enable one person to operate several machines.

For an FMS cell to work, a host computer is needed to control the sequencing of jobs, and to monitor the status and performance of each machine in the cell. This host computer will download CNC part programs according to customer orders. Due to the fact that the machines are flexible, it is possible to have several different programs running and, therefore, different products can be made in the same cell at any one time.

■ ICT in manufacturing

Introduction

The use of computers in manufacturing is a subject that you should investigate.

You should have a thorough understanding of the use of ICT in industry, and be able to recall some specific examples of how and why ICT is used.

Scales of production

Products are made in a range of quantities: from a one-off to large-scale production runs, depending on demand. The numbers produced indicate the scale of production for a product.

↻ One-offs

One-offs refer to those products that have been designed and manufactured for a single, specific situation. For example, a pair of wrought-iron gates specially designed for the gap they are to fill, or a custom-made bicycle frame for a competition rider. Other examples include murals and sculptures that have been designed and made for specific areas, a made-to-measure suit or a bespoke piece of jewellery for a special occasion.

Most one-off products are, generally, hand-made using a wide variety of equipment and techniques. You will probably find this is the case with the final product you have designed and manufactured for your coursework. As a result, one-off or commissioned work is usually very expensive.

Batch production

Batch production is the name given to the manufacture of a set number of products, ranging from just a few items to thousands. Ceramics is an area where products are produced in batches. Producers such as Wedgwood and Royal Doulton rely on orders coming in from customers to determine what will be produced. Within a week they may produce so many thousand 10-inch plates, so many thousand 8-inch, so many 6-inch plates, and so on. These orders will be sent to the manufacturing departments, where specialist equipment is used to manufacture the items. As these products move through the manufacturing processes they will be decorated with patterns and lines on more specialised equipment, again according to the orders they have received.

For a single suit to be manufactured, a good deal of measuring is required to provide the tailor with sufficient information to create patterns for each part of the garment. The patterns will then be set out on the cloth that is then cut manually with scissors. For the manufacture of off-the-peg suits, patterns have already been established to cover a range of heights and waist sizes. Instead of a single layer of cloth being cut, multi-layers can be cut at the same time, usually on a kind of band saw. This means that a number of suits can be made to the same sizes but with different coloured and patterned cloths.

A piece of bespoke jewellery

A jig in use

Activity

Go back to your list of techniques you would need to use to manufacture the one-off product for your coursework. Now consider what changes you would make to the manufacture of the product for batch production. What do you consider to be the main benefits of making these changes?

AQA Examiner's tip

You should show that you have a good understanding of manufacturing systems by using correct terms in your answers to exam questions.

◤ *Using jigs*

Where a number of the same product are to be manufactured, the range of techniques used are usually (i) different, and (ii) less time consuming in the long run. For example, where a number of wrought-iron gates are required to be made all of the same size, then a jig could be used to ensure all lengths cut are of the correct size, reducing the need for additional measuring. A further jig could be set up to hold the pieces in the correct place while being joined, again avoiding the need for fiddly adjustments to be made to the set-up. The joining techniques may well be less refined, for example, a single product may well have solid riveted joints but for speedier manufacture of a number of gates then electric arc welding may be used.

Car manufacturers produce cars in batches, again as a response to demand from customer orders placed in showrooms. As cars travel along the production line, they are sprayed the colour required by the customer and may have different internal features such as air conditioning. The manufacture of cars is a highly specialised business, with equipment designed to manufacture just one kind of product; you will not find many general types of tool like spanners, drills, etc. on a production line.

◤ Mass production (high-volume production)

The standard components used in the building of a car, are, in general, produced in high volume – in some cases, very high volume. For example, for one car there may be in excess of 1,000 nuts, bolts, washers and screws. Light bulbs, seat belt clips, windscreen wiper blades are all produced in high volume, otherwise known as 'mass production'.

There are very few products that are truly mass produced. Most products are produced to order. This, in turn, will reduce the need for storage of over-produced products and associated costs. However, if there is one product that comes very close to mass production, it is the manufacture of polystyrene cups for vending machines. Once used they are discarded and (hopefully) recycled, and the material used again to produce more of the cups. These are produced on dedicated machines. The moulds used are very expensive, but this cost is offset by the huge quantity of cups that can be produced from them.

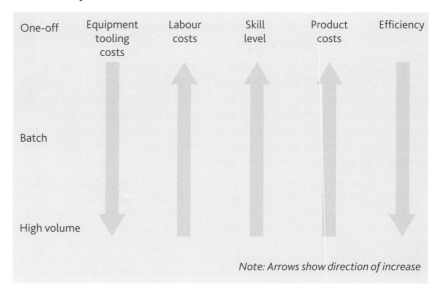

Note: Arrows show direction of increase

Level of production

Continuous production

This term refers to the processes where the product is continuously being manufactured. This applies to a very few processes where stopping would cause a problem (to the steel industry, for example, where the hot steel is continuously being cast into ingots for rolling into various sections).

The petro-chemical industry relies on continuous refinement of crude oil to produce fuel oils, such as petrol and diesel, lubricants and materials to produce plastics.

■ ICT applications in product design and manufacture

Computer-aided design (CAD)

CAD involves using computers to generate either 2-D line drawings or 3-D, photo-realistic, colour-rendered drawings.

Product designers use CAD software to speed up the designing process.

■ Case study: Josiah Wedgwood and Sons

The use of CAD in pottery

Designers at Wedgwood, a pottery company based in Staffordshire, usually create CAD drawings of pottery after creating 'mood boards' with clients and doing some initial concept sketching.

Having decided on a particular pattern, the designer may produce a small sample of the pattern by hand, using pen, ink and paints. This pattern will then be digitally scanned so that it can be used later in CAD drawings and in the design and manufacture of decorative transfers.

The designer can then use CAD in the following ways:

- The range of standard pottery pieces used by Wedgwood, i.e. cups, plates, bowls, etc., can be drawn in both 2-D and 3-D and stored on the CAD system for later use. This allows designers to use these standard designs with different clients, by simply applying their pattern motif or other decoration as required. Alternatively, the designer can easily modify existing product shapes. (This can be quicker than starting from scratch.)

- Using editing features such as mirror, copy, rotate, move, and pattern array: patterns can be repeated and arranged around pre-drawn standard components such as vases, jugs, plates, etc. This saves time; to produce such patterns by hand could take weeks.

- Three-dimensional drawing tools enable the designer to draw bespoke designs rapidly. These can be colour rendered, have patterns and decoration applied and enhanced with lighting effects. This 3-D drawing can then be tumbled so that it can be viewed from any angle. These photo-realistic images can also be placed in photo-realistic backgrounds, such as shop point-of-sale displays, table settings and so on, to give the client a realistic impression of the final design.

Rapid prototyping technology (RPT)

Three-dimensional CAD drawings can be downloaded to a machine that will make a prototype model of a design. There are many

Rapid prototyping (RPT): the use of CNC machines that create 3-D objects using lasers to solidify liquid polymers, known as stereo-lithography.

Layered object modelling (LOM): a type of rapid prototyping machine that cuts layers of self-adhesive card or paper, which are then assembled into a 3-D model.

Fused deposition modelling (FDM): a type of rapid prototyping machine that extrudes layers of liquid polymer to build up a model.

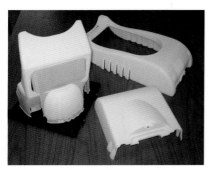

RPT products

Lead time: the time a customer must wait to receive a product after placing an order.

Virtual reality (VR): the use of 3-D simulation software that enables designers to produce photo-realistic images of products in lifelike settings and to interact with them.

different **rapid prototyping** machines available today. Here are some common types:

- **Layered object modelling (LOM)** is similar to a plotter/cutter which would cut the design layer by layer in thin card or self-adhesive film. The layers are then assembled rather like a 3-D jigsaw.
- **Fused deposition modelling (FDM)** is similar to a glue gun. A nozzle extrudes molten plastic and builds up the design layer by layer as it solidifies. Plastics such as ABS are often used.
- Stereo-lithographic modelling involves a bath of liquid resin, which uses lasers to solidify the plastic in the shape of the design.

Designers at Wedgwood produce an FDM rapid prototype model of their designs in ABS (acrylonitrile butadiene styrene – see Table 1: Common polymers on p3). This takes approximately 24 hours. The model can then be painted to give a glazed appearance and finished with printed transfers. The end result is an extremely realistic 3-D model that designers can use with clients and in planning meetings with manufacturing engineers.

Rapid prototyping greatly reduces the **'lead time'** of products (the time taken from design concept to manufacture of a product). For Wedgwood, the lead time for a six-setting dinner service can be reduced from what would have been months to a matter of a few weeks. Before the use of RPT, products would have been prototyped by making them in clay. This is a highly skilled task and required the item to be dried, fired, glazed, re-fired, decorated with paints/transfers and fired again. This was a very lengthy and expensive process.

Virtual reality modelling (VR)

Virtual reality modelling allows designers the opportunity to see and manipulate their designs in a photo-realistic, 3D environment. At Wedgwood, designers can use software that enables them to see and 'handle' products in the environment for which they are intended. This can be very useful when talking to clients who can see their products in restaurant interiors, at table settings, shop displays, and so on.

At Jaguar Cars, designers and production engineers use VR systems to plan how production cells will work. The layout of work cells, the interaction of employees working on an operation together, and the sequence of an assembly operation can all be planned in a virtual model. This makes tremendous cost savings for the company and, again, helps to dramatically reduce the lead-time of new models.

Computer-integrated manufacture (CIM)

Traditionally, the design and development of a product is organised in a sequential, linear pattern. For example, a marketing department within a company passes a brief to the design department, the designers pass the designs to production engineers, who in turn pass the design to materials purchasing, and so on. If departments involved in the design and development of products work in isolation from each other, several problems can arise. For example, the designers may not interpret the original brief or product specification correctly, they may design a product that is difficult to manufacture, or the materials may be expensive and difficult to obtain. This can then ultimately result in a product that is not quite what the client had intended it to be.

Best practice in modern manufacturing work is a system known as 'concurrent manufacturing'. This is where all of the groups involved in the design and development of a product work together, right through the project.

Computers are used to assist concurrent manufacturing. Usually, those working on a project would share marketing data, specification criteria, designs and development drawings, materials specifications and production planning over a centrally controlled database. As each member of the team works on the project, the database is updated. The use of ICT in this way leads to faster development of a product and one that meets client requirements.

CIM can also involve the central control of computer systems that organise production scheduling (the timing and sequence of production operations). This includes the management of stock levels for raw materials and component parts and 'just in time' distribution of these around a factory.

Computer-aided engineering (CAE)

Computer-aided engineering is the use of computers to test components prior to manufacturing. Examples of this can be seen in the automotive industry, where computer models can be used to test vehicle engine or suspension parts under simulated loads. This will usually be supported with computer-controlled tests run on real components assembled in a 'test rig'.

 Product analysis exercise 1: ICT applications in product design and manufacture

CAD

1 Study the pictures below and answer the following questions:

  a Explain the purpose of wire frame CAD drawings like the one shown.

  b What are the benefits of producing CAD drawings in wire frame?

2 a Explain the purpose of surface models.

  b What are the benefits of producing CAD drawings as a surface model?

3 The third CAD model is a solid model. What is the purpose of a solid model?

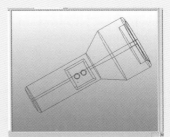
Wire frame model

Surface model

Solid model

◤ Computer-aided manufacturing

Introduction

You should have a good knowledge of some specific industrial examples of CAM in use, and be able to present a balanced argument for the advantages and disadvantages of its use. You should also be able to describe how robots are used in specific industries, and have an insight into the benefits and drawbacks of using robots.

■ **Key terms**

Wire frame model: CAD drawings of products using a range of lines, arcs and points. They take up very little memory and, in wire frames, image-processing time is kept to a minimum. However, as there are no visible surfaces, they do not show any surface or solid properties. They can also be difficult to understand.

Surface models: CAD drawings that provide a more realistic 3-D image than wire frame. They can be used to show machining tool paths and data, and are quicker to re-process than solid models.

CAM and product development

In order to speed up the design and development of products, computer numerically controlled machines, such as five-axis milling machines, can be used to machine moulds or for tooling directly from the data generated from a 3-D CAD drawing.

Example 1: Wedgwood Wedgwood uses software CAD/CAM to convert 3-D CAD drawings of its designs into machining data. This data is then used to machine 'blocks', which are highly accurate master moulds. The blocks are then used to make plaster moulds, which will later be filled with clay slip, in the production of hollow ware. Again, the use of CAD/CAM greatly reduces product development time, because it would take a skilled craftsman considerably longer to make a 'block' by hand.

Example 2: JCB In other industries, CAM may be used to process materials. For example, at JCB Bamford, Excavators, CNC lathes are used to machine highly accurate steel pivot pins (used in the articulating joints of the back hoe). In the production of the vehicle chassis for back-hoe excavators, JCB uses CNC laser cutters to precision cut steel plate. Following this, the steel plate is pressed and folded into shape using computer-controlled hydraulic presses. It would also use computer-controlled robots to carry out precision welding operations, such as in assembling parts to the chassis.

Three-dimensional scanners

Three-dimensional scanners measure an object by tracing a series of points over the surface of the object. The measurements are used to build up a 3-D digital map of the item. This data can then be imported into CAD software and edited to make 3-D rendered drawings.

At Wedgwood, 3-D scanners are used to scan ceramic objects stored in the company's archives. Some objects are up to 200 years old, and may have designs and engravings that can be used on modern products. These can be digitally captured and therefore manipulated. Images or patterns can be reversed, designs 'embossed' below the surface, or relief images created to any size – all from one scanned item.

Wedgwood uses two types of 3-D scanner:

Contact scanner This is large, using a probe that makes physical contact with the object. The probe is driven by a CNC program, which ensures that the object being scanned is measured precisely. Such scanners are normally used for fairly large items and can take some time to scan an object.

■ **Activity**

With reference to other industries you may be familiar with, write a bullet-point list outlining the benefits of using CAM.

Non-contact scanners The most common non-contact scanners use lasers to measure an object. Wedgwood uses this type of scanner to scan very detailed (often small) items, such as those that might have an engraved, or relief, pattern. Laser scanners are extremely accurate and very fast. As they do not make contact with the item being scanned, there is also no risk of damaging the surface.

Robotics

The categories of robots are:

■ **first generation**

■ **second generation**

■ **third generation**.

First generation

This type of robot responds to a pre-set program and will carry on regardless of any external changes. For example, if the robot was packing eggs into a carton, and one egg broke, the robot wouldn't know and would just continue packing. This type of robot is becoming obsolete, as it has limited use in modern industries.

Second generation

This type of robot is fitted with sensors, which are used to feed back information to a central control computer. This information is then used to monitor the operation of the robot and to automate the work cell.

For example, robots placing steel blanks into a press would first collect the blanks from a pallet. Sensors would need to be used:

- to ensure that the pallet is loaded with blanks
- to ensure that the blank is being presented into the press the correct way around
- to check that it has been pressed correctly.

The most common sensing method today in robotics is the use of digital cameras. Pictures of components being worked on can be automatically compared to reference pictures stored on the host computer. The host computer can then automatically stop a work cell, if it detects an error.

Third generation

Third-generation robots use sophisticated sensors and computer programming to create '**artificial intelligence**' or **AI**. This type of robot is able not only to detect changes to the environment in which it is working, but also modify its own program and therefore its actions in response to the changes. So far, AI robots are still generally only in experimental stages but, for industry, there is the potential to develop robots that can detect faults, diagnose the problem and rectify it.

Robot configurations

There are three main types of robot used in industry today:

- beam transfer
- arm
- **automatic guided vehicle (AGV)**.

Beam transfer

These are relatively simple robots that operate on parallel slides or beams. The robot will move along x- and y-axes, and are generally used to pick up a component from one machine or a pallet and place it in another. This type of robot operates in what is sometimes called a 'pick and place' system.

Beam transfer robots can be seen in the car industry, where they are used to pick up press-formed body panels and move them along the manufacturing line.

Arm

This type of robot configuration is the most versatile. Robot arms are jointed in a similar way to the human arm, having a shoulder, elbow and wrist. These joints, and the directions they can move in, are known as '**degrees of freedom**'. The more degrees of freedom a robot has, the more useful it is. The hand of a robot arm is known as the 'end effector'. This can be fitted with a wide range of tools, including:

Beam transfer robot

Robot arm

- air guns for spraying
- spot welders
- laser or flame cutters
- manipulators (often pneumatic suction cups) for picking items up.

Automatic guided vehicles

Automatic guided vehicles, or AGVs, are rather like a fork-lift truck without a driver. They are robots that are used to carry components and finished items around factories.

AGVs navigate either by using sensors, (which follow a wire that is buried under or stuck to the surface of a factory floor), or by using lasers, which bounce off reflectors placed high up on walls. In the latter, the robot takes three measurements at any one time, and can triangulate its position according to a map of the factory layout stored in its memory.

AGVs are often programmed to interface with factory 'just in time' (JIT) systems, so that they deliver materials and components to the right place, at the right time. They are often integrated with Automatic Storage and Retrieval Systems (ASRS) to fully automate the process of collecting materials and components from stores and delivering the finished product to despatch.

Programming methods

There are three main ways to program robots:

- **Teach pendant** Similar to using a remote control, where an operator will use the control or teach pendant to guide the robot through a series of movements. The control computer stores and converts the movements into a control program.

- **Walkthrough** Where an operator will physically pull the robot through the required movements, whilst the control computer records and converts these movements into a control program. This type of programming is useful to 'train' robots in operations such as welding or spray painting.

- **Off-line** One of the most popular ways to program robots. Virtual reality simulations of a work cell can be used to program a robot and to test the program, without the risk of damaging the robot or anything else in the work cell. They can also be used to rehearse dangerous operations, such as maintenance tasks in the nuclear power industry.

The benefits of using robots

Robots can:

- carry out mundane, repetitive tasks that humans dislike, e.g. loading or unloading components from machines
- carry out physically demanding jobs where there might be a risk of repetitive strain injury, for example when lifting and moving heavy components
- work in hazardous areas, such as in work cells where spot welding, arc welding, laser cutting, spraying, is taking place; or in the nuclear industry, to carry out inspection and maintenance on radioactive components
- work to high levels of accuracy, consistently and quickly. For example, in spot welding car body panels, robots will place the correct number of welds in the correct place, every time. Human operators cannot work consistently with such accuracy while having to work at speed

work for long periods of time without the need to stop (apart from maintenance). Maintenance stops can be programmed in to avoid machine breakdown or faults on the product occurring. For example, at MG Rover, robot spot welders will automatically clean their copper electrodes every few welding cycles. The electrodes will then adjust to compensate for any copper that wears away.

The drawbacks of using robots

There are several problems associated with using robots. They are:

- poor mobility and flexibility
- limited degrees of freedom
- high set-up costs
- employment issues.

Mobility and flexibility

Robots have poor mobility and flexibility compared to human workers. A human worker can move easily from one manufacturing cell to another and work on entirely different tasks, if required. Robots, on the other hand, can be difficult to relocate because of their size and, in order to carry out different tasks, they have to be re-programmed and often re-tooled. Humans can pick up different components and different tools easily, whereas a robot's end effector tends to be dedicated to doing one or two tasks.

Degrees of freedom

Humans can work in tight spaces and move in and out of those spaces relatively easily. For example, when installing dashboard or steering wheel assemblies, humans can do the job much more easily than robots.

Set-up costs

Robotic cells are extremely expensive to purchase and, depending on the tasks they are to perform, can be hugely expensive to program and set up so that they function correctly.

Employment issues

Robots are often used to replace labour and, therefore, there can be some loss of jobs. This can lead to poor labour relations, and so on. In addition to this, employees need to be able to adapt to working with the new technology. They need to be willing to train on the use of such technology and be flexible to work in different ways (often taking responsibility to supervise work cells and problem-solve on their own initiative).

Activity

Using the internet, research two different types of robot used in industry. Make notes on how the two robots are used in specific companies.

Further reading

- www.21stcentury.co.uk/robotics
- www.kawasakirobot.uk.com

 Product analysis exercise 2

Computer-aided manufacturing

Study the sketch of the engineering components shown and answer the following questions:

1. The engine part shown has been manufactured using CAM. Name the type of machine that could have been used.

2. Explain why the part would have been manufactured using CAM.

3. What are the disadvantages of using CAM in the manufacture of products?

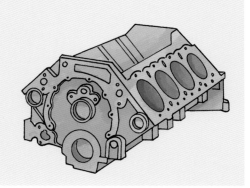

AQA Examiner's tip

As you are answering the exam question it is a good idea to remind yourself where the marks are allocated. In the first question here 2 x 7 marks suggests that two examples are required each of which will provide 7 marks.

AQA Examiner's tip

When answering the type of question shown in 2 you should take care to note that the answer you provide in part (a) will need to be carried through to part (b).

✓ Examination-style questions

1 With reference to specific industries, explain how ICT is used. Your answer should refer to each of the following:

- design and development
- production planning
- control of manufacturing
- quality control   *(2 × 7 marks)*

2 a Describe how computer aided manufacture (CAM) is used in the production of one of the following industries:

- flat-pack furniture
- automotive
- graphics and packaging.   *(14 marks)*

b For your chosen industry (listed in (a) above), explain the benefits and disadvantages of using computer-aided manufacture (CAM).   *(14 marks)*

✓ *After studying this chapter it is hoped that you will:*

- have gained an understanding of the criteria for choosing a manufacturing process

- have become aware of a range of modern manufacturing systems

- have considered scale of production and its effect on choice of manufacturing process

- have appreciated the diversity of industrial robotics from first to third generation

- have understood how ICT, including rapid prototyping, is used in industrial and commercial manufacturing.

Index

Headings in **bold** are key terms

A

acid pickling **141**
acids and metal corrosion **106**
adaptation **155**
adapted products **129–30, 176**
additives, for plastics **4**
adhesives **89, 101, 103–4**
aeroply **86**
aesthetics **56, 60, 147, 201**
age hardening **36**
alloys **28, 29, 32–3, 77–8, 143**
aluminium **26, 30, 31, 120, 137, 206**
   joining **94–5, 97, 106**
analogue television **182–3**
analogy and design **156**
Anglepoise lamp **203–4**
annealing **35, 62**
anodising **111**
anthropometrics **127, 173–5**
anthropomorphism **202**
applied finishes 108, 109
Art Deco **198–9**
Art Nouveau **196–7**
artificial intelligence (AI) 217
Arts and Crafts Movement **196, 202**
associative thinking **155**
automated guided vehicle (AGV) 217, 218

B

batch production **211–12**
batteries **76, 181–2**
Bauhaus **197–8**
bauxite **31**
beam transfer robots **217**
Bell, Alexander Graeme **184–5**
bio diesel **166–7**
bio power **167**
biodegradable materials 5–6
biopol **5**
blanking, metal **38–9**
blobjects **202**
blow moulding 8–9, 16
blowing, **glass 61**
blueing technique 110
boards **69, 75, 115**
bodystorming **153**
boro-silicate glass 63
brass **32, 137**
brazing **91, 95**
briefs, design **150**

Brinell test **138**
British Standards Institution (BSI) 130–1
burrs **110**

C

calendaring **11–12**
carbon **30, 35**
carbon fibre **20, 22–3, 28, 83**
carburising **36**
cards **69, 75, 115**
cars **164–8, 190**
carton board **69**
case hardening **36–7**
casein **2**
casting processes **43–9**
catalysts **13**
cathode ray tube (CRT) 162
catseyes **155, 203**
cellular manufacturing **210–11**
cellulose **2, 55**
ceramics **64–7, 103, 211**
cermets **26**
Charpy test **140**
clay **15, 16, 65, 84**
clients **145, 150**
Cliff, Clarice **198–9**
clothing **80, 84–5, 190**
coatings *see* finishes and finishing
composite materials **20, 21**
   fibre-reinforced **20–5, 82–3**
   particle-based **25–6**
   quantum tunnelling **80**
   replacing traditional materials **27–8**
   sheet-based **20, 21, 26–7, 59–60, 85–6**
compression moulding 13–14, 137
Computer Numerical Control (CNC) 40, 209–10
computer-aided design (CAD) 159, 210, 213–14, 216
computer-aided engineering (CAE) 215
computer-aided manufacture (CAM) 210, 215–19
computer-integrated manufacture (CIM) 214–15
concretes **16, 24–5, 25–6**
consumer profiles **146**
continuous production **213**
Control of Substances Hazardous to Health Regulations (COSHH) 170

conversion of timber 55
copper **31, 32, 137**
copyright **70**
correx boards **69**
corrosion **26, 105–6**
coupling model **193**
crimping **91**
cross-links **13, 14**
crystals (in metals) 30, 34, 36
cullet **61, 63**
cutting of metals **38–40**
cycle times 9

D

deathwatch beetle 56, 107
deburring **110**
decay, wood 56, 106–7
deciduous trees 54
deep drawing **42, 206–7**
defect detection **141–2**
degradation, polymer 5–6, 107–8
degrees of freedom 217, 218, 219
demand pull 193
density **119**
design process
   choice of materials **133–7**
   communication methods **158–9**
   development **153–4**
   environmental issues **124–6, 147–8, 160–8**
   ergonomics **126–7, 173–5**
   ICT and **213–14**
   ideas and starting points **148–9, 153, 154–6**
   inclusive design **129–30, 176**
   in industrial context **149–53**
   protecting designs **156–8**
   roles within **145–6**
   safety issues **131–2, 169–73**
designer-makers **145, 154**
designers **126, 145, 146, 156, 195–204**
destructive tests **138**
Deutsche Werkbund **197**
dichroic glass **85**
die casting **45–7**
die cutting, paper or board **75**
digital printing 74
digitalisation **183, 187**
disabled people **129, 176–7**
drop forging **51–3**
dry rot 106, 107
ductility **118, 121, 138**
durability **119**

duralumin 32, 36
dye sublimation printing 74
Dyson vacuum cleaner 104, 157

E

ecodesign 125–6, 161, 162–3, 164–5
Ecolabel 160
elasticity 118, 138
elastomers 2, 14–15
elderly people 129–30
electric arc welding 97
electric cars 166
electrical properties of materials 119–20
electro-photographic printing 74
electrochemical cells 106
electrodeless induction lamps 164
electroluminescent wires 79
electronic data interchange/ exchange (EDI/EDE) 208
electronic point of sale (EPOS) 208
electroplating 110–11
electrostatic spray painting 113
embossing 42
enamelling 111–12
end effectors 210, 217–18
End-of-Life Vehicle Directive (ELVD) 160
Energy Labelling Directive 160
environmental issues 124–6, 147–8, 160–8
epoxy resin 103
ergonomics 126–7, 173–5
EU directives 160, 172
evergreen trees 54
exploded views 159
extrusion 10–11

F

fabrics 80, 84–5, 190
fashion, influence of 194–5
fastenings 104
fatigue tests 140–1
ferrous alloys 29
ferrous metals 29, 30–1, 105
fibre optics 15, 81
fibre-reinforced composites 20, 20–5
fibre-reinforced polymers (FRPs) 20, 20–4
50th percentile 127, 130
filler rods 88
fine bone china 65
finishes and finishing 108–9
    glass 63–4
    metals 83, 110, 110–14
    paper and cards 115
    plastics 109, 115–16
    wood 110, 114–15

first generation robots 217
flame hardening 37
flexible manufacturing systems (FMS) 209–11
flexography 72–3
flight 202–3
float glass 61
flooring 27–8, 58
fluidic self assembly (FSA) 189
fluids, smart 79
flux 45
foam boards 69
foams, metal 83
forging 50–2
function 19, 117–18
fused deposition modelling (FDM) 214
fusibility 119

G

glass 61
    manufacturing with 35, 61–2
    properties 62–4
    smart and modern 80–1, 85
    thermoplasticity 15, 16
    versus polymers 64
glass-reinforced plastics (GRPs) 20, 22
global manufacturing 145, 154
global warming 124, 125
glowsticks 79–80
glulam 82
grain of timber 54
Grange, Kenneth 200
graphical user interface (GUI) 180
gravity die casting 45–6
gravure 73–4
grease, smart 78–9
green design 161, 161–2, 164–5
green timbers 56
greenhouse **gases 125**

H

hard solders 91, 92
hardening of steels 35
hardness 119, 121, 138
hardwoods 54, 57, 114
Health and Safety Executive (HSE) 170
heat sources 98
heat treatments 4, 34–7
hexaboard 86
high definition TV (HDTV) 183
Houndsfield test 140
hybrid cars 165
hydrogen fuel cells 165–6

I

impact tests 139–40
inclusive design 129–30, 176

induction hardening 37
Industrial Revolution 195
information and communication technology (ICT) 186–9, 213–19
injection moulding 7, 16, 116, 135
inkjet printing 74
integrated circuits (ICs) 180, 187
intellectual property 156–7
internet 188
inventors 145, 148–9, 155, 156
investment casting 48–9
ions 181
iron 30
Izod test 140

J

jiggering 65, 66
jigs 212
joining processes 88–90
    ceramics 103
    metals 91–8
    polymers 101–3
    using adhesives 103–4
    wood 99–101
just in time (JIT) system 208

K

kanbans 208
Kevlar 20, 23–4, 82
kiln drying of timber 56
knock-down (KD) fittings 89, 100
knots (in wood) 55

L

laminates 26, 57–9, 63, 81, 82
laminating paper 115
laser cutting 40, 110
lasers 149
layered object modelling (LOM) 214
laying up 22
layout 68
lead glass 63
lead times 214
lehr 62
letterpress 71
life cycle design *see* ecodesign
light bulbs 162–4
light-emitting diodes (LEDs) 163–4
lignin resin 54, 55
lime-soda glass 61
line bending 12
liquid crystal displays (LCDs) 81, 82
liquid crystals 76, 82
liquid silicon rubber (LSR) 15
lithography 71–2
long-chain molecules 1, 14

M

machine age 195
Mackintosh, C.R. 196–7, 202
magnetic tests 141
magnetism 120
malleability 118, 121, 138
man-made boards 20, 21, 59–60, 85–6
manufacturers 124, 145, 146, 153–4
manufacturing 154
  choice of materials 133–7
  ICT and 213–19
  modern systems 207–11
  safety legislation 170–1
  scales of production 211–13
manufacturing processes
  ceramics 65–7
  glass 61–2
  metals 37–52
  paper and boards 69
  plastics 6–12, 13–14
  selection 206–7
maplex 86
market pull model 192
market research 146, 151–2
marketing mix 146–8
mass production 212–13
master production schedule (MPS) 208–9
materials
  choice of 133–7
  properties of 117–20
  smart and modern 76–86
  testing 120–2, 137–43
  see also ceramics; glass; metals; paper; plastics; wood
materials requirement planning (MRP) 209
matt 23
MDF board 21, 85–6
mechanical properties of materials 118–19
Memphis Group 201
metals 29–32
  alloys and alloying 32–3
  composites 26–7, 80
  corrosion of 105–6
  finishing 110, 110–14
  joining 91–8, 101
  manufacturing with 37–52
  modern 83–4
  testing 120
  thermoplasticity 15, 16
  work hardening and heat treatments 34–7
microchips 180, 187
microfibres 84–5
MIG (metal inert gas) welding 95, 97

miniaturisation 187
mobile phones 125–6, 188
mock-ups 153, 159
models 159
modern materials 76, 81–6
Modernism 198
moisture content of timber 56
mood boards 69, 158
Morris, William 196, 202
MP3 180–1
multi-slide die casting 47

N

N-type semi-conductor 179
nanotechnology 189–91
natural barriers 110
nature, inspiration from 202–4
95th percentile 127, 130
nitriding 37
non-destructive tests 141
non-ferrous alloys 29
non-ferrous metals 29, 31–2
normalising 34, 36
nuts and bolts 89, 101

O

obsolescence 193, 194
off-line programming 218
offset lithography 71–2
one-off products 211
optical properties of materials 120
organic light-emitting diodes (OLEDs) 190
orthographic drawings 158–9
overmoulding 116
oxidation 33
oxo-degradable polymers 5
oxy-acetylene welding 95–6

P

P-type semi-conductor 179
packaging 18–19, 160, 162
paints and painting 112–13, 114
Pantone colours 70
paper 15, 16, 67–9, 75, 115
parisons 8
particle-based composites 20, 25–6
patents 156–8
patterned glass 62
performance 19
permanent joints 88, 90
perspective drawings 159
PHAs (polyhydroxyalkanoates) 5
phase change materials (PCMs) 85
PHBs (poly-beta-hydroxybutyrates) 5
phosphorescent pigments 77
physical properties of materials 119–20
piercing, metal 38–9

piezoelectric devices 76, 78
planishing 34
plasma cutting 39, 40, 110
plastic coating of metals 83
plastic dip coating 113–14
plasticity 118
plastics (polymers) 1–4
  additives 4
  biodegradable 5–6
  in cars 167–8
  composites 20–4, 26–7, 80
  degradation of 107–8
  elastomers 2, 14–15
  finishing 109, 115–16
  glass versus 64
  identifying 121
  identifying processes 16–17
  international symbols 17
  joining 101, 102–3
  modern 84, 84–5
  thermoplastics 2, 3, 4–5, 6–12, 14, 18–19
  thermosets 2, 3, 12–14
plate glass 61
plugs, electrical 136–7, 172–3
plywood 21, 58, 86
polyactides (PLA) 5
polymers *see* plastics
polymorph 84
Post Modernism 200–1
powder coating 113
powder processing 49–50
precious metal clays (PMCs) 84
presentation boards 69, 159
press-forming 41, 42–3, 209
pressure die casting 46–7
print runs 74
printing 70–4
process colours 70
product age 195
product life cycle 162, 193–4
projection television 183–4
properties of materials 117–20
prototypes 153, 154, 159
Pyrex 63

Q

quantum tunnelling composites 80
quarter sawn timber 55
quenching 35–6
quick response manufacturing (QRM) 207

R

radio 149, 178–81
radio frequency identification (RFID) tags 188–9
rapid prototyping (RPT) 213–14
razors 148
rebound effect 167

redistribution techniques,
    metal **40–52**
reduce, reuse, recycle **124–5**
registration marks 71
reinforced concrete **24–5**
renderings **67**, **158**, **159**
renewables **5**
research **151–3**
resistance welding 90
Restriction of Hazardous Substances
    Directive (RoSH) **160**
rheological effects 79
rigid cross-links 14
risk assessments 169, **170–1**
robots **210**, **216–19**
Rockwell test **138**
rot **56**, **106**, **107**
rotational moulding 9–10, **17**
rust **105–6**

S

safety **130–2**, **169–73**
sand casting **44–5**
scale models 153
scales of production **211–13**
screen printing **73**
seam welding 98
seasoning of timber **56**
second generation robots 217
self-assembly furniture **99–100**
self-coloured materials **109**
self-finishing materials **109**
self-tapping screws **89**, **90**
semi-conductor materials 79, **120**,
    179
shape memory alloys 77–8
sheet-based composites **20**, **21**,
    26–7, **59–60**, **85–6**
shrinkage of timber **56**
silver **31**, **32**, **84**, **92–4**
Sinclair C5 **192**
sintering **49–50**
slab sawn timber 55
slip **65**, **103**
slip casting 65, **66**, **67**
slumping, glass **61–2**
smart materials 76–81
software **187**
softwoods **54**
soldering **91–5**
solvents **101**
Sony Walkman **180**, **191–2**
specifications, design **150**
spinning, metal **42–3**

splits in timber 55
spot welding 90, **98**
sprues **16**
stability **119**
steam bending of wood **59**
steel **30**, **31**, **33**
    corrosion **105–6**, **110**
    hardening **35**, **36–7**
    testing **120**, **143**
strength **119**, **121–2**, **138–9**
strip bending 12
structure of materials **117**
surface models 216
surface mount components 186
surveys **151–2**
sustainability **124–6**, **161**
swatches **158**

T

tanalising **115**
teach pendant 218
technological developments **178–91**
technology push 149, **191–2**
telematics **209**
telephones **125–6**, **184–6**, **188**
television (TV) **162**, **182–4**
tempered **glass 35**
tempering **35**
temporary joints 88, **89**
tests and testing **120–2**, **137–43**,
    154
textiles, smart **80**
textures **9**, **10**, **109**
thermal properties of materials **120**
thermal transfer printing **74**
thermochromic pigments 76
thermoforming **10**, **17**
thermoplastic elastomers
    (TPEs) **14–15**, **135**
thermoplastic materials **15**, **16**
thermoplastics **2**, **3**, **14**
    applications for **4–5**
    processing **6–12**
    welding **102**
thermosets **2**, **3**, **14**
    applications for **12–13**
    processing **6**, **13–14**
thermosetting materials **15–16**
thin-film transistor (TFT) 183
third generation robots 217
three-dimensional scanners **216**
thumbnail sketches 158
TIG (tungsten inert gas)
    welding 95, **97**

timber *see* wood
titanium **32**, **84**, **112**
toothbrushes **134–6**
total design approach 150–1
toughened **glass 35**, **62**
toughness **118–19**, **122**
tracheids **54**
Trading Standards Agency **172**
transfer of technology **155**
transistors **179**, **181**, **187**
twisting of timber 56

U

ultrasonic welding 101–2
urea formaldehyde **12–13**, **136**
users **146**, **150**, **152–3**
UV radiation and plastics **107–8**

V

vacuum forming 10, **17**
van de Waals bonds 14, **15**
varnishes **110**, **114**, **115**
Velcro **155**, **203**
veneers **57**
Vickers test **138**
video conferencing 154
virtual reality (VR) modelling 214

W

walkthrough programming 218
warping of timber 20, **56**
Waste Electrical and Electronic
    Equipment (WEEE) Directive **160**
wasting processes, metal **38–40**
wear resistance tests **140**
web-fed printing 71, **72**
welding **39**, **90**, **95–8**, **101–2**
wet rot 106, **107**
wire frame models 216
wood **54**, **120–1**
    decay **56**, **106–7**
    finishing **110**, **114–15**
    joining **99–101**
    structure **54–6**
    veneers, laminates and
        composites **20**, **21**, **57–60**,
        82, **85–6**
wood joints 89, **99**
wood preservatives 115
wood products 58
wood screws 89
woodworm **107**
work hardening 34